Economic Policies
and
Unemployment Dynamics
in Europe

Economic Policies
and
Unemployment Dynamics
in Europe

Editors
S.G.B. Henry
Dennis J. Snower

International Monetary Fund
1996

© 1996 International Monetary Fund

Library of Congress Cataloging-in-Publication Data

Economic policies and unemployment dynamics in Europe / S.G.B.
  Henry, Dennis J. Snower, editors.
    p. cm.
    Includes bibliographical references.
    ISBN 1-55775-578-7
    1. Unemployment — Europe. 2. Labor policy — Europe.
3. Labor Market — Europe I. Henry, S.G.B. II. Snower, Dennis J.
HD5764.A6E27 1996   96-45174
331.13'794—DC21   CIP

The cover and interior of this book were designed by the IMF Graphics Section.

Price: $24.00
Address orders to:
International Monetary Fund, Publication Services
700 19th Street, N.W., Washington, D.C. 20431, U.S.A.
Tel.: (202) 623-7430   Telefax: (202) 623-7201
Internet: publications@imf.org

recycled paper

Contents

Preface
  Massimo Russo • vii

1. The Dynamics of European Unemployment
   S.G.B. Henry and Dennis J. Snower • 1

2. Adjustment Dynamics in the German Labor Market
   Paolo Mauro and Tessa van der Willigen • 39

3. Labor Market Dynamics and Economic Policy in France
   Karl F. Habermeier and S.G.B. Henry • 66

4. Italian Unemployment, 1975–95: An Analysis
   of Macroeconomic Shocks and Policies
   Charalambos A. Christofides • 96

5. The U.K. Labor Market: Analysis of Recent Reforms
   S.G.B. Henry and Marika Karanassou • 150

6. Labor Market Policies and Unemployment Dynamics
   in Spain
   Jeffrey R. Franks • 175

The Authors • 216

Preface

OVER THE LAST two decades, there has been a marked and persistent increase in unemployment in many Western European countries. Joblessness has risen with every cyclical downturn, but has failed to decline back to its prerecession levels during the subsequent economic recoveries, leading to a gradual ratcheting up of the unemployment rate. The high unemployment that now prevails in most of Western Europe has many costs: forgone output, loss of human capital, and a heavy burden on the public finances. From the perspective of the IMF, another important concern would be that a failure to solve the problems in European labor markets might eventually undermine the present commitment to sound monetary and fiscal policies. While a return to the more active macroeconomic policies of the past would be met with no enduring success in reducing unemployment, it would significantly increase economic and financial instability.

The studies in this volume attempt to advance the understanding of the relationship between economic policies and the dynamics of unemployment in five large European countries within a common methodological framework, in the hope of contributing to the design of policies aimed at durably reducing unemployment. While the studies generally confirm earlier findings of a link between unemployment and policies that increase labor market rigidities and blunt incentives, they also highlight the fact that the labor market often responds to changes in policies with a surprisingly long lag. Thus, both the detrimental effects of increasing labor market rigidities, and the beneficial effects of reducing them, typically take a considerable time to make themselves felt. We believe that in the public debate on policies to reduce unemployment, a greater awareness of these lags would help to shift the focus away from "quick fixes" and toward a more patient and steady approach to implementing labor market reforms.

In addition to the editors and the other authors of the papers, many people in the IMF have contributed to the production of this book. In particular, I wish to thank Jacques Artus, Willem Buiter, Flemming Larsen, and Leslie Lipschitz for their comments on the papers and Susan J. Becker, Patricia Gillett-Lorusso, Xiaoning Gong, Alison McCaul, Luzmaria Monasi, Fritz Pierre-Louis, and Jolanta Stefanska for research assistance. Thanks are also due to Elisa Diehl of the External Relations Department, who provided editorial assistance and coordinated production.

MASSIMO RUSSO
Director
European I Department

1

The Dynamics of European Unemployment

S.G.B. Henry and Dennis J. Snower

THIS BOOK EXAMINES how the dynamic interactions among labor market activities—employment, wage setting, and labor force participation—have contributed to the high levels of unemployment in five European countries—France, Germany, Italy, Spain, and the United Kingdom. It also investigates how labor market policies have affected the resilience of these countries' labor markets.

This approach differs substantially in emphasis from the dominant way of analyzing unemployment nowadays, which concentrates on long-term labor market equilibrium. According to this latter approach, movements of unemployment over time may be understood as random variations around a reasonably stable long-run rate, the "nonaccelerating inflation rate of unemployment" (NAIRU), or the "natural rate of unemployment." The major policy implication of this theory is that, barring some temporary policy shocks that may contribute to the random variations of unemployment, the effectiveness of labor market measures depends entirely on how they influence unemployment in the long run.

What motivates the book is the view that, although the concept of a NAIRU has helped identify many important determinants of unemployment, it does not capture an important European phenomenon, namely, those mechanisms in many European labor markets that prevent employers and employees from adjusting promptly to changing market opportunities and that keep these labor markets from recovering quickly after recessions. It is well known that unemployment is a serious problem in Europe not just because it rises in times of recession, but also because it does not fall readily when the recessions are over. It is this aspect of European unemployment that is the focus of the present study.

1

The book explores the labor market implications of lagged responses of employers, employees, the unemployed, and the inactive to new economic circumstances. In the countries investigated, these lagged responses—in employment, wage setting, and labor force participation—can make unemployment diverge from its long-run rate for substantial periods of time. The policy implication is that labor market measures not only change unemployment in the long run (as highlighted by equilibrium theory), but also affect the process whereby unemployment approaches its long-run rate. This book suggests that unemployment rates may diverge significantly from their long-run values for a decade or more, and it implies that policies that improve the flexibility of labor markets can play an important role in tackling the European unemployment problem, even if they are ineffective in the long run.

The purpose of this book is to give a more balanced appraisal of the sources of European unemployment. In addition to oil prices, interest rates, taxes, and unemployment benefits, which have tended to raise the long-run unemployment rate, there are important dynamic features of unemployment—such as inertia and overshooting—that have contributed significantly to the European unemployment problem over the past 25 years.

The five countries studied in this book are analyzed in the same methodological way, using a broadly common model as the starting point. The resulting empirical models of course differ between countries, but by following a generally common methodology in each country, the differences can be attributed to underlying differences in country behavior. The empirical results for each of the countries are reported in Chapters 2–6 of this book. This chapter presents the reasoning underlying the study and the methods used and gives a short overview of the results of the countries studied.

European Unemployment Problem

In the European Union (EU) as constituted in 1994, unemployment rose rapidly from about 3 percent in the early 1970s to reach about 6 percent at the end of the 1970s, reaching a local peak of over 10 percent in the mid-1980s before falling to a little under 9 percent at the end of the 1980s. By 1994, it had risen again to stand at just under 12 percent. In this respect, its behavior contrasts with that in the United States, where unemployment also rose rapidly in the 1980s, but has since declined to levels seen at the end of the 1970s (see Chart 1). But it would be wrong to assume that the pattern of unemployment changes in Europe was homogeneous. Austria, Switzerland, and the Nordic countries maintained unemployment at relatively low levels over much of the 1970s and 1980s. Even within the EU,

Chart 1. *Unemployment in the European Union and the United States*
(In percent)

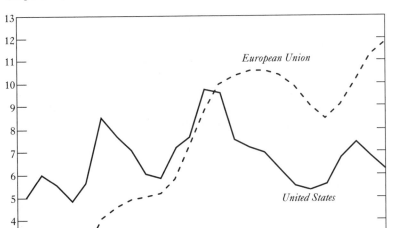

unemployment experiences differed substantially during the 1980s. In the United Kingdom, unemployment fell from about 11 percent in the early 1980s to about 6 percent toward the end of the 1980s. In west Germany, unemployment remained more stable over the same period, declining to about 5.5 percent at the beginning of the 1990s from its peak of 8 percent in the early to mid-1980s. The reduction in unemployment in France (where it fell from 11 percent to 9 percent) was similarly relatively small as it was in Italy (unemployment there only falling from 12 percent to 9.5 percent). Experiences in Spain were rather different, with unemployment peaking at 21 percent in 1985, before falling to 15.5 percent at the beginning of the 1990s. Subsequently, unemployment rose again in each of these countries as recession took hold, falling noticeably more recently only in the United Kingdom, where recovery predated that in the rest of the countries reviewed here.

Since unemployment is the difference between the labor force and employment, cross-country differences in unemployment movements can, by definition, be attributed to intercountry differences in employment creation and labor force adjustment. In the United States, for example, employment grew on average by 1.6 percent a year during the 1980s, compared with 0.5 percent in the EU (see Organization for Economic Cooperation and Development (1994)). But intercountry differences in the degree to which the labor force responds to employment opportunities have also affected unemployment patterns over the business cycle. In Europe, movements of participation rates have differed markedly: France, Spain, and, until quite recently, Germany have had steady increases in the overall labor force, owing in part to increases in female participation rates. The rapid increase in the participation rate for women in the United Kingdom from the end of the 1980s may have contributed to increased unemployment during this period. More recently, declining U.K. participation appears to account for the more rapid onset of falling unemployment in this recovery when compared with previous ones. In Italy, the labor force has declined rapidly during the recession, following substantial increases in female participation in the 1970s and 1980s.

These contrasts have been commented upon at length.[1] In much of this discussion, considerable emphasis has been given to the purported "inflexibility" of European labor markets compared with the U.S. market as the explanation of these broad continental differences (see, for example, International Monetary Fund (1994)). This book takes a more precise look at the phenomenon of inflexibility by identifying the factors that affect the process whereby unemployment adjusts to the long-run equilibrium rate over time.

Considerable attention has been lavished on the role of structural factors, such as the restrictive practices of European trade unions, the relative generosity of European unemployment benefits, and the regulation of European product markets, in bringing about high equilibrium unemployment rates. Relatively little attention, however, has thus far been devoted to the ability of labor markets to respond readily to changing economic circumstances in the aftermath of recessions. This book is a step toward righting the balance, by focusing not only on the structural deterioration of European labor markets (as in Layard, Nickell, and Jackman (1991)), but also on the determinants of sluggish labor market adjustment.

Thus far, the literature on unemployment has concentrated on two polar extremes of unemployment dynamics: the natural rate and hysteresis models. According to the natural rate models, unemployment can be divided into two major components: (1) the long-run equilibrium rate of unemployment, which is the unemployment rate determined by the structural characteristics of the economy: technologies, endowments, preferences, and the degree of competition; and (2) random short-run deviations from that rate caused by temporary frictions.

---

[1]See Organization for Economic Cooperation and Development (1994) and the Commission of the European Communities (1993), both of which give a comprehensive survey of evidence and potential explanations. An influential academic study covering this ground is Layard, Nickell, and Jackman (1991).

In contrast, the hysteresis hypothesis asserts that the unemployment rate tends to "get stuck" at whatever its current rate happens to be. (More precisely, the current unemployment rate is asserted to be the best predictor of the future unemployment rate.) Here every unemployment rate can be a long-run rate and the effects of temporary labor market shocks persist indefinitely.

We will argue that neither of these hypotheses squares well with the central features of European unemployment experience. On the one hand, European unemployment rates can diverge from their long-run "natural" rates for substantial periods of time; on the other, unemployment rates show too great a tendency to return to a limited range of values to be explained by pure hysteresis. The argument we advance is that adjustment dynamics are a neglected dimension of the unemployment problem. Following Snower and Karanassou (1995), this chapter contends that the sluggishness with which the labor market responds to shocks can be a major force keeping unemployment high following a shock, and this tendency often persists for long periods of time. To improve one's understanding of the importance of labor market dynamics and to design appropriate policy responses, one must explore how the major lags in labor market activities arise, identify how they interact with each other, and establish how labor market policies may affect them.

The model used in the individual country studies to advance this argument is grounded fully in real terms and thus focuses exclusively on the dynamics of the labor market following *real* shocks. An important question that the chapter ignores, therefore, is the role of nominal-real interactions, where nominal shocks may have long-lasting real effects owing to sluggish adjustment of wages, prices, or other nominal variables. This source of labor market sluggishness lies beyond the scope of this study, as does the possibility that labor markets may not respond symmetrically to favorable and unfavorable shocks.[2]

This chapter builds on the theoretical and empirical research in labor economics, which suggests that there are significant lagged responses in various labor market decisions. Among the most important examples of "within equation" lagged responses are the presence of lagged employment responses attributable to employment adjustment costs, wage staggering effects attributable to the presence of overlapping wage contracts,

---

[2]We believe that the conventional treatment, which concentrates on price inflation "surprises" as the sole source of short-run nominal-real interaction, is oversimplified. However, to treat this issue fully would involve considerably more complex models than are presented here and would need to include equations for nominal exchange rates and the multiple stages of the pricing process.

insider-outsider effects in wage setting, and labor force lags attributable to costs of entering the labor force. The model of employment, real wages, and the labor force in this chapter covers these and other dynamic effects.

Present Approach Compared with Some Alternatives

Much recent discussion about the source of high unemployment in Europe has emphasized the long-run equilibrium properties of the labor market, leading, arguably, to a lack of recognition of the importance of the adjustment of the labor market when subject to shocks. Those who pursue long-run equilibrium in the labor market have also tended to draw attention to the supply side of the labor market as being the most likely area where the explanation of high unemployment is to be found. Hence "structural" supply-side changes play a major role in this proposed explanation. The structuralist interpretation emphasizes the notion that the higher rates of unemployment actually observed are largely due to changes in its long-run equilibrium rate. In other words, the steady state or nontransitory part of unemployment has risen because of worsening structural factors, such as increasing trade union power, increases in out-of-work benefits, or an increasing dislocation—or mismatch—of unemployed workers to available jobs. A prominent version of this view is the NAIRU equilibrium, where the long-run equilibrium unemployment rate is that achieved in the absence of misperceptions and adjustment costs. Deviations of unemployment from its NAIRU are generally explained in terms of errors in wage-price expectations or intertemporal substitution.

The NAIRU theory leads to a clear-cut diagnosis of European unemployment. Since the long climb in European unemployment over the past two decades cannot realistically be ascribed to growing wage-price misperceptions or to long-term intertemporal substitution of leisure for work, the theory implies that it must be due to changes in the factors determining the long-run equilibrium rate, that is, to a structural worsening of the sort noted earlier.

One of the main reasons for adopting an approach different from the NAIRU is that, over the past two decades, this hypothesis has found it increasingly difficult to explain the movements of European unemployment. As noted in Chapter 5, estimates of the NAIRU for the United Kingdom are surprisingly variable over time. Chapter 6 questions whether the NAIRU in Spain can be as high as the 18 percent at which some recent estimates place it. The European unemployment rate increased markedly with the first oil price shock of 1973 and remained at unprecedentedly high postwar levels until the second oil price shock of 1979, when it rose to yet higher levels. The level of unemployment has gone up again following the 1990s recession. It has been difficult, if not impossible, to find reasons why the NAIRU should have risen by so much during this period. Thus, the model does not seem to provide a satisfactory *empirical* explanation for these changes in unemployment in European countries when the NAIRU is treated as the sole explanation of high unemployment. This is simply because the major variables used to account for the changes in long-run equilibrium unemployment, such as union power, changes in replacement ratios (working through an effect on the reservation wage), taxes on employers and employees, and mismatch, do not move enough to provide a satisfactory quantitative account of the trend increase in unemployment that has actually occurred.[3] The large demographic changes that could have raised the NAIRU—the increase in female labor force participation and the influx of young people into the labor force—did not occur during the time of largest unemployment increases. The important institutional changes pulling in the same direction—the expansion of the unemployment benefit systems and associated welfare state benefits and the rise of union power—occurred, for the most part, in the 1960s. Extremely long lags in people's adjustment to institutional changes, combined with significant overshooting behavior, would be required to rationalize the upward climb of European unemployment between the mid-1970s and mid-1980s for these to be an explanation.[4]

It has been increasingly recognized that the persistence of the labor market is an important aspect of its behavior. First, in some labor markets it is becoming evident that the effects of temporary shocks may last for years. Second, it is clear from recent international comparisons that different economies have differing degrees of persistence (see, for example, Barrell, Morgan, and Pain (1995) and Nickell (1995)). These features point to the need to account for not only the presence of such inertia in the labor market, but also for the degree of persistence in any national labor market in terms of its institutional and other features, such as the degree of centrality of its bargaining structure (Calmfors and Driffill (1987)) and the importance of overlapping in wage contracts in different sectors (or bargaining units) in the economy. In this light, a rigid distinction between structuralist and persistence explanations of rising unemployment is difficult to sustain. For example, if bargaining structure affects persistence, as it appears to, this is evidently a "structural" factor, which affects both the persistence and the long-run equilibrium level of unemployment.

---

[3]Hall and Henry (1987) and Henry, Payne, and Trinder (1985) give some early evidence of this.

[4]See, for example, Organization for Economic Cooperation and Development (1994), Lindbeck (1995), and Phelps (1994) for arguments along these lines.

Furthermore, international differences in persistence imply that it is crucial to investigate persistence mechanisms using behavioral models of the labor market rather than to simply rely on a time-series analysis of the unemployment rate itself. It is sometimes concluded that, when relating unemployment to its lagged values, the coefficients in the autoregression estimate the degree of persistence. (See Blanchard and Summers (1986) and Alogoskoufis and Manning (1988) for examples of this.) But this technique almost certainly leads to an underestimate of persistence, because considering unemployment alone does not allow for the possible influence on it of other variables.[5]

At the opposite extreme from the NAIRU in the literature on unemployment dynamics is the hysteresis approach, whereby every unemployment rate that the labor market produces is a long-run equilibrium rate. An adverse temporary labor demand shock, such as an oil price increase or an exchange rate appreciation, simply pushes the economy from one long-run equilibrium unemployment rate to a new, higher one. Consequently, temporary shocks have permanent unemployment effects.

The hysteresis approach, like the NAIRU, is also at variance with some important facts of unemployment experience in the United States, Europe, and elsewhere. Most important, if unemployment were to depend on its past value with a unit root plus a random error, then the variance of unemployment would clearly be unbounded. This means that unemployment would eventually hit zero or 100 percent with certainty. There is, needless to say, no evidence of such behavior anywhere. In practice, unemployment in the member countries of the Organization for Economic Cooperation and Development (OECD) tends to return repeatedly to values lying within a narrow range of between, say, 2 percent and 12 percent over the long run. The hysteresis approach is unable to account for this tendency.

The approach here builds on these considerations and postulates that, although a long-run equilibrium value of unemployment exists, the actual unemployment rate may deviate from it for substantial periods of time. In practice, it must be recognized that it is difficult to distinguish between protracted persistence and the case where unemployment is responding to permanent changes in structural factors, Z (the basis of NAIRU models). Models built around a long-run equilibrium view attribute all permanent changes in unemployment to the permanent components of Z and serial correlation in unemployment to serial correlation in these exogenous variables. In this way, equilibrium models have tended to understate the role of labor market lags in accounting for dynamic features of unemployment.

---

[5]It rules out the possibility that unemployment may be nonstationary or I(1) and that a cointegrating vector exists between unemployment and other I(1) variables.

As we previously suggested, it is important to recognize that these two alternatives—long-run equilibrium and persistence—are not mutually exclusive; European labor markets may have undergone structural worsening *and* exhibit prolonged persistence. Indeed, one of the more important findings in the present study is that of differing degrees of persistence versus structural change among the countries under review. France is at one end of the scale with relatively short persistence, while Germany is estimated to have considerable persistence, being possibly twice as persistent in the face of shocks. The main point is that it is difficult to identify these two developments—structural change and changes to persistence—unless the model used postulates that both are occurring.

The degree to which sluggish labor market behavior is due to labor market lags as distinct from changes in structural variables is a matter of serious policy concern. Different policies may be required to alter the equilibrium levels of unemployment models (such as the duration and size of social security benefits and union density), than are needed to reduce the dependence of wages, employment, and the labor force on their past values. Policies directed toward altering the long-run equilibrium level of employment in an economy where a high degree of unemployment persistence is actually the problem risk at best being ineffective in reducing high unemployment. That said, there are examples where each approach points to similar factors; the degree of centralization in wage bargaining, for example, probably affects both.

As emphasized already, there has recently been growing awareness of the importance of persistence, and the possibility that it may be a major part of the explanation of rising unemployment in Europe. What, then, does the present study provide that the existing literature does not? The main answer is that the present research analyzes the *dynamics* in each of the labor markets while providing a statistically acceptable explanation of their *long-run* behavior using cointegration analysis. This marks it out from other studies. Alogoskoufis and Manning (1988) take the long-run equilibrium rate to be exogenous in their model. The thoughtful statistical analysis of the sources of persistence by Nickell (1995) concentrates on correlating measures of labor market inertia, including employment sluggishness and change effects of unemployment in wage inflation, with intercountry measures of labor market tenure, severance conditions, and indices of union and employer coordination. His measures of persistence in employment and wage setting (the dependent variables in his regressions) are, however, those previously reported in Layard, Nickell, and Jackman (1991). It is not evident that these earlier estimates are based on acceptable econometric estimates of long-run behavior, because they combine stationary and nonstationary variables. The long-run part of the relevant equations does not cointegrate (that is, the implied equilibrium relationships may not have stationary errors), and hence the estimated short-run dynamics of the models may well be misleading.

As well as providing an econometric explanation of transitional and long-run unemployment dynamics, the study also derives summary statistics of the dynamic unemployment responses to temporary and permanent shocks. These statistics draw attention to the movement of unemployment through time, which depends not only on the constellation of lags in labor market behavior, but also on the interaction between this constellation of lags and the dynamic structure of the shocks to which the labor market is subject. These shocks—such as oil price changes, movements in the exchange rate and interest rates, changes in taxes, and so on—have both temporary and permanent components. The existing literature on persistence and hysteresis has, however, focused almost exclusively on temporary shocks.

The present study attempts to right the balance by considering not only the persistent unemployment effects of temporary shocks, but also the delayed unemployment effects of permanent shocks. We will call the former phenomenon "unemployment persistence" and the latter "imperfect unemployment responsiveness." We will derive measures of these phenomena in the countries under consideration.

Behavioral Lags and Unemployment Dynamics

Earlier, we criticized simple autoregressions of unemployment as ways of estimating persistence. Suppose, for example, that unemployment can be characterized by the first-order autoregressive AR(1) model,

$$U_t = \rho \, U_{t-1} + \epsilon_t, \tag{1}$$

where ρ is the measure of persistence. This usually shows values insignificantly different from unity for the five countries under consideration. Table 1 shows typical results.

Table 1. *AR(1) Models of Unemployment*

	ρ	DF	Sample[1]
France	1.00	2.00	1972Q4–1993Q4
Germany, west	0.98	−2.24	1970Q1–1994Q2
Italy	0.97	−1.30	1970Q1–1994Q2
United Kingdom	0.98	−1.50	1960Q1–1994Q3
Spain	1.00	0.36	1970Q1–1994Q1

[1]Equations run with constants, where DF is the Dickey-Fuller test of the hypothesis that $(\rho-1)$ is zero. (The DF is −2.89 at the 95 percent level.)

Such tests are highly fallible of course, and we do not rely on them here.[6] Moreover, autoregressions are themselves not particularly helpful in understanding the causes of high unemployment. A finding of persistence in a simple autoregression is of little help in formulating policy, because the model would not identify the reasons underlying that persistence. Thus, a behavioral dynamic model is necessary, and the basic form of the one used in the country studies in this project is described below.

It is a commonplace of empirical research that employment, wage determination, and labor force participation include significant lagged effects.[7] We argue that such lags—and particularly the interactions among them and with shocks containing temporary and permanent components—play a key role in determining persistent movements of European unemployment rates in the aftermath of severe labor market shocks, such as the oil-price shocks of the mid- and late 1970s.

This feature—which arises from our multiequation approach—mirrors the insight from early business cycle models that emphasized dynamic interactions, such as multiplier-accelerator mechanisms, in accounting for macroeconomic cycles. The interactions among lags may be analyzed in terms of the model we use, which takes the following general form:

$$\beta_0 Y_t = \beta_1 Y_{t-1} + \ldots + \beta_n Y_{t-n} + \Gamma_1 X_t + \ldots + \Gamma_m X_{t-m} + \eta_t, \qquad (2)$$

where Y is a vector of labor market variables—employment, the real wage, and the labor force. X is a vector of exogenous variables, such as labor market policy variables, the real oil price, and the real interest rate; η_t is a vector of white-noise error terms. This model allows for within-equation and between-equation dynamics. The classic distinction by Frisch of "impulse" and "propagation" mechanisms in producing economic fluctuations plays the same role in this model. The dynamics inherent in equation (2) determine the propagation mechanisms of the labor market, which parallel the same concept in business cycle models. This chapter focuses on the reasons for, and the importance of, these propagation mechanisms.

We describe next a portfolio of the important behavioral lags that, we argue, have played a significant role in determining unemployment dynamics, and these lags will be the centerpiece of the empirical work that

---

[6]Apart from the reasons advanced earlier, the tests themselves are problematic. Such tests based on Dickey-Fuller tests have been widely used in tests for unit roots in aggregate output. Apart from other problems, they may not be appropriate when the series is affected by a structural break.

[7]The potential list of contributors would be extensive. But studies relevant to what is reported here are Sargent (1978), Taylor (1980), Hall and Henry (1988), Lindbeck and Snower (1987a), Alogoskoufis and Manning (1988), Bean and Layard (1987), and Layard, Nickell, and Jackman (1991).

follows. For convenience, lags are grouped under five headings, the names of which refer to their common microeconomic causes. They are not of course intended to be a comprehensive description of these causes—lagged variables may occur in equations for reasons other than the ones we describe, but the headings are proposed merely as a labeling device.

Employment Adjustment Effect

The employment adjustment effect is represented by the lagged employment terms in the employment equation. This is the familiar lagged response in employment, often caused by the presence of adjustment costs on labor inputs. The underlying idea is straightforward: when firms face costs of adjusting their employment—such as hiring, training, and firing costs—their current employment will depend on their past levels of employment. The literature on optimal intertemporal employment plans in the presence of quadratic adjustment costs on employment is extensive. Sargent (1978) provides an extension to the case where firms are assumed to have rational expectations. Berndt and Fuss (1986) survey recent theory and applications of temporary equilibrium models in which factor demand equations for quasi-fixed factors such as employment are subject to adjustment costs. The traditional literature in this area focused exclusively on continuous and infinitely divisible adjustment costs, whereby the costs approached zero as the size of the employment adjustment fell. More recent literature, however, also considers "lumpy" adjustment costs that are of finite size for each worker (for example, Lindbeck and Snower (1988)). The assumption of lumpy adjustment costs introduces discontinuities into firms' employment decisions: there is now a range of productivities over which it is in the firms' best interests to remain inactive (refraining from both hiring and firing), whereas hiring and firing occur at productivities lying above and beneath this range, respectively. However, with the assumption of either divisible or lumpy adjustment costs, current employment depends on past employment.[8]

---

[8]Under quadratic adjustment costs, current employment is a linear function of lagged employment. Under other forms of divisible adjustment costs, the relation is generally non-linear, and, in this case, the linear employment equations in the empirical models below may be interpreted as linear approximations of such nonlinear functions. Under lumpy adjustment costs, current employment depends on past employment only in the range of inaction; but when the employment decisions of heterogeneous firms are aggregated under stochastic conditions, a standard employment equation—in which current employment again depends on lagged employment—can be derived. There are also good reasons for believing that adjustment costs are asymmetric and that hiring new employees in a cyclical upturn can be more costly than reducing the workforce as output falls. The employment-output relationship may thus be nonlinear for this reason also.

Insider Membership Effect

The insider membership effect can be proxied by lagged employment terms in the wage setting equation. The underlying hypothesis is that past employment determines the size of the current incumbent workforce (that is, the current stock of "insiders"), which, in turn, affects the insiders' objectives in wage bargaining. This effect may be positive or negative, depending on the relative strength of two countervailing effects: (1) for any given distribution of labor demand shocks, the smaller the insider workforce of a firm, the greater the insiders' job security at any given real wage, and consequently the higher the negotiated wage (see, for example, Blanchard and Summers (1986) and Lindbeck and Snower (1987a)); (2) the smaller the insider workforce, the smaller the bargaining power of the insiders (because, for example, the weaker the threats that the insiders make to the firms in case of bargaining disagreement), and therefore the lower the negotiated wage (see, for example, Lindbeck and Snower (1987b)). If the size of the current insider workforce depends on past employment, the negotiated wage will depend on past employment as well.

Wage Staggering Effect

This effect is represented by lagged wage terms in the wage setting equation. It has been recognized from at least the time of Taylor's (1980) seminal article that current wages may depend on lagged wages, through the effects of overlapping wage contracts, where one set of bargainers makes a wage claim in the light of past and expected future settlements by comparator wage bargainers. In practice, these effects may reflect concerns with the maintenance of wage differentials. To take one of many examples, Wadhwani (1985) explores this hypothesis at length in estimated aggregate wage equations for the United Kingdom. (See also Foster and Henry (1984), who estimate sectoral wage equations—again for the United Kingdom—where they identify intersectoral wage effects as evidence of such overlapping wage contracts.[9]) Future expected real wage effects are not explicitly included in these specifications, although, on the assumption of the rational expectations hypothesis (REH), where real wages can be characterized by an autoregressive process, according to the substitution

---

[9]In our applications, we allow for the possibility that current real wages may depend on past real wages, reflecting this wage comparison phenomenon. Since the models cover the medium run, in which price misperceptions play no significant role, nominal wage staggering effects translate directly into real wage staggering effects.

method of estimating an REH model, lagged real wages include effects of expected future real wages.

Long-Term Unemployment Effect

The long-term unemployment effect is represented by lagged unemployment terms in the wage equation. There has been considerable discussion of the weakening of the unemployment effect on wage outcomes as the duration of unemployment increases. This diminished effect occurs for several reasons: the skills of the unemployed deteriorate as their unemployment lengthens, making them less attractive to employers; the motivation to search for employment may also wane the longer the unemployment spell; and, finally, the employer may prefer to hire an individual who has been unemployed for only a short period.

A number of empirical studies have found support for the existence of weakening effects on wage settlements as unemployment duration increases. Hall and Henry (1987) and Layard, Nickell, and Jackman (1991) show there is a significant decrease in the bargaining power of the long-term unemployed in the United Kingdom.

Labor Force Adjustment Effect

This effect is represented by the lagged labor force terms in the labor force equation. These terms can be explained by the costs of entering and exiting the labor force. The costs of entering include the costs of registering as unemployed, of engaging in job search activities, and—perhaps most important—of changing one's lifestyle to adopt the characteristics necessary to become employable (for example, reliability, punctuality, and initiative) as well as acquiring the basic skills needed in the workplace. These costs—whether infinitely divisible or lumpy—make people's current labor force participation decisions depend on their past decisions in much the same way that the costs of employment adjustment make firms' current employment decisions depend on past employment.

Interaction Among the Lagged Effects

An obvious but neglected point is that the lags above can operate much more powerfully in conjunction with one another than in isolation. Treating each of the lags described above *alone* as the principal source of unemployment persistence is, in our judgment, quite wrong. An example of this is provided in the otherwise excellent survey by Bean (1994), which, after describing persistence mechanism in seriatim, concludes that each alone does not appear to be large enough to account for Europe's unemployment. While this inference appears to be valid, it is important to add the qualification that *together* these mechanisms may indeed be an important reason why unemployment is so high. Moreover, the approach followed in this book should be distinguished from those in many previous studies of unemployment persistence, which are highly aggregative;[10] they generally take the form of autoregressions of the aggregate unemployment rate alone, rather than decomposing the constituent lags into the lagged effects on employment, wage determination, and labor force participation. Consequently, as previously emphasized, these studies can do little more than provide a summary description of sluggish unemployment adjustment; they cannot shed light on the economic causes of such sluggish adjustment.

This has serious consequences for policy analysis. It is impossible to derive valid policy conclusions from the mere fact that the unemployment rate displays a high degree of serial correlation. Policies must be designed from an empirical assessment of the individual dynamic effects that interact to produce the observed serial correlation in unemployment. In the latter case, different employment policy instruments may be identified that give the policymaker scope to influence different lagged effects. For example, changes in job security legislation may be expected to affect the degree to which current employment depends on past employment, while tax breaks for hiring the long-term unemployed will influence the degree to which current wages depend on past unemployment.

For this reason, it is important to identify the behavioral lags in labor market activity and analyze how the various lags interact with one another and with the dynamic structure of labor market shocks in generating the time path for unemployment. Charts 2 and 3 illustrate lagged interactions between employment and wage setting. The employment equation, representing the aggregate level of employment at any given real wage, is pictured as the downward-sloping labor demand curve *LD* in Chart 2. The wage setting equation, representing the negotiated wage at any given level of employment, is given by the upward-sloping *WS* curve. Finally, the labor force participation equation, representing the aggregate labor force at any given real wage, is given by the *LF* curve. The intersection of the labor demand curve *(LD)* and the wage setting curve *(WS)* yields the equilibrium

---

[10]For example, Alogoskoufis and Manning (1988), Blanchard and Summers (1986), and Phelps (1994).

Chart 2. *Labor Market Equilibrium*

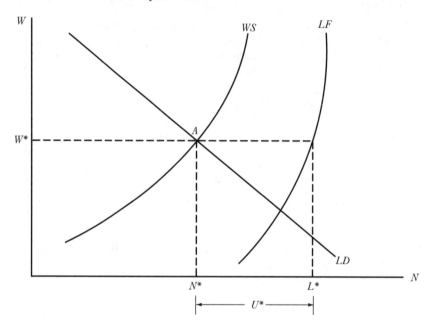

Chart 3. *Labor Market Response to Adverse Shocks*

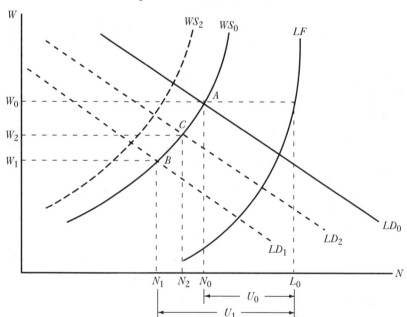

real wage *(w*)* and the equilibrium level of employment *(N*)*. The size of the labor force at the equilibrium real wage is the equilibrium labor force *(L*)*. The difference between the equilibrium labor force *(L*)* and the equilibrium level of employment *(N*)* is the equilibrium level of unemployment *(U*)*.

In this context, lags in employment adjustment owing to hiring and firing costs make the position of the labor demand curve *(LD)* depend on last period's level of employment. Similarly, the labor force may be subject to adjustment lags that make the position of the labor force participation curve *(LF)* depend on last period's labor force. Furthermore, there can be wage staggering, insider membership, and long-term unemployment effects that, in turn, make the wage setting curve depend on last period's wage, employment, and unemployment, respectively.

Suppose that the labor market is initially (in period 0) at its long-run stationary state, denoted by point A in Chart 3, and then (in period 1) a temporary, adverse labor demand shock occurs, shifting the labor demand curve downward from LD_0 to LD_1 for one period. Thus, employment declines from N_0 to N_1. In the following period (period 2), when the adverse shock has disappeared, the labor demand does not shift all the way back to LD_0 again; rather, it shifts part of the way back, say, to LD_2, on account of lagged employment adjustment (the employment adjustment effect). The resulting equilibrium level of employment in period 2 is N_2, and the process of adjustment continues in subsequent periods. This illustrates how the employment adjustment effect causes a temporary labor demand shock to have persistent effects on employment.

But that is not all. The adverse labor demand shock raises the level of unemployment from U_0 to U_1 in period 1. This may be expected to raise the unemployment durations of those without jobs. If effort on job search declines as the average unemployment duration rises (the "long-term unemployment" effect), then the rise in unemployment will raise the wage setting curve in period 2, for now the unemployed have become less effective in competing for jobs, and thus a higher wage is negotiated at any given level of employment. The rise in the wage setting curve, say, from WS_0 to WS_2 in Chart 3, puts further downward pressure on employment. Thus, employment will rise by less than the distance from N_1 to N_2 in Chart 3, and may even fall. This shows how the long-term unemployment effect reinforces the employment adjustment effect in prolonging the effects of a temporary shock.

Furthermore, the temporary labor demand shock reduces the real wage from w_0 in period 0 to w_1 in period 1. If current wage setting depends on lagged wages (the "wage staggering effect"), the wage setting function in period 2 will be lower than it would otherwise have been. Consequently, the wage setting function will rise by less than the previously described shift from WS_0 to WS_2. In this way, the wage staggering effect can be seen to dampen the influence of the employment adjustment effect, reducing the degree to which the effects of a temporary shock persist.

The influence of the insider membership effect in this context obviously depends on the relative strengths of its components. If the job security component dominates the bargaining component, then the fall in employment from N_0 to N_1 will push the wage setting function upward (because the reduced number of insiders now have greater job security than previously and are thus in a position to make more ambitious wage claims). In this case, the insider membership effect reinforces the employment adjustment effect, augmenting the persistent effects of the temporary shock. Conversely, if the bargaining component dominates the job security component, then the fall in employment in response to the adverse shock will push the wage setting function downward (since the reduction in the size of the insider workforce reduces the insiders' bargaining power), and then the insider membership effect dampens the employment adjustment effect.

The illustration above was conducted entirely in response to a temporary shock. A permanent shock could elicit a quite different set of dynamic responses. There is no one-to-one relationship between the dynamic responses of unemployment to temporary and to permanent shocks. Economies in which temporary shocks have comparatively persistent effects on unemployment are not necessarily also the economies in which the full unemployment effects of permanent shocks are comparatively slow to manifest themselves. In short, inertia in the aftermath of temporary shocks does not necessarily imply inertia in the aftermath of permanent ones (see Karanassou and Snower (1993) and Snower and Karanassou (1995)).

This example illustrates our view that a fruitful way to understand the movement of unemployment in different European countries is by estimating the lags in employment, wage setting, and labor force participation equations, investigating how these lags interact with one another, and analyzing the implications of these interactions in the presence of shocks with both temporary and permanent components.

Empirical Model

This section specifies the empirical model that underlies the studies reported in the companion country studies, providing the basis for measures of unemployment persistence and responsiveness presented next.

As already anticipated, the model used is consciously synthetic, building on much previous work on the labor market. The framework is a one-sector model of the labor market with emphasis on dynamics. It comprises the following equations.[11]

Employment Equation

This employment equation is the empirical representation of the aggregate short-run labor demand curve. In general, it can be expressed as

$$A_0(L)n_t = A_1(L)Y_{1t} + A_2(L)X_{1t} + \epsilon_{1t}, \tag{3}$$

where n_t is total employment, Y_1 is other endogenous variables (including the real product wage), X_1 is a vector of exogenous variables, and ϵ_1 is a white-noise error term. $A_i(L)$ ($i = 0, 1, 2$) is a polynomial in the lag operator L. The lagged employment terms in this equation are the "employment adjustment effect." The underlying model is based on familiar dynamic optimizing models of the firm, where the firm faces adjustment costs on labor. Assuming quadratic adjustment costs coupled with assumptions that employment comprises several types (such as insiders and entrants) with differing cost functions, second-order lagged equations in employment result (see Sargent (1978), and Nickell (1978) for further discussion). With imperfect competition, the first-order profit-maximizing conditions may, under specific circumstances, lead to an employment equation conditioned on aggregate demand, among other things, and hence aggregate demand would then be a natural variable to include in the Y vector in equation (3).[12] In the light of the endogeneity of real demand, an instrumental variable (IV) estimation would be needed. Alternatively, aggregate demand may be modeled using other exogenous variables, such as measures of aggregate policy and the external environment. (See Henry and Wren-Lewis (1983) for an early example. See also Bean (1994).)

Wage Setting Equation

This equation represents the real wage that emerges from bargaining between employers and employees. It can be written in general as

$$B_0(L)w_t = B_1(L)X_{2t} + B_2(L)Y_{2t} + \epsilon_{2t}, \tag{4}$$

---

[11]All variables that follow, except the unemployment rate, are in logs.
[12]See, for example, Lindbeck and Snower (1994).

where w is the real consumption wage; Y_2 represents other endogenous variables, including unemployment and employment; X_{2t} is a vector of exogenous variables; and ϵ_{2t} is the error term. Again, this model encompasses models that have been extensively used in empirical work. Specifically, X_2 could include tax and price wedge terms, and other structural factors, such as union membership or mismatch. The employment terms in the equation are associated with the insider membership effect, since the size of the firms' insider workforce affects the insiders' objectives in the wage setting process. The set of lagged real wage terms can reflect effects of overlapping wage contracts and produces the wage staggering effect, because staggered wage setting makes current real wages depend on their past values. Finally, current unemployment can capture the effect of an excess supply of labor on bargains, and lagged unemployment terms in the equation can proxy long-term unemployment effects, because the long-term unemployed tend to search less intensively for jobs and thus have less influence on the wage setting process than the short-term unemployed.

Labor Force Participation Equation

This equation describes the size of the labor force and takes the following form:

$$\Gamma_0(L)l_t = \Gamma_1(L)X_{3t} + \Gamma_2(L)Y_{3t} + \epsilon_{3t}, \tag{5}$$

where l_t is the size of the labor force, and X_3 represents exogenous variables such as the working population, and Y_3 represents endogenous variables including unemployment and the real wage. The lagged labor force terms in the equation may be associated with the "labor force adjustment effect," since costs of entry to and exit from the labor force often make the current labor force depend on its past magnitudes. Discouraged-worker effects are proxied by unemployment. Thus, if unemployment is high, fewer workers are expected to enter the workplace because the probability of finding a job is low.

Definition of Unemployment

While unemployment is the difference between the labor force and employment, to preserve the linearity of our system, we take the following approximation:

$$u_t = l_t - n_t. \tag{6}$$

The lags identified above are not the only ones that may be significant in labor demand, wage setting, and labor force participation decisions, but they occupy a particularly prominent place in the empirical and theoretical labor market literature, which is one reason they are emphasized here.

Estimation Methods and Overall Model Behavior

Estimating the Labor Market Model

The models described in this study are joint models of employment, wages, and labor force determination. A number of issues need to be addressed, including the following:

- At least some of the labor market variables are nonstationary (namely, I(1), needing to be differenced once to render them stationary). To allow for this, equilibrium relationships between the nonstationary variables need to be sought so that, in combination, the variables have a stationary error (the combination of the variables are then cointegrating vectors). Using these results, the dynamic relationship between all the relevant variables—whether stationary or nonstationary—can be estimated in a statistically consistent way.
- The labor market models entail the solution of simultaneous equations, with employment depending on current values of the real wage, for example. To avoid possibly biased estimates of the coefficients in the model, these simultaneous effects need to be explicitly allowed for. There are a large number of possible ways of dealing with this, depending on the precise forms of model involved, and some of these are illustrated in the country papers.

Some of the technical issues arising in estimating models of this sort are discussed more fully in the appendix.

Indices of Unemployment Persistence and Imperfect Responsiveness

The literature on unemployment persistence and hysteresis[13] has concentrated almost exclusively on temporary shocks. In practice, however, labor market shocks have both temporary and permanent components. For

---

[13]See, for example, Blanchard and Summers (1986) and Lindbeck and Snower (1987a).

example, whereas some exchange rate fluctuations and movements in the prices of raw materials are temporary, some changes in productivity, taxes, and real interest rates are long lasting. Supply-side changes such as deregulation, the decline of union power, and the easing of job security legislation are further examples of longer-term shocks.

The study provides a methodology for exploring these issues. It recognizes two dimensions of the unemployment problem: (1) the persistent effects of temporary labor market shocks, or unemployment persistence, and (2) the delayed effects of permanent shocks, or imperfect unemployment responsiveness.

While it is possible to get some idea of the effects of lags in particular equations, interest is primarily in the dynamic behavior of the entire model. It is standard to use dynamic simulations of temporary and permanent shocks to estimate how long it takes for unemployment to reach the neighborhood of equilibrium (for example, the half-life of a delay is often used, being the time taken to get halfway to equilibrium).

The simulations reported are fully dynamic ones. These first solve the complete model forward in time, treating the exogenous variables as fixed at their 1994Q2 values. This gives a base solution. Next, a further simulation applies a shock of a 0.01005 reduction in the constant term of the employment equation, which is equivalent to a 1 percent reduction in the level of employment, and recomputes the solution. This simulation can be thought of as an exogenous productivity shock to the system. The difference in the two solutions then gives the full model dynamic response to the exogenous shock. We report two sets of summary indices concerning unemployment persistence and imperfect unemployment responsiveness. The first indicates how long the model's predicted unemployment rate takes to get halfway back to equilibrium after it has been disturbed by a temporary shock (that is, one that lasts for only one quarter) or a permanent one. The second set is the sum of the deviations of the predicted unemployment rate from its long-run equilibrium value normalized by the size of the shock, whereas the first set focuses on how long the behavioral lags keep unemployment from its stationary state. The second set is a proxy for the resulting waste of labor resources over time.

Overview of Country Results

Country results are described at length in Chapters 2–6. Here, we draw together the key results, highlight the differences that have been found between the countries, and discuss their policy implications.

There is a growing awareness of the possible importance of employment and unemployment dynamics as key features of OECD unemployment. It is increasingly recognized that an explanation of the response of employment and unemployment to shocks is crucial to the understanding of high levels of unemployment in Europe. In comparisons with the United States, European countries show considerable persistence (see Table 2), and there are significant differences in the pattern of persistence among European countries themselves.

Why is there such an apparent profound difference between the United States and Europe on the one hand, and what is the explanation of inter-European differences on the other? Before turning to the results of our empirical work, we note that the literature on European labor market inflexibility tends to have concentrated on a number of distinct themes: hiring/firing regulations and other costs of adjusting employment, wage rigidities, and the structure of bargaining (specifically with respect to its degree of centralization). These phenomena affect unemployment dynamics in that they are responsible for generating lags in labor market behavior.

The evidence that hiring/firing regulations interfere with the functioning of most European labor markets is relatively unambiguous. About 50 percent of employers in most EU countries claim that these costs constitute a serious impediment to increasing employment (see Table 3 and Pujol (1995) for further discussion). Interestingly, the United Kingdom appears to be an exception in this sample.

The findings from existing empirical studies analyzing the influence of wage rigidities have been more contentious. Layard, Nickell, and Jackman (1991) adopt a fairly simple measure of real wage rigidity in terms of the effects of unemployment on the real wage and the markup of prices over wages. The aggregative nature of this study and others makes it difficult to assess what the sources of this rigidity may be—in terms of lagged responses of labor market decisions to external shocks—and how these sources interact with one another. Other studies are somewhat more precise. Alogoskoufis and Manning (1988), for example, attempt to identify the importance of insider effects in wage setting, with the recently employed changing the unemployment effect on real wages. They find that this insider effect is not important. Nickell (1995), on the other hand, relates cross-sectional estimates of the effect of wages on the change in the unemployment rate (as an effect from the change in unemployment on wages is often taken as a measure of wage inertia) to a number of indices of insider power and bargaining coordination. He finds, in contrast, that insider power is important in accounting for real wage persistence.

As noted previously, none of these studies systematically analyzes the time-series evidence, such as presented here. What the studies cited so far confirm, however, is that variations in persistence are substantial between

Table 2. *Persistence Measures of Selected European Countries and the United States*
(Mean lag in years)

Country		Model			
		Snower and Karanassou[1] (1993)	Nickell (1995)	Anderton and Soteri (1995)	Alogoskoufis and Manning (1988)
United States	Unemployment	3.0	n.a.	n.a.	2.0
	Employment (manufacturing)	n.a.	n.a.	n.a.	n.a.
France	Employment	n.a.	1.6	n.a.	n.a.
	Unemployment	n.a.	3.8	n.a.	pure hysteresis
Italy	Employment	n.a.	5.2	n.a.	n.a.
	Unemployment	n.a.	n.a.	n.a.	20.0
Germany	Unemployment	25.0	n.a.	n.a.	n.a.
	Employment (manufacturing)	n.a.	n.a.	n.a.	n.a.
Germany, west	Employment	n.a.	7.0	n.a.	n.a.
	Unemployment	n.a.	n.a.	n.a.	17.0
United Kingdom	Unemployment	13.0	n.a.	n.a.	11.0
	Employment	n.a.	3.3	6.7	n.a.

[1] These are ϵ neighborhood calculations, not mean lags. They are thus higher than the mean lag, which gives the time taken to go halfway to equilibrium.

Table 3. *Firms Citing Hiring/Firing Procedures as a Factor for Not Hiring*
(In percent)

Country	Number of Firms
Belgium	46
France	53
Germany	44
Greece	51
Ireland	45
Italy	62
Netherlands	58
Portugal	42
Spain	63
United Kingdom	27

Source: Pujol (1995).

Europe and the United States. For example, Nickell (1995) estimates a mean lag of just over three years in unemployment following a shock for the United States, whereas it is between seven and nine years for the United Kingdom (p. 31). See also Karanassou and Snower (1993).

Table 2 places these results in a wider context, presenting summary statistics on persistence measures in selected European countries and in the United States. The table illustrates the familiar result that persistence in unemployment is estimated to be much lower in the United States than in European countries. Although the above calculations are based on different models, estimation methods, and sample sizes, each is nonetheless consistent with this general pattern.[14] In turn, employment is estimated to be more responsive in the United States, a finding that appears to be an important determinant of low unemployment persistence there. In similar fashion, there is some evidence that the persistence of German unemployment may be higher than in other European countries.

Summary of Findings on Labor Market Dynamics

For the five countries studied, the findings suggest that labor market lags play an important role in determining how unemployment responds to labor market shocks. This conclusion is supported by the econometric results for single equations, which have significant lagged effects, implying

---

[14]The Alogoskoufis and Manning results are probably overestimates, for reasons described earlier.

Table 4. *Unemployment: Indices of Persistence*

	Mean Lag (in years)	Sum of Absolute Deviations
France	3.0	15
Germany	6.5	26
Italy	5.0	24
United Kingdom	5.0	32
Spain (A)	8.0	33
(B)	3.0	10

Note: The mean lag is the familiar half-life of the response to the shock. The sum of the absolute changes of unemployment from the base following the shock is given as an alternative. For Spain, (A) refers to the basic model, (B) to the policy model. (See Chapter 6 for the definitions of these two scenarios.)

slow responses in employment, wages, and the labor force following a shock when each of these variables is considered separately. Single-equation information, of course, is only a rough guide to the dynamics of the whole model, because it does not include interequation dynamics. Only full model simulations account for all the dynamic feedbacks in the model, and these are reported next.

Model simulations of a temporary labor demand shock in France show that unemployment takes approximately three years to recover halfway to equilibrium.[15] For Germany, this response may take as long as six and a half years. Equilibrium unemployment may be higher in France, however. In Italy and the United Kingdom, the response appears to be about the same at five years. (See Chapters 2–6 and Table 4.)

These results indicate that considerable dispersion exists in the overall dynamic behavior of these selected European economies. France appears to respond quickly to shocks, but Germany appears to be at the other end of the scale, with Italy and the United Kingdom somewhere in between. Although other researchers have drawn attention to the differences between European and U.S. persistence, the empirical results given here show that intra-European differences are also profound.

The empirical results for German employment, wage, and unemployment equations are consistent with the existence of relatively strong persistence mechanisms there; that is, the tests reveal significant employment persistence, wage staggering, and labor force adjustment effects. More

---

[15]In what follows, half-lives are taken to be the time taken to get halfway to full equilibrium; in the case of a temporary shock, this means halfway to the base solution.

generally, these findings appear consistent with institutional features of the German labor market, namely, its centralized bargaining system and strong employment protection (which is probably coupled with the presence of extensive risk sharing by employers, thus ensuring that employees are shielded from adverse temporary real shocks).

The five countries' responses to permanent shocks reveal important differences between Italy and the United Kingdom. (See Chart 4 and Table 5.) In both countries, the equilibrium level of unemployment rises, but it rises much more in the United Kingdom than in Italy. For a protracted interval (of more than a decade), the increase in unemployment in Italy exceeds its long-run effect. Gradually, the level of unemployment adjusts downward, largely because of falling participation rates, but these processes take a long time to work through. For the United Kingdom, although increases in unemployment appear more regular, the timescale of the change is significant. Thus, it takes about five years to get halfway to the full equilibrium effect. The pattern of unemployment in France following the shock is also one of overshooting, so that the worsening of short-run unemployment exceeds that of long-run unemployment (as with Italy). The process is much quicker in France, also because the persistence of unemployment appears short lived. Germany shows a most singular oscillating response to the productivity shock, with unemployment over- rather than undershooting its long-run value. The time taken to get to the new equilibrium is also very long, with the labor market approaching equilibrium in a cycling manner, with cycles each lasting over a decade.

Finally, in Spain, the response to a permanent shock is estimated to take a very long time in the "basic" model, but appears much shorter in the "policy" model. This point is discussed further in the next section.

Are Labor Market Lags Affected by Policy?

The research described in the country studies shows that important differences may have emerged between European countries during the 1980s as a result of labor reforms introduced in certain countries. The United Kingdom reformed its industrial relations procedures in the 1980s to improve both wage bargaining and the flexibility of hiring and firing regulations. In Italy, far-reaching reforms were initiated in the mid-1980s and again at the beginning of the 1990s, both times to reform wage bargaining procedures and, in the 1990s, hiring and firing regulations. Spain has experienced profound changes in its labor market structure. After the demise of the Franco regime in 1975, labor relations and social protection changed

Chart 4. *European Union: Imperfect Responsiveness*

—— *DU*   ······ *DL*

DU = (unemployment rate with the permanent shock) – (unemployment rate without the shock)

DL = (long-run unemployment rate with the shock) – (long-run unemployment rate without the shock)

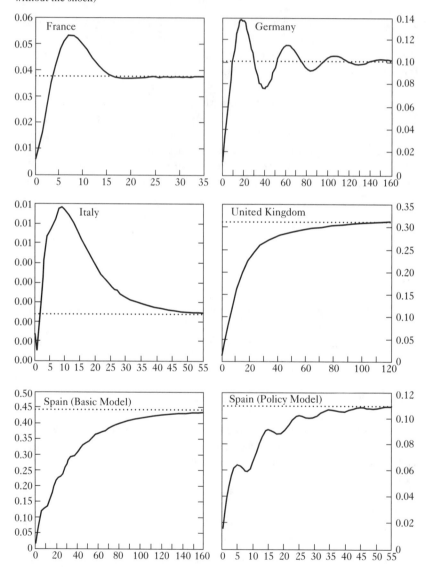

Table 5. *Unemployment: Indices of Imperfect Responsiveness*

Country	Index
France	3.50
Germany	−17.26
Italy	176
United Kingdom	−578
Spain (Basic)	−1085
Spain (Policy)	−83.22

significantly, although restrictions on working conditions and labor mobility continued. The power of unions increased dramatically and entailed substantial severance costs. The country has an active minimum wage policy, although the real value of wages did not grow in the 1980s at rates achieved in the 1970s. In the last couple of years, Spain has undertaken reforms to reduce unemployment compensation and increase labor mobility, in part by reducing firing costs. Last, and in contrast to the previous examples, France and Germany have attempted relatively little deep-seated reform of the labor market.

Although any results must be regarded as tentative, some quantitative assessment of the effects of these reforms is possible. According to our econometric results, there appears to have been little change in the underlying behavior of employment, wage setting, or labor force participation in France and Germany. In Italy, Spain, and the United Kingdom, however, reforms implemented over the last decade or so appear to have discernable, quantitative effects on certain aspects of labor market behavior.

The case of Italy provides two examples of policies designed to reform the labor market: policies that were undertaken in 1984 and those undertaken in 1991. According to results reported in the study on Spain (Chapter 6), the policy initiatives in 1984 failed (in the sense that they appear not to have affected underlying behavior), whereas those of 1991 appear thus far to have succeeded. Although tentative, these latter results suggest that

- the employment adjustment effect has declined;
- the responsiveness of employment to output variations has fallen, and that with respect to wages has increased;
- the wage staggering effect has fallen (although it is too early to judge whether this is a significant change); and
- the labor force is significantly less prone to discouraged-worker effects.

These changes all point to more flexibility in the labor market. The changes in the effect of lagged employment and output on current employment are consistent with a decrease in labor hoarding as well as with the hypothesis that employment adjustment costs, both actual and implicit, have fallen.[16] Increases in the elasticity of employment with respect to real wage changes also point to increasing flexibility in the labor market. In turn, the decline in the discouraged-worker effect and the decrease in lagged employment effects in the labor force equation indicate possible increases in the flexibility of labor supply. Finally, wage bargaining patterns may have changed, as the evidence suggests that wage staggering effects have decreased.

The United Kingdom also shows that the underlying patterns of behavior in the labor market seem to have changed under the impetus of policy initiatives taken during the 1980s. These were mainly in the sphere of reform of industrial relations, which raised the costs of strikes, eased hiring and firing costs, and promoted the decentralization of wage bargaining (see Henry and Karanassou (Chapter 5) for details). These reforms might be expected to affect both employment flexibility and the responsiveness of wages.

Unlike in Italy, labor market reforms in the United Kingdom have been in place long enough to enable direct tests of structural change in employment and wage equations to be made. The results of these tests show that the principal effects of the reforms have been on employment. This is consistent with there being some easing of hiring and firing constraints on firms. Ascertaining the scale of this improvement is not straightforward, however. The evidence from the employment demand equation is that the overall effect, although not statistically significant on conventional tests, may nonetheless be quantitatively important. This result may be affected by the level of aggregation used, however, and effects at the manufacturing level, for example—where adjustment costs are probably significantly larger than elsewhere—could be larger.

Tests were also conducted of possible effects of the reforms on wage bargaining. These concentrated on whether there is evidence of a change in the wage-unemployment relationship. Whereas in a more flexible labor market, the unemployment effect might be expected to increase, little evidence of a discernable change in the effect of unemployment on real wage developments is found. Our tests thus support the interpretation of no change in underlying wage behavior.

---

[16]This needs to be interpreted with care, however, because the other contending explanation—that expected real demand has fallen—has not been formally tested in this work.

France and Spain fall into a different category in that policy is found to have important effects on the equilibrium level of unemployment. In Spain, policy also appears to have had important effects on the dynamic behavior of the labor market. In France, social security spending is found to have an important effect on unemployment through its effect on employment, reducing this below what it would otherwise be. This appears to operate directly on employment, not, as might be expected, through an effect on the real wage. The analysis is further complicated by the finding of an important effect on the aggregate real wage of the minimum wage level. At the same time, persistence in France is among the lowest of the countries reviewed here. Thus, although France appears to be suffering from policies that lead to a high equilibrium level of unemployment, it appears to respond quickly to shocks.

Spain is not only the country with the highest rate of unemployment in the countries investigated but its labor market is the most complex. The judgment on developments in Spain (see Chapter 6) is that over the 1980s a number of changes in the labor market raised the equilibrium rate of unemployment and probably decreased its (substantial) persistence. It seems that the increases to disability pensions, higher levels of unemployment benefits, and the increased incidence of industrial disputes tended to lower employment and that the minimum wage tended to raise the aggregate wage. All these factors tend to raise the trend rate of unemployment. Some amelioration in these tendencies is due to the increased share of the salaried workforce on temporary contracts, which appear to reduce the real wage. This reduction is small, however, and affects only a small part of the workforce. Overall, these factors appear to have decreased the persistence of the labor market as well. Nonetheless, it appears a reasonable characterization of developments in the Spanish labor market to interpret the policy changes over the 1980s as both leading to higher equilibrium rates and, through effects on employment and wage adjustment, reducing persistence.

Conclusions

While it is important not to overstate the conclusions drawn from our models, most of the major European economies exhibit a substantial degree of unemployment persistence and imperfect responsiveness. Although preliminary, the empirical results suggest that the degree to which each country is characterized by these features differs, apparently quite significantly. One finding of this study is that there appear to be substantial differences in these countries' dynamic responses to shocks. It is therefore misleading to lump them together as having common dynamics of a single "European" variety. In turn, the analysis suggests some of the key areas of the labor market in which these differences arise. Although in a study such as this it is difficult to quantify the effects that particular institutions and policy characteristics have upon the dynamic behavior of the labor market as a whole, some indications of the role that policy may play can be obtained. In France, persistence seems relatively low, but the minimum wage and social security policy have probably led to high trend rates of unemployment. Over the 1980s, unemployment in Spain has risen, but persistence has declined. In Germany, on the other hand, labor market policy has changed little, and the responsiveness of the general labor market to shocks appears slow despite, for example, the coordination of pay bargaining and the level of training, which might be expected to lead to low persistence.

Italy and the United Kingdom exemplify policy initiatives that can improve the resilience of the economy to shocks. The evidence that this is happening is not clear, however, even in the United Kingdom, where reform has been in train for over a decade. This finding, by itself, suggests that improving the patterns of dynamic responses in labor markets may be a very long process.

Appendix: Issues in Estimating Dynamic Systems

This appendix discusses issues in estimating the models described in this chapter and used in the country studies, which are in the traditional form of structural dynamic models. Repeating equation (2) from p. 11 for convenience, they are of the following general form:

$$\beta_0 Y_t = \beta_1 Y_{t-1} + \ldots + \beta_p Y_{t-p} + \Gamma_1 X_t + \ldots + \Gamma_q X_{t-q} + \eta_t, \qquad (2')$$

where Y_t is an m-dimensional vector of endogenous variables, X_t is a k-dimensional vector of exogenous variables, and η_t is an m-dimensional vector of independently and identically distributed (iid) random disturbances. The model allows for the possible presence of simultaneous effects between the endogenous variables; hence, the matrix β_0 will have restrictions that derive from economic theory (that is, $\beta_0 \neq I$, the unit matrix). To estimate this model, appropriate simultaneous estimators of either a limited-information or a full-information variety are required. (This is discussed further below.)

In estimating the models in the country papers, a sequence of steps is followed:

(1)   The relevant variables are tested for orders of integration, and tests are conducted for the presence of cointegration in the subset of I(1) variables.

(2) Cointegrating vectors are estimated, using either Johansen's maximum likelihood procedure or Pesaran and Shin's (1995a) autoregressive distributed lag (ARDL) approach.

(3) The model is estimated in its I(0) form, as a vector error correction model (VECM).

Step (1) is clearly necessary to ensure that issues of spurious regression and inconsistent estimation are avoided; it is familiar enough not to require extensive justification. The justification behind step (2) involves identifying cointegrating vectors and is more unfamiliar. Step (3) is also a familiar procedure, most often involving the two-step procedure originated by Engle and Granger (1987), where cointegrating residuals are entered into a dynamic equation that, by construction, is composed of I(0) variables. In a single-equation ARDL (1,1) model

$$y_t = \alpha_0 + \alpha_1 + y_{t-1} + \beta_0 x_t + \beta_1 x_{t-1} + \epsilon_t, \tag{1}$$

where y_t and x_t are scalar I(1) variables. In a two-step procedure, estimates of the long-run relation are based on the presence of a cointegrating vector between y_t and x_t. Then, equation (1) may be estimated in its ECM form as

$$y_t = \alpha_0 - (1 - \alpha_1)(y_{t-1} - \theta x_{t-1}) + \beta_0 \Delta x_t + \epsilon_t. \tag{2}$$

The long-run multiplier y_t with respect to x_t,

$$\theta = (\beta_0 + \beta_1)/(1 - \alpha_1),$$

is estimated directly from equation (1) by Pesaran and Shin (1995a), who have shown that by estimating a suitably augmented ARDL, all the short-run parameters (α_0, α_1, β_0, β_1) are $\sqrt{T}$-consistent, while the long-run parameter, θ, is T-consistent. Equation (1) can then be used to produce standard errors of the model's short-run parameters as well as the long-run parameters such that standard inference on both parameters is possible.

Integrability

Dividing by β_0, equation (2′) can be written as

$$Y_t = \Phi_1 Y_{t-1} + \ldots + \Phi_p Y_{t-p} + \Psi_0 X_t + \ldots + \Psi_q X_{t-q} + \mu_t, \tag{3}$$

where $\Phi_i = \beta_0^{-1} \beta_i$, $i = 1, \ldots, p$, $\Psi_j = \beta_0^{-1} \Gamma_j$, $j = 0, \ldots, q$, and $\mu_t = \beta_0^{-1} \eta_t$. At this point, it is important to define the order of integrability of the variables in the model. If they are all I(0) stationary variables, then equation (2′) or, if the model is just identified, equation (3) may be estimated directly, either by using a simultaneous estimator on equation (2′) if the model is overidentified or by using indirect least squares on equation (3) in the just-identified case. If all the identifying restrictions from the reduced form are ignored, the model can be consistently estimated by single-equation least squares, although it has no structural interpretation.

This vector autoregression (VAR) model is then the theoretic model proposed by Sims (1980), for which he recommended the application of "minimal" restrictions in order to identify shocks. Where the variables are nonstationary, they may be rendered stationary by differencing, which is standard practice for estimating both structural models like that in equation (2′) or, in the unrestricted case, VAR models of the same general form as in equation (3), with the change that all variables are now replaced by first differences (ΔY_t, ΔX_t). Inducing stationarity by differencing the relevant variables the appropriate number of times loses potential information and is not appropriate where there is potential cointegration between the nonstationary variables. Where the I(1) variables are cointegrated, estimating the model in first differences is invalid and will result in misspecification and inefficiency (see Robertson and Wickens (1994)).

The appropriate form of model is then a VECM. Assuming that the k-dimensional exogenous variables, X_t, follow the multivariate independent unit root processes, $\Delta X_t = e_t$, and $p = q$, we can write equation (2′) as the VAR(p) model,

$$A(L)Z_t = u_t,\tag{4}$$

$$A(L) = \begin{bmatrix} \beta(L) & \Gamma(L) \\ 0 & 1-L \end{bmatrix},$$

where $\beta(L) = \beta_0 - \beta_1 L - \ldots - \beta_p L^p$, $\Gamma(L) = -\Gamma_0 - \Gamma_1 L - \ldots - \Gamma_p L^p$, $u_t = (\eta_t',$ $e_t')'$, and $Z_t = (Y_t', X_t')'$ is the n (= $m + k$)-dimensional vector of combined endogenous and exogenous variables. Noting that $A(L) = A_0 - A_1 L - \ldots$ $- A_p L^p$, and dividing equation (4) by A_0, we obtain

$$\Pi(L)Z_t = v_t,\tag{4'}$$

where $\Pi(L) = I_n - \Pi_1 L - \ldots - \Pi_p L^p$, $\Pi_i = A_0^{-1} A_i$, $i = 1, \ldots, p$, and $v_t = A_0^{-1} u_t$. Reparameterizing equation (4′) we finally obtain the (reduced-form) VECM as

$$\Delta Z_t = -\Pi(1)Z_{t-1} + \Pi_1^* \Delta Z_{t-1} + \ldots + \Pi_{p-1}^* \Delta Z_{t-p+1} + v_t,\tag{5}$$

where $\Pi(1) = I_n - \Pi_1 - \ldots - \Pi_p$ and $\Pi_i^* = -\Sigma_{j=i+1}^{p}\Pi_j$. If there are r cointegrating vectors between the n-dimensional Z_t variables, then the rank of $\Pi(1)$ is r, and $\Pi(1)$ can be decomposed as $\alpha\beta'$, where β is the $n \times r$ matrix of r cointegrating vectors, and α is the corresponding matrix of factor loadings (see Engle and Granger (1987)). If $h_t = \beta'Z_t$ is the r-vector of cointegrating residuals, then the appropriate stationary form for estimating the model is

$$\Delta Z_t = -\alpha h_{t-1} + \Pi_1^* \Delta Z_{t-1} + \ldots + \Pi_{p-1}^* \Delta Z_{t-p+1} + v_t. \tag{6}$$

Structural Versus Reduced-Form Models

Reorganizing the model above into a VECM can be done directly on the structural form of the model (2'). Thus, if we take the simpler first-order model for convenience

$$\beta_0 Y_t = \beta_1 Y_{t-1} + \Gamma_0 X_1 + \Gamma_1 X_{t-1} + \eta_t, \tag{7}$$

an ECM with endogenous regressors results, that is,

$$\beta_0 \Delta Y_t = -(\beta_0 - \beta_1)(Y_{t-1} - \theta X_{t-1}) + \Gamma_0 \Delta X_t + \eta_t, \tag{8}$$

where $\theta = (\beta_0 - \beta_1)^{-1}(\Gamma_0 + \Gamma_1)$.

Estimation of equation (8) then needs to allow for the possible presence of simultaneously determined variables in each equation. In the examples provided in the country papers, equations with endogenous regressors have been estimated using instrumental variables to ensure independence of right-hand-side variables and the equation error. An alternative is to use full-information methods, although the trade-off between these and limited-information methods is well known (full information is sensitive to misspecification of any single equation, whereas limited information is robust to this). However, there is no clear-cut way to resolve these differences, and examples of each approach are given in the country papers.

Identification

The principal method of estimating the model, Johansen's maximum likelihood approach, gives the long-run relations $h_t = \beta'Z_t$, the r linear combinations of the Z_t variables, which are cointegrated. This, however, is a purely "empirical" identification scheme. For identification, estimation, and hypothesis testing under the general nonhomogeneous and possibly nonlinear overidentifying restrictions on the cointegrating vectors, see Pesaran and Shin (1995b). In addition, in Johansen's VAR approach, the lag length on each variable is assumed to be the same, and in many cases this lag length may be long, thereby severely constraining degrees of freedom. This is one justification for estimating the long-run parameters using the ARDL approach. Pesaran and Shin (1995a) have shown that this approach is appropriate even when the variables are I(1), provided that the lag lengths are appropriate as judged by information criteria. This procedure may be an advantage over the Johansen one because it is clearly possible to both incorporate a priori information readily on signs of individual parameters and to allow differing lag lengths to be estimated for individual variables. Pesaran and Shin show that such ARDL models can yield superconsistent estimates of the model's long-run parameters.

There are arguments, however, in favor of using a system maximum likelihood approach, because the set of cointegrating vectors it identifies may then be tested for economic-theoretic restrictions (see Johansen (1991) and Pesaran and Shin (1995b)).

References

Alogoskoufis, George S., and Alan Manning, 1988, "On the Persistence of Unemployment," *Economic Policy: A European Forum*, Vol. 3 (October), pp. 428–69.

Barrell, R., J. Morgan, and N. Pain, 1995, "Employment, Inequality and Flexibility: A Comparative Study of Labour Markets in North America and Europe" (unpublished; London: National Institute of Economic and Social Research).

Bean, Charles, 1994, "European Unemployment: A Survey," *Journal of Economic Literature*, Vol. 32 (June), pp. 573–619.

———, and Richard Layard, eds., 1987, *The Rise in Unemployment* (New York: Blackwell).

Berndt, Ernst, and Melvyn Fuss, 1986, "Productivity Measurement with Adjustments for Variations in Capacity Utilization and Other Forms of Temporary Equilibrium," *Journal of Econometrics*, Vol. 33, pp. 7–29.

Blanchard, Olivier J., and Lawrence H. Summers, 1986, "Hysteresis and the European Unemployment Problem," *NBER Macroeconomics Annual*, Vol. 1 (Cambridge, Massachusetts: MIT Press).

Calmfors, Lars, and John Driffill, 1987, "Centralization of Wage Bargaining and Macroeconomic Performance," Seminar Paper No. 402 (Stockholm: University of Stockholm Institute for International Economic Studies).

Commission of the European Communities, 1993, *Growth, Competitiveness, Employment: The Challenges and Ways Forward into the 21st Century* (Luxembourg: Office for Official Publications of the European Communities).

Engle, Robert F., and C.W.J. Granger, 1987, "Cointegration and Error Correction: Representation, Estimation, and Testing," *Econometrica*, Vol. 55 (March), pp. 251–76.

Foster, N., and S.G.B. Henry, 1984, "Public and Private Sector Pay: A Partly Disaggregated Study," *National Institute Economic Review*, No. 107 (February), pp. 63–73.

Hall, S., and S. Henry, 1987, "Wage Models," *National Institute Economic Review*, No. 119 (February), pp. 70–75.

———, 1988, *Macroeconomic Modelling* (Amsterdam; New York: North-Holland).

Henry, S., and S. Wren-Lewis, 1983, "The Aggregate Labour Market in the U.K.: Some Experiments with Rational Expectation Models," in *Contributions to Modern Macroeconomics*, ed. by P. Muet and P. Malgrange (London: Basil Blackwell).

Henry, S., J. Payne, and C. Trinder, 1985, "Unemployment and Real Wages: The Role of Unemployment, Social Security Benefits and Unionisation," *Oxford Economic Papers*, Vol. 37 (June), pp. 330–38.

International Monetary Fund, 1994, "Fostering Job Creation, Growth, and Price Stability in Industrial Countries," in *World Economic Outlook* (Washington), pp. 34–53.

Johansen, Soren, 1991, "Estimation and Hypothesis Testing of Cointegration Vectors in Gaussian Vector Autoregressive Models," *Econometrica*, Vol. 59 (November), pp. 1551–80.

Karanassou, Marika, and Dennis J. Snower, 1993, "Explaining Disparities in European Unemployment Dynamics," *Rivista di Politica Economica*, No. 2, pp. 37–62.

Layard, R., S. Nickell, and R. Jackman, 1991, *Unemployment* (New York: Oxford University Press).

Lindbeck, Assar, 1995, "Hazardous Welfare-State Dynamics," *American Economic Review, Papers and Proceedings*, Vol. 84 (May), pp. 9–15.

———, and Dennis J. Snower, 1987a, "Union Activity, Unemployment Persistence, and Wage-Employment Ratchets," *European Economic Review*, Vol. 31 (February), pp. 157–67.

———, 1987b, "Strike and Lock-out Threats and Fiscal Policy," *Oxford Economic Papers*, Vol. 39 (December), pp. 760–84.

———, 1988, "Cooperation, Harassment, and Involuntary Unemployment: An Insider-Outsider Approach," *American Economic Review*, Vol. 78 (March), pp. 167–88.

———, 1994, "How Are Product Demand Changes Transmitted to the Labour Market?" *Economic Journal*, No. 104 (March), pp. 386–98.

Nickell, S., 1978, "Fixed Costs, Employment, and Labour Demand over the Cycle," *Economica*, Vol. 45 (November), pp. 329–45.

————, 1995, "Labor Market Dynamics in OECD Countries," Discussion Paper No. 255 (London: Centre for Economic Performance, London School of Economics).

Organization for Economic Cooperation and Development, 1994, *The OECD Jobs Study, Part 2, The Adjustment Potential of the Labor Market* (Paris).

Pesaran, M. Hashem, and Yonagcheol Shin, 1995a, "An Autoregressive Distributed Lag Modelling Approach to Co-integration Analysis," Working Paper No. 9514 (Cambridge, England: Department of Applied Economics, University of Cambridge).

————, 1995b, "Long-Run Structural Modelling," Working Paper No. 9419 (Cambridge, England: Department of Applied Economics, University of Cambridge).

Phelps, Edmund S., in collaboration with Hian Teckltoon, George Kanaginis, and Gylfi Zoega, 1994, *Structural Slumps: The Modern Equilibrium Theory of Unemployment, Interest and Assets* (Cambridge, Massachusetts: Harvard University Press).

Pujol, T., 1995, "Labor Demand and Turnover with Adjustment Costs" (unpublished; Washington: International Monetary Fund).

Robertson, Donald, and Michael Wickens, 1994, "VAR Modelling," in *Applied Economic Forecasting Techniques*, ed. by Stephen Hall (New York: Harvester Wheatsheaf).

Sargent, Thomas, 1978, "Estimation of Dynamic Labor Demand Schedules Under Rational Expectations," *Journal of Political Economy*, Vol. 86 (December), pp. 1009–44.

Sims, Christopher, 1980, "Macroeconomics and Reality," *Econometrica*, Vol. 48 (January), pp. 1–48.

Snower, Dennis J., and Marika Karanassou, 1995, "A Contribution to Unemployment Dynamics," CEPR Discussion Paper No. 1176 (London: Centre for Economic Policy Research).

Taylor, John B., 1980, "Aggregate Dynamics and Staggered Contracts," *Journal of Political Economy*, Vol. 88 (February), pp. 1–23.

Wadhwani, S., 1985, "Wage Inflation in the United Kingdom," *Economica*, Vol. 52 (May), pp. 195–207.

2

Adjustment Dynamics in the German Labor Market

Paolo Mauro and Tessa van der Willigen

UNEMPLOYMENT IN (WEST) Germany remains low compared with that in other European countries. Nevertheless, as elsewhere, it has risen considerably since the 1970s, because employment growth has failed to keep pace with a steady rise in the labor force (Chart 1). Much of the literature has focused on the possible rise in the "equilibrium" rate of unemployment that may underlie this increase. This paper takes a rather different approach, focusing instead on adjustment dynamics in the labor market. Slow adjustment of the labor market means that the effects of temporary shocks will be persistent and the effects of permanent shocks will be delayed. An understanding of why adjustment is slow should point to policies that could speed it up—a particularly important question in Germany in light of the danger of persistent high unemployment in the new Länder.

This paper reports the results of a set of estimates based on data on the west German labor market for 1970–94.[1] Broadly following the methodology in Karanassou and Snower (1994), a system of labor demand, labor supply, and wage determination equations is estimated, using current and, most important, lagged aggregate variables, such as employment, labor force, and wages, as well as policy indicators. The study singles out the effects of lagged variables, including the ways in which they may have changed over the last two and a half decades, as objects of attention. A number of sources of adjustment lags are identified and are related to specific features of labor market institutions and policies. In addition, the study pays particular attention to the way the effects of different lagged variables interact, and the response of the system to various types of shocks

---

[1]Insufficient data preclude the inclusion of east Germany, but the wholesale extension of west German labor market institutions to east Germany means the results should also be relevant to the new Länder.

Chart 1. *West Germany: Unemployment and Employment*
(In thousands)

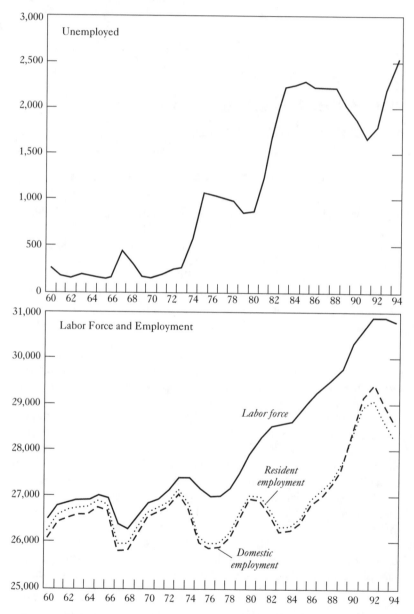

Sources: Federal Bureau of Statistics, *Volkswirtschaftliche Gesamtrechnungen;* and
Deutsche Bundesbank, *Monthly Report.*

is simulated over time. As will be seen, the results—tentative as they are— suggest that unemployment may remain far from its long-run equilibrium for a long time, so that the long-run equilibrium itself may lose much of its relevance over any time horizon of practical significance.

Developments in
Labor Market Institutions and Policies Since 1970

The German labor market is characterized by a centralized system of collective bargaining and by rather extensive social protection.[2] Its institutions and policies have remained relatively stable throughout the postwar period, although some trend toward greater government activism in labor market matters can be discerned after 1970, when the Government proclaimed an unconditional "full employment guarantee" (Soltwedel (1988)).

The following paragraphs describe a number of important labor market institutions and policies as they stand at present, and note significant changes that have occurred since 1970. In each case an attempt is also made to identify the ways in which the institutions and policies described may affect the equilibrium rate of unemployment and the speed with which unemployment moves to its equilibrium.

The basic principles governing wage bargaining in Germany date back to the 1920s. The partners to the negotiations are industrywide employers' federations and trade unions. Negotiations take place at the regional level, but national demands are publicized in advance of the wage round, and wage contracts within a sector are typically identical nationwide. Wage agreements specify a set of minimum tariff wages; minimum wages are established by law. The coverage of collective bargaining is very broad. Although the unionization rate is only about 40 percent (up only a little from about 35 percent in 1970), the majority of west German employers belong to employers' federations and are obliged to pay at least the union-negotiated wage.[3] Individual firms are free to pay wages higher than the tariff, and most do. However, in practice, perhaps in part because industrial action is prohibited in firm-level negotiations, increases in actual wages tend to follow the increase in the tariff, and "wage drift" from year to year is small.

---

[2]For a detailed discussion of three key features of the German labor market—the wage bargaining system, income support for the unemployed, and employment protection—see van der Willigen (1995).

[3]The Minister of Labor has the authority, under certain conditions, to extend the validity of collective agreements to employers who are not members of employers' federations, through a "declaration of general validity." However, these declarations involve a minority of contracts, usually relating to working conditions rather than to wages.

In practice, the system operates more like a centralized one than these bare facts suggest. Not only is there little regional differentiation between wage contracts within sectors, but coordination mechanisms between sectors include the employers' and unions' umbrella organizations and a system of "pattern bargaining" whereby certain sectors—metalworking in particular (represented by the largest of the unions), followed by construction and the public sector—set the standard for each wage round.

There has been no significant change in either the operation or the coverage of the bargaining system since 1970. Something of a watershed was reached in 1984, with a nine-week strike by the metalworkers' union, affecting about half a million workers by the end—the biggest and arguably most embittered strike in the history of west Germany (Streeck (1988)). Remarkably, the traditional consensual pattern of west German industrial relations survived this strike, and, unlike in other countries in the 1980s, there was no determined effort by employers or the Government to roll back union power.[4]

The generally consensual patterns evident in collective bargaining also prevail at firm and plant level. "Industrial democracy" in Germany has a long history, but was strengthened significantly with the 1972 Works Constitution Act (*Betriebsverfassungsgesetz*) and the 1976 Codetermination Act. These laws established the rights of Works Councils (*Betriebsräte*, representing the workforce) to approve decisions on most aspects of working practices and to be consulted or at least informed on other matters. They also strengthened worker representation on supervisory boards (*Aufsichtsräte*), which guide long-term company strategy.

The high degree of coverage of collective bargaining and the influence of employees over firm-level working practices suggest a potential role for "insider-outsider" effects in German labor markets.[5] Both the unions and the firms' own workforces represent primarily the interests of the employed, so that high unemployment may have only a weak tendency to correct itself through wage restraint. This effect may be magnified by centralized bargaining, which will tend to make all wages in the economy

---

[4]The only legislative change—much debated but, in the final analysis, rather minor—was the passage of Section 116 in 1986. Previously, unions had been able to conserve strike funds by striking only at selected firms and counting on other firms in their sector having to shut down for lack of supplies, but Section 116 made workers at the latter firms (who stand to benefit directly from the industrial agreement at stake) ineligible for unemployment benefit.

[5]This is not to deny the benefits of centralized bargaining, which many authors have theorized includes greater overall wage restraint. See van der Willigen (1995) for a detailed discussion of the advantages and disadvantages of the German system of collective bargaining.

move together and, hence, may prevent wages in particularly weak segments of the labor market from adjusting to eliminate unemployment.[6] Pattern bargaining in Germany may introduce a further element of persistence in the form of wage staggering, even though most of the agreements are concluded over a time span of only a few months: adjustment to a labor market shock may be delayed by the heavy influence exerted on contracts concluded later in the wage round by contracts concluded earlier in the round.[7]

A unique feature of the German labor market is the prominence of apprenticeship programs, which provide employment for over half of all 16- to 19-year-olds and which combine practical training with compulsory part-time education at vocational schools. Practical training has long been provided in private firms, but since 1969 it has been regulated by the Vocational Training Act (*Berufsbildungsgesetz*). In 1976, fears of free-rider problems led the Government to introduce fines for employers for a collective failure to create enough apprenticeships to absorb all those leaving school. Although the relevant law was struck down as unconstitutional in 1980, apprenticeship programs expanded considerably during the 1970s and 1980s. These programs are undoubtedly a major reason why Germany does not suffer from the widespread youth unemployment prevalent in other countries; in addition, they may contribute to reducing insider power because they "enfranchise" outsiders in the wage determination process. Another factor is Germany's educational system, which helps keep the proportion of unskilled workers in the population low.

Germany places considerable emphasis on active labor market policies—an emphasis that has increased since 1970. The precursor of the Federal Labor Office was created as early as 1927, with responsibilities for job placement in addition to the compulsory unemployment insurance system, but the Labor Promotion Act (*Arbeitsförderungsgesetz*) of 1969 set the stage for an expansion of vocational training and counseling and job creation programs.

---

[6]This is true whether the labor market is broken down by region, sector, or skill level. In the last case, it is the usually egalitarian objectives of the unions that make all wages tend to move together. See van der Willigen (1995) for a detailed discussion of wage differentiation in Germany.

[7]An interesting example is provided by the 1995 wage round. The key metalworkers' agreement was signed just before a sharp appreciation of the deutsche mark. Commentators generally agree that wage increases in the (export-oriented) metalworking sector would probably have been lower had the appreciation occurred before the agreement was concluded, but these wage increases nevertheless set the standard for other sectoral agreements, concluded after the appreciation.

Table 1. *Germany: Unemployment Insurance Statutory Replacement Ratios*
(In percent)

	1970–74	1975–83	1984–93	1994
Unemployment benefit				
With child(ren)	63	68	68	67
Without child(ren)	63	68	63	60
Unemployment assistance				
With child(ren)	53	58	58	57
Without child(ren)	53	58	56	53

Source: German authorities.

Note: Statutory replacement ratios were constant over the periods indicated. Replacement ratios apply to previous after-tax earnings, excluding the typical thirteenth-month wage; thus, as a proportion of total annual earnings, replacement ratios are a little lower.

To the extent that the expansion of both apprenticeship programs and active labor market policies has mitigated skill mismatches, it would be expected to have reduced equilibrium unemployment (at least compared with what it might have been otherwise). At the same time, retraining and job creation programs may help smooth adjustment by ensuring that the unemployed remain in touch with the labor market.

Income maintenance for the unemployed is provided under the headings of unemployment benefit (*Arbeitslosengeld*, typically for the first year of unemployment), unemployment assistance (*Arbeitslosenhilfe*, thereafter and indefinitely, subject to means-testing), and social assistance (*Sozialhilfe*, available to all whose income is inadequate).[8] Replacement ratios rose in 1975, but were reduced in 1984 and again in 1994 (Table 1). At the same time, from the beginning of the 1980s, eligibility requirements for unemployment insurance payments—in particular the minimum contribution period and the penalties for turning down job offers—were gradually tightened.

An exception to the trend of decreasing generosity of benefits from the mid-1980s occurred in 1986, when the period of eligibility of older workers for unemployment benefits was extended from one year to, depending on age and tenure, up to 32 months. Because unemployment in Germany is disproportionately concentrated among older workers, unlike in many other European countries, the significance of this change should not be underestimated: in 1994, 40 percent of the unemployed in west Germany

---

[8]A government proposal to limit the duration of unemployment assistance to two years was recently rejected by the Parliament.

were 45 or older (up from about 30 percent in the early 1980s), compared with 30 percent of those in dependent employment.

From an international perspective, Germany's replacement ratios for unemployment insurance are not unusually high, at least in the first few years of unemployment. However, Germany is unusual in that it provides unemployment insurance benefits (albeit at a slightly reduced level, in the form of unemployment assistance) indefinitely.

From a theoretical point of view, the more generous the unemployment insurance, the less intense the job search by the unemployed and the downward pressure unemployment puts on wages. The result could be not only higher equilibrium unemployment, but also higher persistence in unemployment following adverse macroeconomic shocks.

The growing cost of both active labor market policies and income support for the unemployed, together with a more general expansion of government activities, has been reflected in rising taxation of labor. Like other major industrial countries, Germany has experienced an enormous rise in the "tax wedge" between net take-home pay and the total cost of labor to employers (Charts 2 and 3). The overall wedge has risen from just over 50 percent (of take-home pay) in 1970 to close to 90 percent in 1994.

Rising taxation of labor would be expected—for given take-home pay— to raise labor costs, reduce employment demand, and hence raise the equilibrium rate of unemployment. Of course, if rising taxation of labor is instead absorbed through a decline in take-home pay, employment demand would be unaffected, and measured unemployment might even fall to the extent that labor supply contracts in response to falling net wages. In either case, changes in the taxation of labor might be expected to affect both long-run equilibrium unemployment and the dynamics of unemployment (as it may take time for agents to adjust fully to the tax changes).

Employment protection in Germany is fairly severe. This may be one reason why the German economy operates with large amounts of overtime even in periods of recession (Franz and König (1986)), and why, as shown by Abraham and Houseman (1993), shocks to labor demand tend to result in changes in the number of hours worked rather than in the number of employees.

For strictness of protection against individual dismissals, Grubb and Wells (1993) rank Germany fifth among 11 countries of the Organization for Economic Cooperation and Development (OECD), directly behind 4 southern European countries (Portugal, Spain, Italy, and Greece). Perhaps even more important, much is left to the discretion of the courts, creating uncertainty for employers. Individual dismissals have to be "fair," but criteria for fairness are only partly laid down in legislation. Similarly, individual redundancies can be implemented only if alternatives are

Chart 2. *West Germany: Labor Costs and Take-Home Pay*

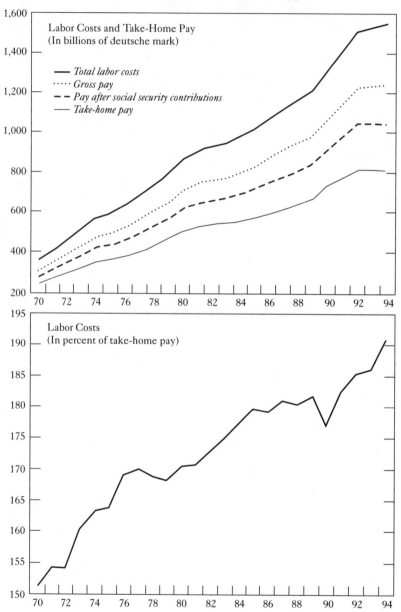

Source: Federal Bureau of Statistics, *Volkswirtschaftliche Gesamtrechnungen.*

Chart 3. *West Germany: Labor Taxes*

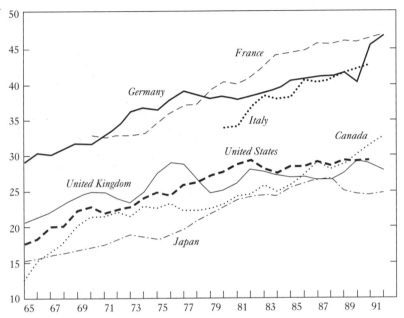

Source: Mendoza, Razin, and Tesar (1993).
Note: All taxes on labor as a percentage of all payments for labor (including both social
security contributions and payroll taxes).

"intolerable," and the choice of redundant workers is subject to "social criteria," but the definitions of these requirements have in practice been left
up to the courts.[9] In addition, large-scale dismissals must be accompanied
by social plans, under which compensation is negotiated.[10]

Although there were no basic legal changes in employment protection
during the 1970s and early 1980s, labor courts over this period increasingly developed the idea of employees' "social property rights" in their
jobs. There is some evidence that in practice average dismissal compensation payments rose considerably over the period (Soltwedel (1988)).
Employment protection legislation was relaxed a little in 1985, with the
passage of the Employment Promotion Act (*Beschäftigungsförderungsgesetz*).
This law expanded the possibilities for fixed-term contracts, increased

[9]Social criteria that have been adduced include wealth, age, health, family responsibilities,
and spouse's income.
[10]For a detailed description of employment protection in Germany, see van der Willigen
(1995).

their maximum duration to 18–24 months from 6 months, and exempted new firms from the social plan requirement. Due to expire in 1995, its validity was recently extended to the year 2000.

While the effects of employment protection are the object of debate, the high costs and uncertainty involved in making workers redundant in Germany are likely to affect the dynamics of adjustment in the labor market, by making current employment depend more strongly on past employment. In addition, the relevance of social criteria to the dismissal decision is likely to magnify long-term unemployment and thus to increase the persistence of unemployment: those who have been long-term unemployed are relatively more likely to be protected by these criteria, and are therefore at still more of a disadvantage in attempting to find employment.

Aside from their direct effects on the speed of adjustment of employment, hiring and firing costs also strengthen the hand of insiders in wage negotiations, and would thereby be expected to delay the adjustment of wages to weak labor market conditions and to result in higher equilibrium unemployment rates overall.

The peculiarities of the German housing market—in particular a relatively high proportion of owner occupancy, together with an underdeveloped market in previously owned houses (owing in part to tax preferences for new housing)—are likely to have contributed substantially to regional unemployment differentials and, thus, to aggregate unemployment rates. The sharp increase in unemployment in Germany during the 1970s and the 1980s coincided with the structural decline of the coal, shipbuilding, and metallurgy industries located in the north of the country, and these areas remain characterized by especially high unemployment rates. However, a study of this phenomenon would require a model disaggregated by region, and the issue thus lies beyond the scope of this study.

In sum, German labor market policies and institutions exhibit a number of features that would be expected to raise equilibrium unemployment and reduce the speed with which unemployment responds to changing conditions. The most important of these features are relatively strict employment protection, high and rising labor taxation, and generous unemployment insurance (with a rising duration of benefits in the 1980s). The most important influences in the opposite direction are likely to be training policies, including the apprenticeship system.

Labor Market Model

The characteristics of the German labor market were analyzed by estimating a model of labor demand, labor supply, and wage determination that allows for a rich lag structure. Its adjustment dynamics were subsequently investigated by simulating the effects of temporary and permanent labor demand shocks.

Description of the Model

The system of equations was specified as follows: a labor demand equation, with employment as a function of total labor costs to the employer and GDP (the latter as a proxy for product demand); a wage bargaining equation, with real take-home pay as a function of productivity and the wedge between real total labor cost to employers and real take-home pay for employees (which consists of the tax and social security wedge between total labor costs and take-home pay, and of the discrepancy between consumer and producer prices); and a labor force equation, with labor force as a function of working-age population and unemployment (the latter as a proxy for the "discouraged-worker" effect). A number of other independent variables were tried in each equation, but proved insignificant.

The potential effects of labor market policies and institutions were analyzed in several ways in this model. First, policy variables were included in the system as exogenous, explanatory variables. Second, the stability of the relationships was analyzed by exploring potential changes in the estimated coefficients for different sample periods, corresponding to changes in labor market policies and institutions. The relative stability of these policies and institutions in Germany over the past twenty-five years sets limits on what either method can achieve. Nevertheless, it is possible to identify important ways in which labor market behavior has changed, ways that in themselves suggest possible policy responses. Finally, the equations themselves, and the effects of lagged variables in particular, point to various possible sources of sluggish adjustment, some of which may be amenable to policy changes.

Estimation

The estimation strategy (autoregressive distributed lag, or ARDL, strategy) was to estimate equations including a number of lags of the independent and dependent variables and to infer the long-run relationships implied by them.[11] The general structure of the approach relies on (1) test-

---

[11]All equations were also estimated using an alternative strategy, which involved the estimation of long-run, cointegrating relationships and the subsequent estimation (both with the ordinary least squares (OLS) and with the three-stage least squares (3SLS) techniques) of error correction models (ECMs) based upon them. The ECM model is a restricted form of the ARDL model, with the restrictions reflecting a priori judgments about the form adjustment dynamics are likely to take. The results of the ECM equations are not presented because they were not used in the final estimation of the measures of persistence and imperfect responsiveness.

ing that the variables are all integrated of order 1,[12] (2) testing for cointegration (also via the Johansen procedure),[13] (3) OLS estimation, (4) misspecification tests and consideration of the possibility of endogeneity, and (5) 3SLS estimation. In principle, the result would be a structural model that is consistent with an underlying cointegrating vector autoregression (VAR), as shown in Karanassou and Snower (1994).

The long-run relationship in the ARDL model drops out of a general dynamic specification, which is estimated directly using a "general to specific" specification search to simplify the lag structure. In each case, the coefficients on the lagged variables provide key information on the speed with which the system adjusts.

The models were estimated through a variety of econometric techniques to counter potential problems, such as simultaneous equation bias. Quarterly data for 1970–94 were used.[14] The results presented here are based on ordinary least squares.[15] Lags of up to eight quarters were used in light of the strong autocorrelation of many of the data series, not only at the first but also at the higher orders.[16]

Results and Implications

Tables 2, 3, and 4 report the individual-equation estimates for the employment, wage, and labor force equations, respectively.

[12]While formal Dickey-Fuller and Augmented Dickey-Fuller unit root tests yield ambiguous results for some of the series, it seems safe to assume that all variables included in the regressions are integrated of order 1.

[13]In all cases, there is tentative evidence that long-run relationships exist among the variables of interest. For the most part, the Dickey-Fuller and Augmented Dickey-Fuller statistics are not far from rejecting the null of no cointegration at the conventional levels. In all cases, the Johansen procedure yields a strictly positive set of cointegrating vectors, which typically do not significantly differ from those of the long-run relationships estimated using both approaches adopted in this study.

[14]The data are drawn from German official sources and the IMF's *International Financial Statistics*. All series refer to west Germany. All variables are in logarithms. Employment includes both dependent employment and self-employment.

[15]The 3SLS estimation technique was not applied to the ARDL model, because the 3SLS results would have been practically identical to the OLS ones, because—in the final specification—none of the equations contained contemporaneous values of any endogenous variable.

[16]The fact that eight lags are required when quarterly data are used is consistent with the finding that two lags are needed when annual data are used, as in Karanassou and Snower (1994).

Table 2. *Employment Equation*

E = number of people employed
w^g = real total labor costs (total labor income per worker, inclusive of taxes and social security payments by employers and employees, divided by the GDP deflator)
y = real GDP
Q1, Q2, Q3 = quarterly dummies
Δ_4 = four-quarter difference operator

Autoregressive distributed lag (ARDL) model

$$\Delta_4 E = 0.219 + 1.20\ E(-1) - 0.51\ E(-2) - 1.06\ E(-5) + 0.46\ E(-6)$$
$$(5.37)\ (13.3)\qquad (-5.57)\qquad (-12.08)\qquad (5.06)$$

$$- 0.17\ E(-8) - 0.018\ w^g(-1) + 0.12\ y - 0.09\ y(-4)$$
$$(-4.21)\qquad (-3.24)\qquad (7.92)\ (-6.39)$$
$$R^2 = 0.98;\quad DW = 1.91;\quad \text{serial correlation statistic} = 1.51\ [0.82]$$

Implied long-run relationship from the ARDL model

$$E = 2.23 - 0.18\ w^g + 0.27\ y$$
$$(20.6)\ (-3.75)\qquad (8.92)$$

$$R^2 = 0.63;\quad DW = 1.91.$$

Note: All variables are in logarithms. *t*-statistics are in parentheses. The serial correlation statistic is a Lagrange multiplier statistic of the null hypothesis that the residuals are serially uncorrelated (up to the fourth order) and is distributed as a χ^2 with 4 degrees of freedom; the rejection level is reported in square brackets.

Employment Equation

Employment (E) is modeled as a function of total labor costs to the employer (w^g) and GDP (y) (the latter as a proxy for product demand):[17]

$$E_t = f_1\ (w_t^g,\ w_{t-1}^g,\ \ldots,\ y_t,\ y_{t-1},\ \ldots,\ E_{t-1},\ \ldots\ ).$$

The results for the employment equation are reported in Table 2.[18]

---

[17]The potential role of a number of other explanatory variables—including real interest rates, competitiveness indicators (the ratio of import prices to the GDP deflator), and (changes in) the real oil price—was explored, with no significant and robust relationship being identified, so that they are not included in the preferred specification.

[18]Little evidence was found of endogeneity bias, related to the two-way causation between (demand for) output and labor input. In fact, in a cointegrating regression in levels, two-stage least squares estimation using trade-weighted foreign partner income—that is, an appropriately exogenous variable that affects the demand for, but not the supply of, domestic output (and/or oil prices) as an instrument for domestic GDP—yielded results very similar to the OLS estimates.

Table 3. *Wage Bargaining Equation*

---

w'' = real net take-home pay (labor income per worker, exclusive of taxes and social
security payments by employers and employees, divided by the CPI)
g = real GDP per person employed
rtw = real tax wedge, or ratio of real total labor cost to real net take-home pay
Q1, Q2, Q3 = quarterly dummies
Δ_4 = four-quarter difference operator

Autoregressive distributed lag (ARDL) model

$$w'' = 0.532 + 0.66 \, w''(-4) + 0.09 \, w''(-8) + 0.26 \, g - 0.10 \, g(-4)$$
$$\quad (6.55) \ (10.3) \qquad\qquad (1.87) \qquad\qquad (4.64) \ (-1.65)$$

$$\qquad - 0.97 \, rtw \ + 0.63 \, rtw \, (-4) - 0.03 \, Q1 - 0.02 \, Q2 - 0.02 \, Q3$$
$$\quad (-19.9) \qquad\quad (11.0) \qquad\qquad (-5.31) \quad (-3.99) \quad\ (4.20)$$

$R^2 = 0.99; \quad DW = 1.47$; serial correlation statistic = 9.62 [0.47]

Implied long-run relationship from the ARDL model

$$w'' = 8.63 \ - \ 1.40 \, rtw + 0.64 \, g - 0.125 \, Q1 - 0.076 \, Q2 - 0.076 \, Q3$$
$$\quad (7.90) \ (-6.03) \qquad (10.1) \ (-10.7) \qquad (-6.06) \qquad\ (-6.60)$$

$R^2 = 0.81; \quad DW = 1.47.$

Note: All variables are in logarithms. *t*-statistics are in parentheses. The serial correlation statistic is a Lagrange multiplier statistic of the null hypothesis that the residuals are serially uncorrelated (up to the fourth order) and is distributed as a χ^2 with 4 degrees of freedom; the rejection level is reported in square brackets.

The signs of the coefficients are as expected if the equation represents a labor demand function: high labor costs reduce employment, while high output demand raises it.[19] The long-run elasticity of employment with respect to the real total labor cost is estimated to be –0.2, using the implied long-run relationship from the distributed lag model.

The results suggest that there is considerable persistence in employment. The sum of the coefficients on lagged values of employment in the distributed lag form of the employment equation is very high (0.92), indicating that employment depends very strongly on its own past values. Strong persistence in employment may be related to the presence of considerable hiring and firing costs in Germany, as described in the section on labor market institutions and policies since 1970.

---

[19]An analysis of the exact mechanisms through which aggregate product demand may affect aggregate labor demand is beyond the scope of this paper.

Table 4. *Labor Force Equation*

L = number of people in employment and unemployment
w^n = real net take-home pay
U = unemployment rate
N = working-age population
Δ = one-quarter difference operator
Δ_4 = four-quarter difference operator

Autoregressive distributed lag (ARDL) model

$$\Delta L = -0.091 - 0.63\Delta L(-2) - 0.12\,L(-8) + 0.45\,N - 0.53\,N(-4) + 0.22\,N(-8) - 0.29\,U$$
$$(-1.47)\,(-7.61)\qquad(-3.40)\qquad(7.11)\quad(-4.58)\qquad(2.59)\qquad(-6.00)$$

$$+\,0.29\Delta U(-1) + 0.57U(-3) - 0.44U(-4) + 0.13U(-8) - 0.02w^n(-1) + 0.01\,Q1 + 0.01\,Q3$$
$$(3.39)\qquad(7.78)\qquad(-6.68)\qquad(3.58)\qquad(-2.88)\qquad(4.36)\qquad(3.76)$$

$R^2 = 0.87;\quad DW = 1.75$; serial correlation statistic = 10.5 [0.03]

Implied long-run relationship from the ARDL model

$$L = -0.75 - 0.28\,U + 1.21N - 0.13\,w^n + 0.51\,Q1 + 0.35\,Q3$$
$$(-2.16)\,(-1.54)\quad(12.8)\quad(-2.12)\qquad(2.99)\qquad(2.52)$$

$R^2 = 0.92;\quad DW = 1.75.$

Note: All variables are in logarithms. *t*-statistics are in parentheses. The serial correlation statistic is a Lagrange multiplier statistic of the null hypothesis that the residuals are serially uncorrelated (up to the fourth order) and is distributed as a χ^2 with 4 degrees of freedom; the rejection level is reported in square brackets.

Recursive estimation of the employment equation yields no evidence of changes in the coefficients on the individual lagged employment terms, or in their sum, so that there is no evidence of changing persistence in employment. In particular, there is no sign of reduced persistence in employment around 1985, the date of the Employment Promotion Act. This finding accords with that of Abraham and Houseman (1993), who analyze the responsiveness of employment to output changes and find no evidence of instability in this relationship around 1985.

Wage Bargaining Equation

Real take-home pay (w^n) is modeled as a function of productivity (g) and the wedge between real total labor cost to employers and real take-home pay for employees (rtw) (which is equal to the ratio of nominal total labor cost to nominal take-home pay divided by the ratio of the GDP deflator to the consumer price index (CPI)):[20]

$$w_t^n = f_2 \left(rtw_t, \, rtw_{t-1}, \, \ldots, \, g_t, \, g_{t-1}, \, \ldots, \, w_{t-1}^n, \, \ldots \right).$$

The results for the wage bargaining equation are reported in Table 3.[21] The coefficients on both the real tax wedge and productivity display the expected signs in the long-run relationship. Real take-home pay responds negatively to the real tax wedge and positively to productivity. In this model, employees bear the whole (indeed, more than the whole) increase in the tax wedge. Anecdotal evidence suggests that the trade unions have not recently sought to "shift forward" increases in the personal income tax burden, although they did in the early 1970s and, on the other hand, that increases in social security contributions tend to be accepted by employers and employees at the statutory levels, that is, 50 percent each.

Although real take-home pay is positively associated with productivity in the long run, the elasticity is estimated to be less than 1. Thus, increases in productivity have not been fully reflected in increases in real take-home pay over the sample period considered, as would be expected in the presence of a rising tax wedge. Chart 4 shows the gross and net labor shares over the sample period.

Perhaps the most important result from the long-run relationships, and one that significantly affects the dynamics of the system, is the small role played by unemployment in wage bargaining. A priori, one would expect unemployment to feature prominently in the wage equation: higher unemployment should dampen wage claims, both by raising fears of unemployment among "insiders," and by increasing competition for jobs from "outsiders." It is, however, difficult to find evidence of such an effect in these regressions. In particular, the unemployment rate (or its change) does not enter significantly into the "levels" form of the wage bargaining equation. The first lag of unemployment was found to be marginally significant, but recursive estimation of this coefficient (Chart 5) suggests that the effect of unemployment on wage settlements diminished in the 1980s.

---

[20]Because much of the impact of unemployment insurance in Germany is thought to come through the intermediary of duration of benefits, rather than their level, statutory replacement ratios were not included in the wage equation. No suitable data could be found for aggregate replacement ratios.

[21]A model in which the tax wedge (defined as the ratio of nominal total labor cost to nominal take-home pay) and the price wedge (defined as the ratio of the CPI to the GDP deflator) were used as separate regressors showed that the coefficients on these two wedges were not significantly different. The preferred specification therefore aggregates the two wedges into a single "real tax wedge" (rtw).

Chart 4. *West Germany: Labor Share*

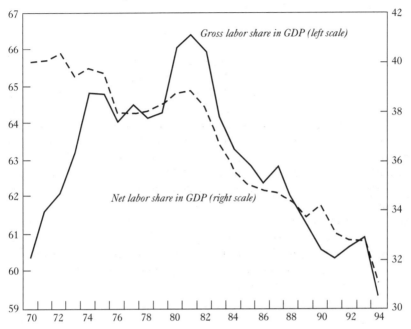

Source: Federal Bureau of Statistics, *Volkswirtschaftliche Gesamtrechnungen.*
Note: Labor shares calculated as percent of GDP at factor cost.

Since the restraining effect of current and lagged unemployment on wages is important for equilibrating labor markets, the weakness of this effect in Germany is a significant finding. It points to hysteresis as a major danger and to insider power as a possible explanation. Certainly, strong worker influence over firms' working practices and generous social protection—for all the other advantages that these institutions bring with them—must help to entrench insider power. In addition, as previously noted, there is some evidence that the effect of unemployment on wages has weakened, suggesting that insider power may have increased over time. With few marked changes in labor market policies and institutions during the period under consideration, it is difficult to pinpoint the sources of the increase. However, the general direction of policy changes toward more government involvement in the labor market may be relevant to this result, as may be the increased duration of unemployment benefits for older workers. Both of these would tend to strengthen insider

Chart 5. *West Germany: The Effect of Unemployment on Wages*

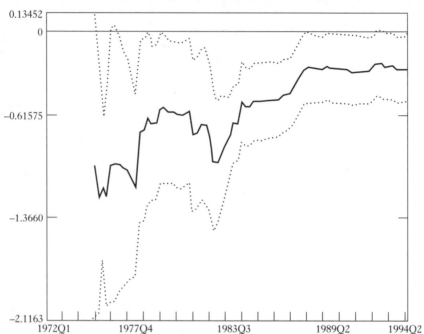

Note: Wage bargaining equation; coefficient of lagged unemployment rate and its two-standard-error bands based on recursive ordinary least squares.

power by reducing the search intensity of the unemployed and tempering insiders' own fear of unemployment.

In addition, the finding of increasing insider power is consistent with the observed growing segmentation of the labor market between high- and low-skilled individuals in particular, with the latter becoming increasingly marginalized.[22] It is widely recognized that skill-biased technological change and skill-biased international trade flows have in recent decades increased the demand for skilled labor in industrial countries relative to

---

[22]While the apprenticeship system in Germany ensures that the majority of people have a qualification, the unemployment rate for the unskilled is still generally at least twice as high as for those with a qualification. In addition, those with low-level skills should be taken to include those whose specific skills have been devalued by structural change, helping to explain the concentration of unemployment in the heavily industrial northern regions of west Germany and among older people. See van der Willigen (1995) for a detailed discussion of labor market segmentation in Germany.

that for unskilled labor. These developments would tend to require a widening of skilled-unskilled wage differentials, whereas the centralized bargaining system in Germany has instead tended to compress wages.

High persistence in wages is suggested by the relatively high (0.75) sum of the coefficients on lagged wages in the wage equation. High persistence in wages may reflect in part staggered wage setting, which will tend to make current wages depend on past wages. Such staggering may be rather prevalent in Germany, with its systems of pattern bargaining.

Labor Force Equation

The labor force is modeled as a function of working-age population (N), unemployment (U), and real take-home pay (w''):

$$L_t = f_3(N_t, N_{t-1}, \ldots, U_t, U_{t-1}, \ldots, w_t^n, w_{t-1}^n, \ldots, L_{t-1}, \ldots).$$

The labor force is positively and significantly associated with working-age population, with an elasticity of about 1 (Table 4). The labor force is also negatively associated with the unemployment rate, perhaps owing to the discouraged-worker effect. While the elasticity is rather small, it is statistically significant at the conventional levels. There is no significant evidence of any effect of real take-home pay on the labor force, perhaps owing to offsetting income and substitution effects. It is also possible to speculate that the decision of whether to enter the labor force is determined by other factors, while wages may play a role in determining effort and the number of hours worked.

Labor supply displays considerable persistence and there is significant evidence that—holding working-age population and other factors constant—past increases in unemployment are negatively associated with increases in the labor force. There is also tentative evidence that changes in working-age population are associated with labor supply changes, although the elasticity is relatively low. Again, there is no evidence that wage changes play a significant part in changes in the labor force.

The labor force exhibits high persistence. The sum of the coefficients on lags of the labor force is 0.88. This suggests that entering and leaving the labor force involve large adjustment costs. The lasting discouraged-worker effects found in these equations suggest that unemployment will be associated not only with lower output today, but also with lower potential output tomorrow, and point to the risk that measured unemployment may not capture total welfare costs. The fact that unemployment enters into the labor force equation in lagged form suggests that it takes some time before it discourages workers from searching for a job, and points to the important role of long-term unemployment. Measures to keep the long-term unemployed in touch with the labor market may thus be particularly important.

Labor Market Dynamics

The importance of lagged effects in the individual equations of the labor market model has been highlighted. These lags, in addition, interact to create more complex dynamics in the system as a whole. To investigate these dynamics, the labor market system[23] was simulated in the presence and absence of, first, a temporary adverse shock to labor demand and, second, a permanent adverse shock to labor demand. Slow adjustment is manifested in the former case in the form of a slow return of unemployment to what its level would have been in the absence of a shock (following Karanassou and Snower (1994), we call this "persistence" of unemployment), and in the latter case in the form of a slow adjustment of unemployment to its new equilibrium level (we call this "imperfect responsiveness" of unemployment).

The simulations show that the effects of a temporary shock are very persistent and that it takes considerable time to reach a new long-run equilibrium following a permanent shock. Each case is analyzed in turn below.

Following a 1 percent *temporary shock* to employment demand, it takes 20 years for the unemployment rate to stabilize within the vicinity of equilibrium (defined as a distance equivalent to one-fourth of the initial shock) (Charts 6 and 7). The results reflect strong and mutually reinforcing persistence in employment, wages, and the labor force. When the negative shock is applied to employment demand, employment falls, thus raising productivity. The rise in productivity raises wages, and this in turn reinforces the initial fall in employment. Also, as employment falls, unemployment rises, and in subsequent periods this puts downward pressure on the labor force, through the discouraged-worker effect. This mechanism slightly mitigates the effects of the fall in employment on the (measured) unemployment rate. The lag structure produces overadjustment, and unemployment oscillates toward its equilibrium level.

Following a *permanent shock* to employment demand, it takes 12 years for the unemployment rate to return to and stabilize in the vicinity of the new

---

[23]Since the labor demand equation contains output (demand) among its explanatory variables, the simulated system included a technical relationship between labor and output, using the coefficients obtained from prior estimation of a Cobb-Douglas production function for the German economy. In addition, two identities were part of the system: first, unemployment was defined as the log-difference between the labor force and employment, and second, productivity was defined as the log-difference between output and employment.

Chart 6. *West Germany: Temporary Shock; Difference in the Unemployment Rate With and Without the Shock*
(In percentage points)

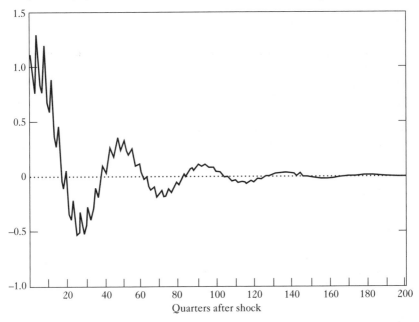

Source: IMF staff estimates.

equilibrium (Charts 8 and 9). Following the permanent rise in the growth rate of employment demand, the same mechanisms as described in the case of a temporary shock raise productivity and wages and reduce the labor force; the overall effect is a rise in unemployment.

Overall, the model suggests that there is considerable sluggishness in German labor markets. This conclusion is further supported by the international comparisons reported in Chapter 1 of this volume. Based on the simulations reported above for Germany and similar ones for other European countries, Henry and Snower present the time taken to recover after temporary and permanent shocks, as well as aggregate measures of persistence and imperfect responsiveness.[24] The time to recover following either a temporary or a permanent shock is longer in Germany than in any of the

[24]The measure of persistence is defined as the sum of deviations of unemployment from its baseline path in response to the temporary shock, and the measure of imperfect responsiveness as the sum of deviations of unemployment from the new long-run equilibrium resulting from the permanent shock.

Chart 7. *West Germany: Temporary Shock; Difference in Each Series With and Without the Shock*
(In percentage points)

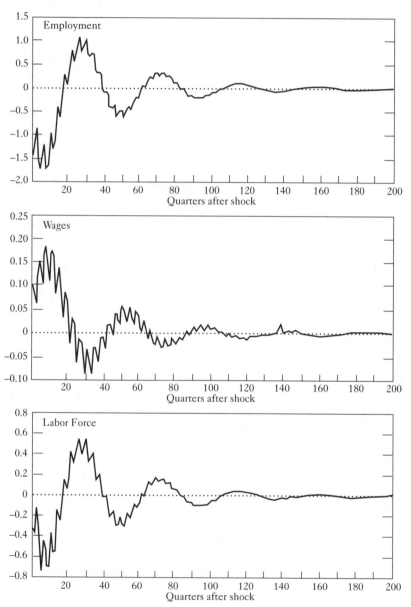

Source: IMF staff estimates.

Chart 8. *West Germany: Permanent Shock; Difference in the Unemployment Rate With and Without the Shock*
(In percentage points)

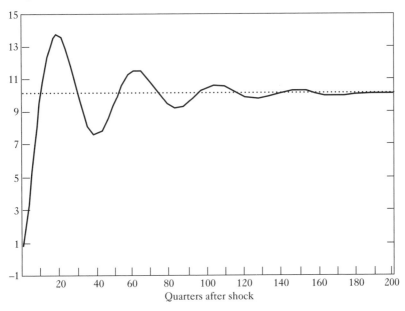

Source: IMF staff estimates.
Note: Dotted line is the difference in long-run equilibrium with and without the shock.

other countries. Similarly, the measure of persistence is higher in Germany than anywhere else, and the measure of imperfect responsiveness indicates that inertia was higher only in the United Kingdom.

These results may appear to be at variance with the traditional view of the German labor market as rather more "flexible" than those of other European countries—a view that is based on Germany's relatively low unemployment rate.[25] However, there is no necessary connection between low equilibrium unemployment and rapid labor market adjustment. Although the results of the present study need to be treated with caution, they suggest that while equilibrium unemployment may be low in (west) Germany, adjustment to that equilibrium may be at least as slow as in the rest of Europe.

---

[25]Layard, Nickell, and Jackman (1991), however, also find more rigidity—in this case, real wage rigidity, interpreted as the extent to which real shocks translate into unemployment at constant inflation rates—in Germany than in France or Italy.

Chart 9. *West Germany: Permanent Shock; Difference in Each Series With and Without the Shock*
(In percentage points)

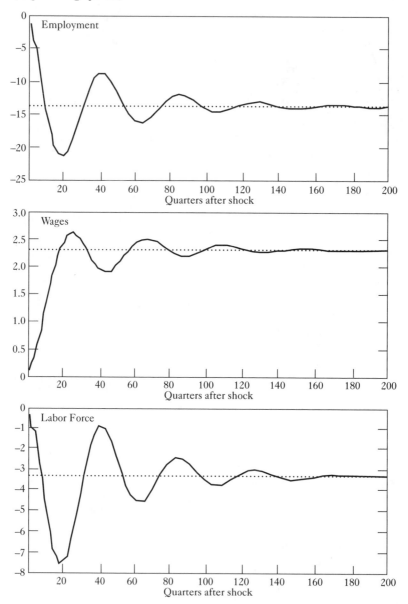

Source: IMF staff estimates.
Note: Dotted line is the difference in long-run equilibrium with and without the shock.

Of course, because the model is by its nature symmetric (responses to rises in employment demand are the exact opposite of responses to falls in employment demand), both persistence in the face of a temporary shock and overshooting in the face of a permanent shock will work to lower unemployment if a shock is favorable, just as they work to raise unemployment if a shock is adverse. In practice, many of the effects identified as sources of sluggish adjustment are likely to have asymmetric effects. An exploration of these asymmetries is beyond the scope of this study. Nonetheless, the presence of considerable sluggishness in German labor markets is sufficient to raise serious concerns about the likely path of unemployment should Germany face serious adverse shocks in the future. To the extent that west German labor market behavior is replicated in east Germany, slow adjustment is also likely to keep unemployment in east Germany higher than it would otherwise be.

Conclusions

The estimation results suggest a number of tentative conclusions on the potential links between institutional features and adjustment dynamics in the German labor market, which may be relevant for the debate on possible policy implications.

The study finds that the German labor market exhibits considerable sluggishness in adjustment. The specific numerical results should be treated with caution, but they are at least suggestive that, in the present model, it takes one to two decades for the effects of a temporary shock to employment demand to disappear, and for employment to adjust to its new equilibrium level following a permanent shock. Adjustment to a temporary shock appears to be particularly slow. It may thus be that unemployment at any given point in time is determined much more by its own history than by its "long-run equilibrium." Such slow adjustment—as in other European countries—may help to explain the rise in unemployment since the early 1980s, and does not bode well for the path of unemployment in the future, including in east Germany. In addition, there is tentative evidence from this and companion studies that the German labor market adjusts more slowly than those of other European countries. Thus, even though the (west) German unemployment rate is relatively low by European standards, structural reform of the labor market may be no less necessary in Germany than elsewhere in Europe. At the same time, strong persistence in unemployment strengthens the presumption that macroeconomic policies should be stability oriented. If inflation is allowed to get out of hand, the rise in unemployment necessary to get it back to acceptable levels may turn out to be very long lived.

The results show that there is substantial persistence in employment in Germany, perhaps related to relatively strict employment protection and to the fact that the courts have considerable discretion in the area of dismissals. Even so, there is no evidence of reduced persistence in employment around the time of the Employment Promotion Act of 1985, which somewhat loosened the restrictions on dismissals. Another factor underlying high persistence in employment and unemployment is a weak effect of unemployment on wage growth. This result may be related to Germany's labor market institutions (widespread collective bargaining, industrial democracy, and generous social protection), which—for all their strengths in other dimensions—would be expected to prevent outsiders from exerting a major influence on wages. The indefinite duration of unemployment assistance, which distinguishes the German unemployment insurance system from that of most other countries, probably plays an important role in this respect.

The fact that collective bargaining is in practice highly centralized may also contribute to the weak effect of unemployment on wage growth, as it reduces the likelihood that wages will adjust to clear segments of the labor market (for example, in particular regions or sectors) that are subject to particularly high unemployment. Although centralized bargaining need not produce a relatively undifferentiated structure of wages across skill levels, in practice it tends to do so, reflecting unions' objectives; thus, high unemployment among particular skill groups may also exert only weak downward pressure on wages overall.

To the extent that any effects of unemployment on wage growth are found, there is evidence that they weakened during the 1980s. An increase in government involvement in the labor market may have contributed to this, as may an increase in the duration of unemployment benefits for older workers (who represent a large and growing fraction of the unemployed). The finding is also consistent with the observed growing segmentation in job opportunities of the German labor market—between regions, ages, and skill levels—during the 1980s. There is also inertia in wage levels, which depend strongly on their own past values, implying slow adjustment to labor market disequilibria. Germany's system of pattern bargaining, whereby the first wage contracts signed each year become the standard for subsequent ones, may contribute to this, as there is little opportunity for changed labor market conditions to be reflected after the first agreements have been concluded.

Rises in measured unemployment tend to be mitigated by declines in the labor force: there is evidence that the labor force responds negatively to unemployment, suggesting that discouraged workers leave the labor force. Thus, the detrimental effects of unemployment may be underestimated if one looks only at the unemployment rate, without considering the loss of the productive potential of discouraged workers. Measures to keep the long-term unemployed in touch with the labor market may be especially important in this respect.

References

Abraham, Katherine G., and Susan S. Houseman, 1993, *Does Employment Protection Inhibit Labor Market Flexibility? Lessons from Germany, France and Belgium*, NBER Working Paper No. 4390 (Cambridge, Massachusetts: National Bureau of Economic Research).

Franz, Wolfgang, and Heinz König, 1986, "The Nature and Causes of Unemployment in the Federal Republic of Germany since the 1970s: An Empirical Investigation," *Economica* (Supplement), pp. S219–S244.

Grubb, David, and William Wells, 1993, "Employment Regulation and Patterns of Work in EC Countries," *OECD Economic Studies*, Vol. 21, pp. 7–58.

Karanassou, Marika, and Dennis J. Snower, 1994, "The Sources of Unemployment Persistence and Responsiveness" (unpublished; London: University of London, Birkbeck College).

Layard, R., S. Nickell, and R. Jackman, 1991, *Unemployment: Macroeconomic Performance and the Labour Market* (Oxford, England: Oxford University Press).

Mendoza, Enrique G., Assaf Razin, and Linda Tesar, 1993, "A Comparative Analysis of the Structure of Tax Systems in Industrial Countries," IMF Working Paper 93/14 (Washington: International Monetary Fund).

Soltwedel, Rüdiger, 1988, "Employment Problems in West Germany: The Role of Institutions, Labor Law, and Government Intervention," *Carnegie-Rochester Conference Series on Public Policy*, Vol. 28 (Spring), pp. 153–220.

Streeck, Wolfgang, 1988, "Industrial Relations in West Germany, 1980–87," *Labour*, Vol. 2 (No. 3), pp. 3–44.

van der Willigen, Tessa, 1995, "Unemployment, Wages, and the Wage Structure," in *United Germany: The First Five Years—Performance and Policy Issues*, ed. by R. Corker and others, IMF Occasional Paper No. 125 (Washington: International Monetary Fund).

3

Labor Market Dynamics and Economic Policy in France

Karl F. Habermeier and S.G.B. Henry

As IN MANY other member countries of the Organization for Economic Cooperation and Development (OECD), the unemployment rate in France has risen during each cyclical downturn, but has not returned to its prerecession levels during the subsequent recoveries. As a result, unemployment has gradually increased over the last 30 years, from about 2 percent of the labor force in the 1960s to about 12 percent in 1993 and 1994 (Table 1 and Chart 1).[1]

The costs of high unemployment have been substantial. First, output has been lost, with real GDP several percentage points lower than its full-employment level. Second, the income support provided to more than 2 million persons (out of about 3 million unemployed) has placed additional strains on public finances.[2] Third, the human and social costs of rising dependency on public assistance cannot be dismissed; these include the depreciation of human capital, the loss of social standing, and the degradation of family structures.

Note: The views expressed are strictly personal. The authors wish to thank Jacques Artus, Willem Buiter, Thierry Pujol, Ramana Ramaswamy, Dennis Snower, and Uli Baumgartner for their comments on earlier drafts.

[1]These issues are discussed in Bean (1994), who provides a useful survey of labor market developments in Europe.

The staff estimates that the portion of the unemployment rate not attributable to the cycle amounts to 9–10 percent of the labor force. In the copious literature on labor market issues, this noncyclical portion of the unemployment rate is generally attributed to structural factors that reduce the incentives of workers to accept employment and of employers to create jobs. These factors are thought to include labor market mismatch, regulations governing hiring or dismissal, minimum wage laws, social benefits (especially unemployment benefits), and the tax system.

[2]The expenditure of the unemployment insurance funds alone came to more than $1\frac{1}{2}$ percent of GDP in 1994. This does not include the amounts allocated for early retirement and social welfare payments.

Table 1. *Unemployment Rates in Industrial Countries*
(In percent of labor force)

	Average			1993	1994
	1960s	1970s	1980s		
France	1.7	3.8	9.0	11.6	12.4
United States	4.8	6.2	7.3	6.8	6.1
Japan	1.3	1.7	2.5	2.5	2.9
Germany	0.8	2.4	6.8	8.8	9.6
Italy	5.2	6.4	10.3	10.3	11.3
United Kingdom	1.8	3.5	9.0	10.3	9.3
Canada	5.0	6.7	9.3	11.2	10.4
Average, seven countries	3.0	4.4	6.9	7.3	7.2

Sources: OECD, Analytical Database; and International Monetary Fund (1995).

This paper establishes a relationship between economic policies and unemployment in France by constructing a macroeconomic model of the labor market. The analysis of the aggregate data suggests that the rise of unemployment has been related mainly to the increasing size of the social security system, which is financed by heavy taxes on labor. More specifically, high levels of social contributions and benefits appear to have severely dampened the growth of employment.[3] A second and equally important result is that the minimum wage has a strong influence on aggregate wages, employment, labor force participation, and unemployment.

Labor Market Developments and Economic Policies: An Overview

A salient feature of the French labor market in the last two decades has been the slow growth of employment relative to population. As shown in

---

[3]Schmitt and Wadsworth (1993) conclude that job searching is not much affected by the level of unemployment benefits. However, their investigation was limited to the United Kingdom and did not take into consideration the broader range of benefits available to non-employed individuals. Other studies, for example, that by Layard and Nickell (1991), show that the duration of benefits, rather than their level, is what most affects the labor market. Many social benefits in France are independent of efforts to participate in the labor market and are of essentially unlimited duration.

Chart 1. *France: Unemployment Rate*
(In percent)

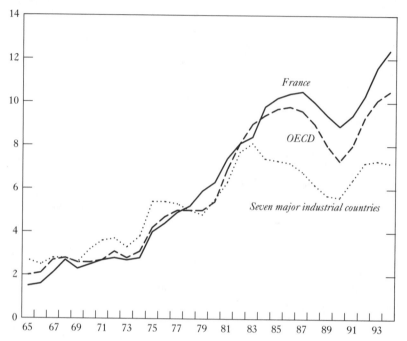

Source: IMF, *World Economic Outlook.*

Table 2, the working-age population of France has increased by about 20 percent since 1970, while employment—especially in the private sector—has grown very little by comparison. Put differently, labor force participation fell while unemployment and nonemployment increased sharply.[4] These developments took place against a backdrop of substantial economic growth. With employment essentially stagnant, the increase in real GDP can be accounted for almost entirely by higher labor productivity, which in turn reflects some combination of capital deepening and technological change (Chart 2).

Wages also increased substantially over this period, although their growth rate at times diverged markedly from that of labor productivity

---

[4]The overall decline in the labor force participation rate masks a strong increase in the rate for females and an even sharper decline in the rate for males.

Table 2. *Demographic and Labor Market Flows*
(In millions of persons, unless otherwise noted)

	1970	1990	Change
Population	50.8	56.7	5.9
Working-age population[1]	31.6	37.4	5.8
Labor force	21.4	24.8	3.4
Employment	20.9	22.6	1.7
Public	3.7	5.1	1.5
Private	17.2	17.5	0.3
Unemployment	0.5	2.2	1.7
Memorandum items			
Unemployment rate[2]	2.5	8.9	6.4
Nonemployment rate[3]	33.9	39.6	5.7
Labor force participation rate[4]	67.8	66.3	−1.5

[1]Individuals aged 16 to 64.
[2]Unemployed persons in percent of labor force.
[3]Persons of working age not employed, in percent of working-age population.
[4]Labor force in percent of working-age population.

(Chart 3). For example, from 1970 to 1983, the ratio of real producer wages to labor productivity (which is equivalent to the share of labor income in GDP) rose markedly. In contrast, during the second half of the 1980s, wages increased much more slowly than productivity. It is not a trivial task to explain these changes in the share of labor. However, they appear to have been strongly correlated with the real price of oil—perhaps because higher energy prices sharply depressed the rate of return on the existing capital stock or because workers succeeded, in the wage bargaining process, in being compensated for the increase in real fuel prices.

The period since 1970 has also been characterized by substantial changes in economic policy, many of which fit into a larger pattern of expanding government social programs (Chart 4). This has been reflected in a remarkable rise in the ratio of general government current expenditure and revenue in relation to GDP. Most of this increase is accounted for by higher social spending—on health care, pensions for regular and early retirement, unemployment compensation, and welfare—and has been financed largely by continuing increases in social security taxes levied on labor income. It is of course legitimate to ask whether higher social spending and higher social security taxes were

Chart 2. *France: Labor Market Indicators and Economic Performance*

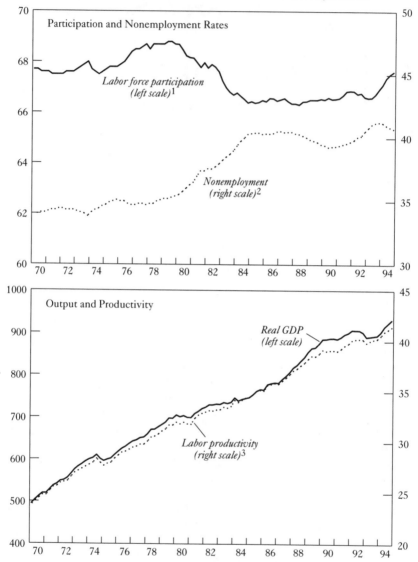

Sources: Institut national de la statistique et des études économiques database;
Organization for Economic Cooperation and Development, analytical database; and IMF
staff calculations.

[1]Labor force in percent of working-age population.

[2]In percent of working-age population.

[3]Real GDP divided by employment.

Chart 3. *France: Wage Developments*

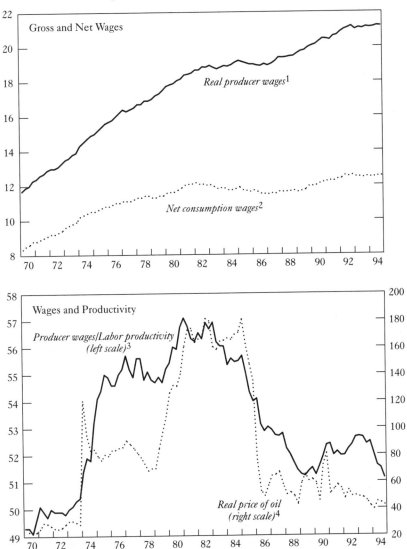

Sources: Institut national de la statistique et des études économiques database; Organization for Economic Cooperation and Development, analytical database; and IMF staff calculations.

[1]Gross income from dependent employment divided by GDP deflator.
[2]Income from dependent employment net of taxes, deflated by consumer price index.
[3]Equivalent to share of labor in GDP.
[4]In francs per barrel, divided by GDP deflator.

principally a cause or an effect of higher unemployment—a question that is further discussed in the next section.

Another way of looking at the expansion of social expenditure is to calculate the ratio of social benefits per capita to the average wage net of social security contributions (Chart 4).[5] It appears that, on average, a French resident (of any age) in 1993 received social support payments equivalent to almost 30 percent of the average net wage and to almost 90 percent of the minimum wage. This represents a massive increase compared with 1970, when these ratios were about half as high as they are now. A possible implication could be that unemployment, or nonwork, has become materially more tolerable than it was a generation ago and may even be an attractive alternative to certain low-paying jobs. The data support this interpretation.

An important example of the trend toward more remunerative government social programs, and one that is thought to affect the labor market directly, is the average replacement rate of the unemployment insurance system.[6] This rate became substantially more generous from 1970 until about 1982 (Chart 5).[7] A sharp turnaround took place under the government of socialist Prime Minister Laurent Fabius in 1983. However, even under the conservative governments that held office from 1986 to 1988 and after 1993, benefits were never scaled back to the levels that prevailed until the early 1970s.

The legal minimum wage has also risen substantially in real terms.[8] However, it has remained in a narrow band relative to average gross producer wages, ranging from a high of 45 percent in 1970 to a low of 40½ percent in 1980 (Chart 5).

[5]Ideally, one would want to calculate the benefits obtained by persons of working age who are not employed and to set them in relation to the net wages (including benefits) received by those persons who are employed. These data are not readily available.

[6]Useful descriptions of changes in labor market policy may be found in Bolot-Gittler and in Cornilleau, Marioni, and Roguet (1990).

[7]The rate is calculated by taking the ratio of unemployment benefits per unemployed person to gross wages per employed person. Of course, the replacement ratio is substantially higher for a newly unemployed person. Under the new system of *allocation unique dégressive* adopted in 1993, the maximal gross replacement ratio is equal to 75 percent (for an individual previously earning the legal minimum wage). See Moghadam (1995) for further details.

[8]The minimum wage rate may be increased for three reasons: (1) automatic increases whenever the consumer price index (CPI) has increased by more than 2 percent; (2) automatic increases equal to one-half the rate of increase in gross real wages; and (3) increases at the discretion of the Government.

Chart 4. *France: Indicators of Public Sector Activity*

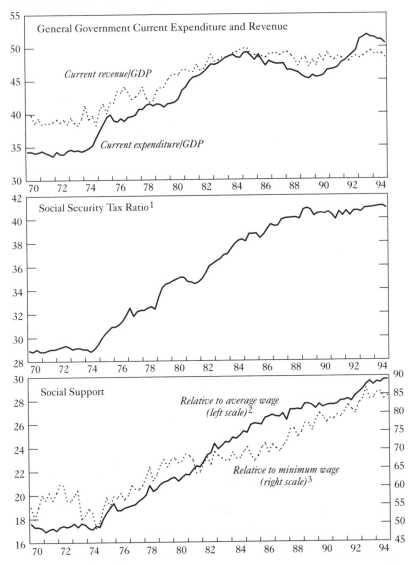

Sources: Institut national de la statistique et des études économiques database; Organization for Economic Cooperation and Development, analytical database; French authorities; and IMF staff calculations.
[1]Ratio of social security taxes to gross income from dependent employment.
[2]Social security benefits per capita in percent of average net wage.
[3]Social security benefits per capita in percent of minimum wage.

Chart 5. *France: Indicators of Labor Market Policy*

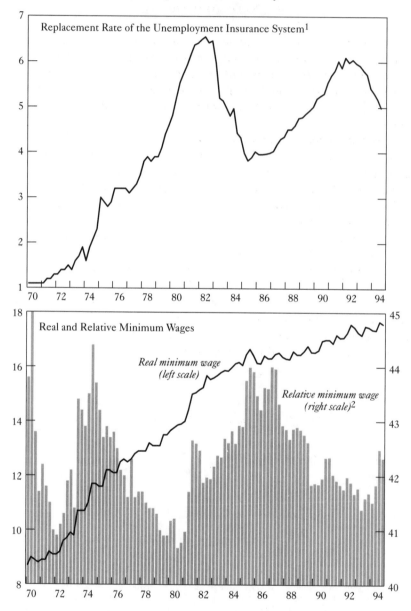

Sources: French authorities; and IMF staff calculations.
[1]Unemployment benefits per unemployed person in percent of average wages.
[2]Minimum wage in percent of average gross wage.

Single-Equation Models of Unemployment and Nonemployment

One way to investigate general economic influences on the unemployment and nonemployment rates is to seek statistically significant correlations between these rates and other economic variables.[9] Such an exercise—based on an ad hoc specification search—is preliminary to the more systematic structural investigation to be described in the next section.[10]

The statistical determinants of the unemployment rate and of the nonemployment rate are analyzed using a general autoregressive distributed lag (ARDL) model that includes a large number of explanatory variables, including real GDP, real interest rates, the employment rate, the real price of oil, social security benefits, the replacement ratio of the unemployment insurance system, and minimum wages.[11]

The principal result is that, for both the unemployment rate and the nonemployment rate, the only policy variable that matters is the ratio of social security expenditure to gross income from dependent employment (the "social benefit ratio"), and this variable has an extremely strong and robust influence.[12] Granger causality tests suggest that the direction of causation runs both from social security expenditure to the dependent variable and the other way around. An equally strong result is obtained if the social expenditure ratio is adjusted for the effects of the business cycle.

A Structural Model of the Labor Market

Modeling Aggregate Labor Market Variables

The single-equation models of unemployment (and nonemployment) presented in the previous section offer an incomplete account of labor market behavior. In particular, the model of the unemployment rate (rela-

---

[9]The nonemployment rate is defined (in levels) as the share of the working-age population that is not employed.

[10]Details are found in appendix.

[11]All variables were tested for order of integration. With only one exception, a unit root cannot be rejected in levels, but is strongly rejected in first differences.

[12]Suitable proxies of this variable, such as the ratio of general government expenditure to GDP, perform similarly well.

tive to the labor force) contained the employment rate (relative to working-age population) as an explanatory variable, while the model of the nonemployment rate included wages. Both of these variables should be viewed as endogenous to the labor market.

This underscores the need for a structural, multiequation model that simultaneously explains labor force participation (labor supply), employment (labor demand), and the wage bargaining process. In deriving and estimating the model, particular attention is given to identifying the dynamics inherent in the labor market, not just in each equation individually, but also in the interactions between the equations. The hope is that modeling these interdependencies will deepen our understanding of the sources of unemployment persistence and imperfect responsiveness. The estimated simultaneous model is later used to examine how the labor market responds to exogenous shocks.

The theoretical basis for the model is the widely used "competing claims" approach, which treats the determination of wages as the outcome of a bargain between unions and firms, where the latter operate in imperfectly competitive markets. Although there is a wide variety of different versions of the union-firm bargaining model, there appears to be a broad similarity in the implications they have for wage and employment behavior (see Bean (1994) on this point). Thus, in these models, the real wage equation is generally of the form

$$(w - \rho) = \alpha U + B'Z + \theta(L)(w - \rho)_{-1}, \tag{1}$$

where unemployment (U) enters the equation as a determinant of the unions' fallback wage and captures the effect on the real wage of excess supply in the labor market. The term $\theta(.)$ is a polynomial in the lag operator, which in turn allows for inertia in the real wage. The most important element in the equation is a set of variables (Z) that typically includes variables from objective functions of unions and firms (and thus depends implicitly on the relative strength of unions in the bargain).

Even if there is a wide consensus in the research that leads to specifications of the general form of equation (1), there is debate about the variables to include in the set Z. For example, there has been much discussion about the statistical importance of the replacement ratio, including how this variable should be measured (see Layard, Nickell, and Jackman (1994)). Earlier, it was noted that the replacement ratio in France had increased, so it might be expected to have an important effect here. It turns out that there is little evidence that the replacement ratio has a direct effect on wage setting. Rather, the data strongly support the view that an indicator of the fiscal weight of the social security system has a powerful effect on employment.

Minimum wage provisions are another potentially important influence upon aggregate wages. There has been considerable controversy about whether minimum wages have deleterious effects on wages and employment. For example, in efficiency wage models it is possible that a minimum wage could help, not hinder, employment. More conventional labor market theory implies that minimum wage provisions, by preventing perfect downward flexibility of wages, raise aggregate wages and hence lower employment. In the wage equation above, this is tested by including a measure of minimum wages in the set of determinants of the real wage. As will be seen below, this variable was highly significant.

Employment is determined within the same imperfectly competitive framework, to which is added the assumption that lagged employment can have an important effect on the current level of employment. This dynamic effect is due to the presence of adjustment costs: the number of persons employed is seen as difficult and costly to change in the short run. In contrast, labor input is somewhat more flexible. For example, the utilization of employees can be changed through variations in the work week or through increasing the intensity of effort.

Finally, the model is closed with a labor force participation equation. This allows for the simultaneous determination of real wages, employment, and unemployment. The labor force equation allows for variations in participation rates in response to changes in demographic factors and wages. Overall, then, the system of equations takes the following form:

$$A(L)\, y_t = B(L)\, z_t + v_t, \tag{2}$$

where y_t is a vector of the three endogenous variables, namely, employment (LE), the labor force participation rate (LFR), and real producer wages ($RWAGR$). $A(L)$ and $B(L)$ are matrix lag polynomials, and z_t is a vector of exogenous variables.[13] The reduced form of this model is simply a vector autoregression (VAR) that also includes contemporaneous and lagged exogenous variables.

The model as a whole may be represented most concisely by the static long-run solution to the three-equation model, written in the following stylized form:

$$LFR = a_0 + a_1\, LERPW + a_2\, WNET$$
$$LE = b_0 + b_1\, WGR + b_2\, Y + b_3\, G$$
$$WGR - LPR = c_0 + c_1\, LUR + c_2\, WMIN + c_3\, POILR, \tag{3}$$

where LFR is the labor force participation rate, $LERPW$ is the ratio of employment to working-age population, $WNET$ is the real wage net of

---

[13]Exogenous here means nonmodeled but not necessarily exogenous in a statistical sense.

social security contributions, LE is employment, WGR is the real gross wage, Y is real GDP, G is the ratio of social security expenditure to gross labor income, LPR is labor productivity, LUR is the unemployment rate, $WMIN$ is the real minimum wage, and $POILR$ is the real oil price. All variables, except the ratio G, are given in terms of natural logarithms.

Thus, labor force participation depends on the prospects of obtaining employment and on net wages. Employment depends on gross real producer wages, real GDP, and the social benefit ratio. Real producer wages depend on labor productivity, the unemployment rate, the minimum wage, and the price of oil.

On the further simplifying assumption that social security taxes are equal to social security benefits (and expressing the ratio appropriately), one obtains the following identities:

$$LFR = LF - LPW$$
$$LERPW = LE - LPW$$
$$LUR = LF - LE$$
$$WNET = WGR\, f(G)$$
$$LPR = Y - LE. \tag{4}$$

Substituting these identities in the system of equations set out above, one obtains a system with a rich structure of simultaneous relationships among the endogenous variables. Thus, wages and employment affect the labor force in the first equation; wages affect employment in the second equation; and employment and the labor force affect wages in the third equation.

Estimation Results

The issues that arise when estimating a model of the kind presented here are discussed at some length in Karanassou and Snower (1993) and Chapter 1 of this volume. Briefly, the main problems are those of dealing with non-stationary variables and of ensuring that the model, which is a simultaneous one, is estimated consistently. To allow for the presence of nonstationary variables, tests of cointegration among these nonstationary variables have been conducted.[14] The estimated models are dynamic structural equations, and each equation is estimated as an "error correction" model (ECM), where the cointegrating relationship between the levels of the variables appears as the long-run equilibrium part of the equation. To allow for the presence of

---

[14]Where nonstationary variables cointegrate, at least one linear combination of these can be found that has a stationary error.

Table 3.   *Tests of Orders of Integration*

Variable	Levels		Differences	
	DF	ADF	DF	ADF
LFR	−1.2	−2.4	−6.1	−3.2
LEPW	−0.9	−2.2	−4.0	−2.6
WNET	−3.1	−3.2	−7.3	−2.2
LE	−0.9	−2.5	−4.3	−2.9
WGR	−2.5	−2.8	−7.7	−2.6
Y	−1.8	−2.6	−7.8	−3.6
G	−2.2	−2.4	−11.0	−4.6
LPR	−1.7	−2.3	−8.2	−3.4
WMIN	−1.8	−3.1	−10.9	−3.3
POILR	−1.8	−2.1	−9.8	−4.9

Note: The 95 percent critical value is 3.45 for the Dickey-Fuller (DF) statistic, and 3.46 for the Augmented Dickey-Fuller (ADF) statistic.

contemporaneous values of other endogenous variables on the right-hand side of an equation (for example, where the current real wage is a determinant of employment), this equation needs to be estimated by a method that allows for this to avoid bias in the parameter estimates. In what follows, this issue is addressed through the use of instrumental variables (IV) estimation. Where appropriate, tests of these and other characteristics of the estimated equations are shown in the tables of empirical results.

All the variables used in this section were first tested for their order of integration.[15] All the relevant variables were found to be nonstationary, although in certain cases, this result was not clear cut (Table 3). Subsequently, tests for the presence of cointegration among the levels of the variables that compare the long-run parts of the participation, employment, and wage equation, respectively, showed that each had one cointegrating vector. The subsequent estimation of the dynamic model equations then builds on this finding. The results for each equation are discussed in somewhat greater detail next.

Labor Force Equation

It is reasonable to hypothesize that the labor force participation rate depends on the probability of obtaining employment and on the prevailing net wage rate. Policy variables may also affect the decision of individuals to

---

[15]For example, an I(1) variable has to be differenced once to make it stationary, and the resulting stationary first difference is referred to as I(0).

join or leave the labor force. For example, minimum wages may induce some individuals to offer their services who might otherwise not find it worthwhile to seek employment. Similarly, the replacement ratio of the unemployment insurance system might increase participation by offering an incentive to stay on the unemployment rolls instead of dropping out of the labor force.

Systematic testing and reduction yielded the model shown in Table 4. In it, the labor force participation rate is positively correlated with the employment rate (or negatively correlated with the unemployment or nonemployment rate). In addition, the findings suggest that higher net wages encourage labor force participation. These variables were found to form a cointegrating set (the Johansen likelihood ratio test was 31.9 compared with a 95 percent critical value of 29.7, confirming the presence of at least one cointegrating vector). However, none of the policy variables considered in this study (social security benefits, social security taxes, direct taxes, real interest rates, minimum wages, or the replacement ratio of the unemployment insurance system) was found to have a significant effect on the labor force participation rate when they were added to the basic economic variables already considered. Only the replacement ratio of the unemployment insurance system comes close to being significant, but it entered the equation with a negative sign—a counterintuitive result—and so was discarded as a probable influence upon participation.

Table 4.   *Labor Force Equation*
(Dependent variable *LFR*; sample period 1970Q3–1991Q4)

Level equation

Variable	Constant	Employment ratio (*LERPW*)	Real consumption wage (*WNET*)
LFR	−0.4	0.39	0.08
	(6.6)	(7.3)	(2.47)

Dynamic equation

Variable	Constant	$\Delta LFR(-1)$	$\Delta LERPW$	$\Delta LERPW(-1)$	$\Delta WNET$	$ECM(-1)$
ΔLFR	0.034	0.52	0.58	−0.41	0.005	−0.09
	(2.73)	(5.8)	(9.3)	(5.4)	(0.3)	(2.7)

$R^2 = 0.6$, $\chi_1^2(4) = 1.68$, $\chi_2^2(1) = 0.3$, $\chi_3^2(2) = 12.9$, $\chi_4^2(1) = 8.0$, $\chi_5^2(1) = 1.6$

Note: In all the reported results, figures in parentheses are *t*-statistics.

Other summary statistics quoted are defined as follows: $\chi_1^2(.)$ is a Lagrange multiplier test of residual correlation; $\chi_2^2(.)$ is the Ramsey RESET test; $\chi_3^2(.)$ is a test for normality of residuals; and $\chi_4^2(.)$ is a test for heteroscedasticity. $\chi_5^2(.)$ is Sargan's test that the instruments are valid. Instruments used were lagged values of the right-hand-side variables.

Employment Equation

As expected, employment is affected negatively by real producer wages and positively by a measure of output. In addition, there is a somewhat unusual result, in that an indicator of the fiscal weight of the social security system has a strong negative effect on employment. This effect might be expected to be intermediated through the real wage, with the social security variable tending to increase real gross wages, which in turn would reduce employment. This issue is discussed more fully below.

Table 5 shows the parameter estimates. Tests confirmed the presence of a single cointegrating vector in this set of variables ($LR = 38.0$ compared with 27.1 at the 95 percent level). As with the other equations presented in this paper, this specification was obtained by systematically testing and reducing a general model. A full set of policy variables was included initially, notably the real interest rate, oil prices, a measure of international competitiveness, the replacement ratio of the unemployment insurance system, and the minimum wage. None of these—with the exception of the social security burden—was found to have a significant influence.

In particular, higher real interest rates appear to have no measurable direct, adverse effect on employment. This result runs counter to the hypothesis that an anti-inflationary monetary policy is associated with higher unemployment, at least in the short run. However, real interest rates may be shown to affect investment and output, and so affect employment indirectly.

From a policy standpoint, the key conclusion would appear to be that labor demand is sharply dampened by an increase in the overall burden

Table 5.   *Employment Equation*
(Dependent variable *LE*; sample period 1970Q3–1991Q4)

Level equation

Variable	Constant	Real product wage (*WGR*)	Output (*Y*)	Fiscal variable (*G*)
LE	1.6	−0.04	0.26	−0.46
	(14.4)	(1.7)	(10.9)	(7.4)

Dynamic equation

Variable	Constant	$\Delta LE(-1)$	ΔWGR	ΔY	ΔG	$ECM(-1)$
ΔLE	0.24	0.57	−0.001	0.08	−0.06	−0.15
	(4.29)	(9.1)	(0.0)	(3.74)	(1.96)	(4.3)

$R^2 = 0.77$, $\chi_1^2(4) = 1.38$, $\chi_2^2(1) = 1.5$, $\chi_3^2(2) = 7.6$, $\chi_4^2(1) = 2.6$, $\chi_5^2(3) = 0.8$

Note: For definitions, see Table 4. Instruments used were lagged values of GDP, the labor force, and wages.

imposed by the social security system. This burden is measured by social security expenditure, which by definition is the sum of social security taxes and the financial balance of the social security system. This result raises several difficult questions. The first two are statistical, while the third concerns the economic interpretation of the result.

First, it is somewhat surprising that the effect of the social security system on employment is not fully captured by producer wages, which already include social security taxes. To investigate this point further, wages net of social security taxes were substituted for gross wages in the employment equation. The result was that the adverse effect of the social security variable on employment became even larger, while the size of the coefficient on wages dropped sharply. The overall size of the effect of the social security system on employment was thus unchanged. There is, according to this result, evidence of a larger (negative) effect on employment of social security payments than is captured by their effect on the gross real product wage alone.

Second, it might be hypothesized that causality runs in the opposite direction, from employment to social security spending. Indeed, when employment declines, as in a cyclical downturn, social security spending tends to increase. However, much of the effect of the cycle on employment is already accounted for by the inclusion of GDP in the equation. Furthermore, the adverse and separate effect of social security spending on employment is still found if the social expenditure variable is adjusted for cyclical deviations of actual GDP from potential GDP.

If it is granted that the effect of social expenditure on employment is statistically robust, what is the channel through which it exercises its influence? In particular, economic theory provides little support for the notion that social security benefits have a direct effect on the hiring decisions of employers. One possible explanation is that the employment equation is not a labor demand equation: this follows from the definition that any equation for employment is also an equation for nonemployment.[16] In the preceding section, the nonemployment rate was shown to depend strongly and positively on social expenditure. The economic rationale for this effect appears straightforward: higher benefits encourage workers to remain nonemployed.[17] This effect, which seems empirically well founded and rests

---

[16]The sum of employment and nonemployment is the working-age population, which is an exogenous variable over the time horizons studied here.

[17]This argument can also be cast in a somewhat different light. Higher social benefits reduce what might be called "effective labor force participation," which is measured labor force participation less those unemployed persons who are voluntarily unemployed (and are therefore not really seeking work). The smaller the effective labor force, the lower is employment in a search and matching framework, since the lower will be the probability that any given employer will find a new recruit (at any given wage offer).

Table 6.   *Wage Equation*
(Dependent variables *WGR*, *LPR*; sample period 1970Q3–1991Q4)

Level equation

Variable	Constant	Unemployment rate (*LUR*)	Minimum wage (*WMIN*)	Real oil price (*POILR*)
WGR − LPR	−1.27	−1.69	0.21	0.05
	(5.8)	(2.63)	(1.97)	(5.5)

Dynamic equation

$\Delta(WGR - LPR)$	Constant	ΔLUR	$\Delta WMIN$	$\Delta POILR$	$ECM(-1)$
	0.21	0.57	−0.04	0.01	−0.16
	(6.17)	(2.05)	(1.0)	(3.19)	(6.17)

$R^2 = 0.39$, $\chi^2_1(4) = 3.1$, $\chi^2_2(1) = 0.0$, $\chi^2_3(2) = 0.86$, $\chi^2_4(1) = 0.76$, $\chi^2_5(2) = 0.0$

Note: For definitions, see Table 4. Instruments used were lagged values of the labor force, the real oil price, unemployment, and the minimum wage.

on a plausible behavioral theory, will therefore also be reflected in the equation for employment.

Wage Equation

In the long run, wage developments in France appear to be accounted for mainly by increases in labor productivity, unemployment, and the minimum wage. Again, it was found that a cointegrating vector exists in this set (*LR* = 30.3 compared with a 95 percent critical value of 29.7). The results of estimating an ECM with this vector as its equilibrium term are shown in Table 6.

The minimum wage appears to have a strong influence on real wages as a whole, tending to raise them above what can be accounted for by productivity and unemployment. This result stands in contrast to some earlier studies of the French labor market.[18] However, the work of other authors supports the conclusion reached in the present paper. Bazen and Martin (1991) show that a higher minimum wage raises the cost of youth labor. Moghadam (1995) finds a direct effect of the minimum wage on the real wage. He notes that the proportion of individuals earning the minimum wage is particularly high for those who are less than 26 years old (35.5

[18]Elmeskov (1993), in a review of explanations for unemployment in the OECD countries, concludes that "most empirical evidence points to rather modest effects [of the minimum wage] on total equilibrium unemployment."

percent of wage earners in 1992), which strongly suggests that the overall effect is transmitted through younger workers.

Finally, the unemployment rate is an indicator of outsider pressure in wage negotiations; higher unemployment tends to act as a constraint on the wage demands of insiders.[19]

Dynamic Analysis

This section presents an analysis of the aggregate dynamics of the labor market. A system consisting of the behavioral equations and the identities described in the previous section was used to conduct a variety of simulations.

A first set of simulations examined the effect on unemployment of both a permanent and a temporary shock to (increase in) labor demand. These shocks took the form of a change in the constant term of the employment equation equal to 1 percent of the equilibrium level of employment. A permanent shock of this type permanently lowers the unemployment rate by about 1¾ percentage points (see Chart 6). As may be seen, the adjustment of employment and the labor force—and hence of unemployment—to a new equilibrium is fairly rapid. The response of wages is considerably slower. The reaction of the system to a temporary shock is somewhat different: the labor force initially responds more strongly than does employment, reflecting the strong effect of higher employment on wages. Thus, the unemployment rate rises before settling back to its equilibrium value (Chart 7).

The dynamic system was also used to simulate the effect on unemployment of a permanent change in the level of social protection. Chart 8 shows the impact on the unemployment rate of a 1 percentage point reduction in the social security tax and benefit ratios (these ratios are computed relative to gross income from dependent employment). There is some overshooting of the unemployment rate early on, reflecting a stronger short-term effect on labor force participation. In the longer run, the effect on employment predominates, and the unemployment rate declines by about 0.2 percentage point. The incidence of the reduction in social security taxes is mainly on workers: producer wages increase by only ½ of 1 percent in the long run, largely reflecting the lower equilibrium unemployment rate, while net consumption wages rise by more than 1½ percent.

The last simulation examined the effect of a permanent 10 percent reduction in the real minimum wage (Chart 9). Again, there is some overshooting of the unemployment rate. In the long run, however, employment rises substantially and the unemployment rate drops about ½ of 1 percentage

---

[19]A systematic treatment of the insider-outsider theory of employment and unemployment may be found in Lindbeck and Snower (1988).

Chart 6. *France: Response of Labor Market to Permanent Labor Demand Shock*

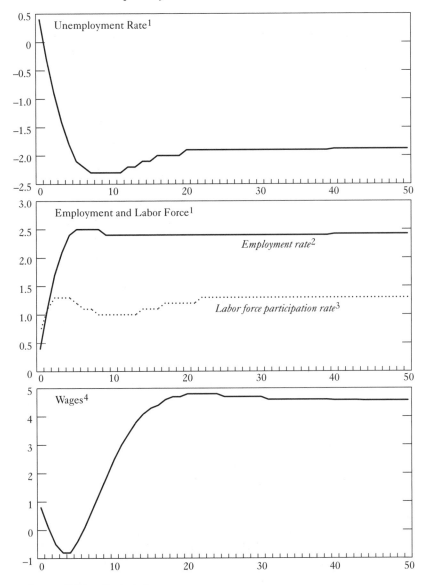

Source: IMF staff calculations.
Note: Shock to labor demand equivalent to 1 percent of employment.
[1]Deviation from baseline; in percentage points.
[2]Employment in percent of working-age population.
[3]Labor force in percent of working-age population.
[4]Real producer wages; percentage deviation from baseline.

Chart 7. *France: Response of Labor Market to Temporary Labor Demand Shock*

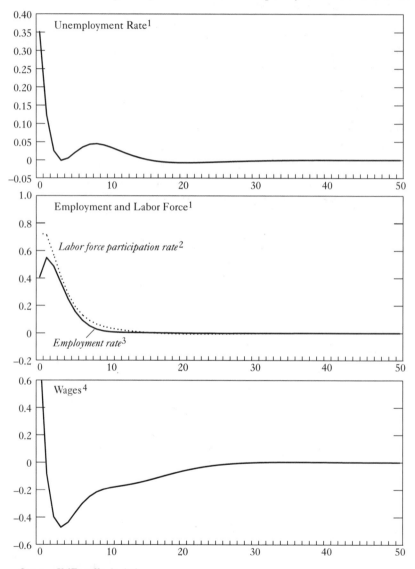

Source: IMF staff calculations.
Note: Shock to labor demand equivalent to 1 percent of employment.
[1]Deviation from baseline; in percentage points.
[2]Labor force in percent of working-age population.
[3]Employment in percent of working-age population.
[4]Real producer wages; percentage deviation from baseline.

Chart 8. *France: Response of Labor Market to Permanent Alleviation of Social Security Taxes and Expenditure*

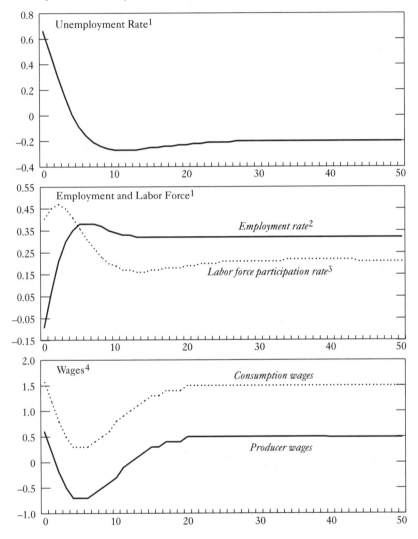

Source: IMF staff calculations.

Note: Reduction in revenue and expenditure by 1 percent of gross income from dependent employment.

[1]Deviation from baseline; in percentage points.

[2]Employment in percent of working-age population.

[3]Labor force in percent of working-age population.

[4]Percentage deviation from baseline.

Chart 9. *France: Response of Labor Market to Permanent Reduction of the Minimum Wage*

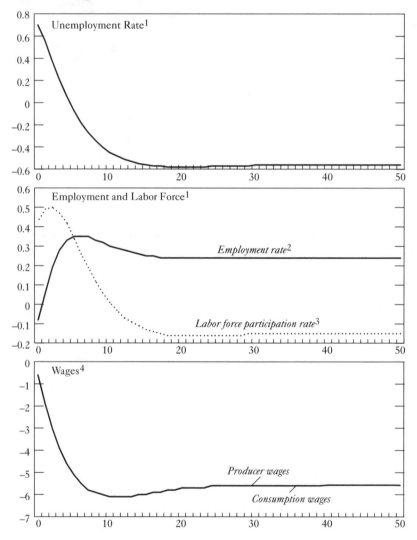

Source: IMF staff calculations.
Note: Reduction by 10 percent in real terms, relative to the baseline.
[1]Deviation from baseline; in percentage points.
[2]Employment in percent of working-age population.
[3]Labor force in percent of working-age population.
[4]Percentage deviation from baseline.

point. As would be predicted by theory, a reduction in the minimum wage leads to a somewhat smaller decline in average wages (the elasticity appears to be in the neighborhood of $\frac{1}{2}$).

Concluding Remarks

The dynamic analysis is revealing, suggesting that dynamic responses to external shocks in France are relatively quick. Unemployment gets close to equilibrium within two years, a much shorter time than it takes other European countries to recover from a similar shock.

This is not a standard finding. Barrell, Morgan, and Pain (1995), for example, report that, if anything, France shows more inertia than do the other major European countries. There are, however, reasons for believing the present results are more likely. The model in this paper reveals powerful effects on the level of employment from social security payments and on wages from the minimum wage provisions. These are characteristics of the French labor market that are not found elsewhere in Europe. Hence, the role for a persistent movement in unemployment away from its equilibrium (NAIRU) rate is that much less in France, and, concomitantly, the structural rate of unemployment appears to have risen more in France than elsewhere.

For policy, these findings suggest that the share of the public sector in the economy, which has grown rapidly in the last quarter century and is now one of the highest among the industrial countries, may need to be reduced. Cutting the tax and social security burden should stimulate labor demand. Lower taxes, along with less generous benefits, can also be expected to give those who are not employed a greater incentive to seek work. The results presented in this study also provide support for a substantial reduction in the real minimum wage. Over time, it would be possible to lower the real minimum wage simply by avoiding any further increase in nominal terms.

Of course, policy recommendations based on macroeconomic results must be supplemented by a more disaggregated, microeconomic analysis. For example, because unemployment in France is concentrated among low-skilled individuals, measures targeted at this group could be relatively more effective. Thus, an across-the-board reduction in the level of social protection may be neither necessary nor sufficient to reduce unemployment.[20] What presumably matters more is the high minimum level of social support,

---

[20]Reducing social contributions and benefits for the top 20 percent of wage earners, or even the top 60 or 80 percent, is likely to have relatively little effect on either their employment or their unemployment.

which is one of the principal determinants of the reservation wage. The level and comprehensiveness of welfare benefits are a key social choice, entailing a trade-off between the generosity of benefits, on the one hand, and employment objectives, on the other. The evidence in this paper suggests that, if unemployment is to be substantially reduced, the generous system of social protection must be trimmed. To be sure, more effective education and training as well as labor and product market liberalization are also called for as part of a comprehensive attack on the unemployment problem.

Appendix: Single-Equation Models of the Unemployment and Nonemployment Rates

Unemployment Rate

Formally, the model of the unemployment rate may be written as

$$LUR_t = a_0 + a(L) \, LUR_{t-1} + \sum_{j=1}^{N} b_j(L) \, Z_{jt} + v_t, \qquad (5)$$

where LUR is the unemployment rate, the Z_j are N explanatory variables, and $a(L)$ and $b_j(L)$ are lag polynomials. The static long-run solution of the model is simply

$$LUR = [1 - a(1)]^{-1} \left[a_0 + \sum_{j=1}^{N} b_j(1) \, Z_j \right]. \qquad (6)$$

This general model was reduced by eliminating variables for which the parameter estimates showed the wrong sign or were statistically insignificant, or both. At each stage, the model reduction was tested using F-tests. While the minimum wage (relative to the average wage) was found to raise unemployment, the effect was small and statistically insignificant ($p = 0.98$), and this variable was rejected in the first stage of model reduction. The real price of oil had a negative effect whenever it was included. However, it was also insignificant ($p = 0.40$) and was rejected in the second stage of model reduction. Other variables that were excluded in subsequent stages generally showed the correct sign but were insignificant statistically and made only small contributions to the overall fit of the equation. Notably, higher real producer wages were associated with a higher unemployment rate, while higher real GDP was associated with a lower unemployment rate.[21]

In the final analysis, only two variables were retained in addition to lagged values of the unemployment rate: the rate of employment in the

---

[21]However, real interest rates at times showed an incorrect sign.

Table 7. *Model of Unemployment Rate*
(Sample period 1970Q1–1993Q4)

Model in levels of *LUR*

Variable	Coefficient	Standard error	t-Value	t-Prob	PartR^2
Constant	−0.011672	0.0060901	−1.916	0.0588	0.0429
LUR_1	1.3912	0.071313	19.509	0.0000	0.8227
LUR_2	−0.45528	0.070501	−6.458	0.0000	0.3371
$LERPW$	−0.38551	0.057870	−6.662	0.0000	0.3512
$LERPW\_1$	0.37387	0.057596	6.491	0.0000	0.3394
$RNYSS$	0.058819	0.027607	2.131	0.0361	0.0525
$RNYSS\_1$	−0.028703	0.027918	−1.028	0.3069	0.0127

Solved static long-run equation

$LUR =$	−0.1823	−0.1818 *LERPW*	+0.4702 *RNYSS*
(SE)	(0.04034)	(0.235)	(0.2041)

$R^2 = 0.998968$
$F(6, 82) = 13224\ [0.0000]$
$\sigma = 0.00103287$
$DW = 1.85$

Source: IMF staff calculations.
Note: The variables are defined as *LUR*, unemployment rate; *LERPW*, employment ratio; and *RNYSS*, social benefit ratio.

working-age population (*LERPW*), which measures the general prospects of obtaining work, and the social benefit ratio (*RNYSS*), which is a measure of the overall level of social support payments provided by the public sector. This model reduction was strongly accepted relative to the most general model ($p = 0.53$). It was also accepted relative to all rival models examined in the course of the reduction ($p = 0.13$ for the nearest rival). In addition to real wages, the nearest rival model also included real interest rates, which, however, again showed the wrong sign.

The parameter estimates for the final model are shown in Table 7. In the long run, a 1 percentage point increase in the employment rate (relative to working-age population) results in a 0.16 percentage point drop in the unemployment rate (the labor force is about two-thirds of the working-age population), while a 1 percentage point increase in the social benefit ratio (relative to wage income) leads to an increase in the unemployment rate of 0.27 percentage point.[22]

The basic model was further tested by adding other variables one by one. The results are presented in Table 8. None of the variables is significant,

[22]The model was also expressed in error correction form in order to confirm the long-run results.

Table 8.   *Effect of Adding Variables to Basic Model of Unemployment Rate*

Variable	Long-Run Elasticity[1]	Significance Level[2]
Real interest rate	−0.21	0.19
Real consumption wages	4.52	0.23
Real producer wages	3.44	0.37
Real oil price	0.41	0.71
Replacement ratio	−0.07	0.75
Relative minimum wage	0.20	0.87
Real GDP	0.50	0.98

Source: IMF staff calculations.
[1]Change in unemployment rate (in percentage points) in response to 1 percent (percentage point) change in dependent variable.
[2]F-test for joint significance of current value and two lags.

even at the 10 percent level. Most show the correct sign, with the exception of real GDP, the real interest rate, and the replacement ratio. Furthermore, both explanatory variables included in the previous model remain significant in all but one case. In summary, the basic model appears to be highly robust.

Similar results were obtained when the overall social support ratio or the ratio of general government current expenditure to GDP (both shown in Chart 4) was substituted for the social benefit ratio in the basic model. The ratio of social security taxes to gross income from dependent employment also had a strong positive effect on the unemployment rate. This is not surprising because all of the substitute variables are highly collinear.

Nonemployment Rate

If it were true that more generous social expenditure has added to unemployment by making it more tolerable or indeed attractive in some cases, the rise of unemployment would in part reflect an increase in voluntary unemployment.[23] In addition, one should be able to observe a decline in labor force participation. Thus, the effect of more generous social expenditure on the labor market might be better captured by the nonemployment rate, which is defined as the percentage of working-age individuals who are not employed.

A single-equation model of the nonemployment rate is presented in Table 9.[24] As with the unemployment rate, there is a strong positive effect

[23]Distinguishing between voluntary and involuntary unemployment is not possible on the basis of existing statistics.

[24]Again, the model was obtained by reducing a general autoregressive distributed lag to a form in which the retained variables were significant (or close to significant in the case of real GDP), and the model reduction could not be rejected at any stage.

Table 9. *Model of Nonemployment Rate*
(Sample period 1970Q3–1993Q4)

Model in levels of *LNER*

Variable	Coefficient	Standard error	t-Value	t-Prob	PartR^2
Constant	4.5868	2.2500	2.039	0.0449	0.0512
LNER_1	1.3174	0.10352	12.727	0.0000	0.6778
LNER_2	−0.45333	0.094257	−4.810	0.0000	0.2310
WNET_1	−4.0421	1.5838	−2.552	0.0127	0.0780
WNET_2	2.9081	1.4651	1.985	0.0507	0.0487
RNYSS	0.069197	0.029745	2.326	0.0226	0.0657
RNYSS_1	0.011646	0.032844	0.355	0.7239	0.0016
Y	−2.5095	1.9594	−1.281	0.2041	0.0209
Y_1	−1.5270	2.7758	−0.550	0.5838	0.0039
Y_2	4.1136	1.9089	2.155	0.0343	0.0569
POILR_1	0.039475	0.059426	0.664	0.5085	0.0057
POILR_2	0.097166	0.059849	1.624	0.1086	0.0331

$R^2 = 0.998773; \quad DW = 2.12$

Solved static long-run equation

$$LNER = \quad +33.75 \quad -8.345\ WNET \quad +0.5949\ RNYSS$$
$$+0.5672\ Y \quad +1.006\ POILR$$

Tests on the significance of each variable

Variable	F(num, denom)		Value	Probability	Unit root t-test
LNER	F(2, 77)	=	261.37	[0.0000] **	−3.5489
Constant	F(1, 77)	=	4.1559	[0.0449] *	2.0386
WNET	F(2, 77)	=	4.0031	[0.0222] *	−2.1041
RNYSS	F(2, 77)	=	5.1853	[0.0077] **	2.902
Y	F(3, 77)	=	2.4446	[0.0703]	0.19427
POILR	F(2, 77)	=	4.839	[0.0105] *	3.0721

Tests on the significance of each lag

Lag	F(num,denom)		Value	Probability
1	F(5, 77)	=	35.261	[0.0000] **
2	F(4, 77)	=	9.7353	[0.0000]**

Source: IMF staff calculations.
Note: The variables are defined as *LNER*, nonemployment rate (in percent of working-age population); *WNET*, real net consumption wage; *RNYSS*, social benefit ratio; *Y*, real GDP; and *POILR*, real price of oil. One asterisk denotes significance at the 5 percent level; two asterisks denote significance at the 1 percent level.

of social benefits, both in the long run (the model in levels) and in the short run (the same model in first differences). Real consumption wages have a negative effect, both in the short run and in the long run, which means that people are drawn into the labor market by the prospect of higher net wages. Although stronger economic growth helps to reduce nonemployment in the short run, in the longer term, this demand effect appears to be outweighed by the tendency of nonemployment to rise in tandem with higher levels of real income. Again, the positive association, both in the short run and in the long run, between social benefits (however measured) and the nonemployment rate is highly robust to changes in the detailed specification of the model.

References

Barrell, R., J. Morgan, and N. Pain, 1995, "Employment, Inequality, and Flexibility: A Comparative Study of Labour Markets in North America and Europe" (unpublished; London: National Institute of Economic and Social Research).

Bazen, Stephen, and John P. Martin, 1991, "The Impact of the Minimum Wage on Earnings and Employment in France," *OECD Economic Studies*, No. 16 (Spring), pp. 199–221.

Bean, Charles R., 1994, "European Unemployment: A Survey," *Journal of Economic Literature*, Vol. 32 (June), pp. 573–619.

Bolot-Gittler, Anne, "Le système d'indemnisation du chômage: évolution de ses caractéristiques entre 1979 et 1991," working document of Ministry of Labor, Paris, France.

Cornilleau, Gérard, Pierre Marioni, and Brigitte Roguet, 1990, "Quinze ans de politique de l'emploi," *Observations et diagnostics économiques*, No. 31 (April), pp. 91–120.

Elmeskov, Jørgen, 1993, "High and Persistent Unemployment," Economics Department Working Paper No. 132 (Paris: Organization for Economic Cooperation and Development).

International Monetary Fund, 1995, *World Economic Outlook, May 1995: A Survey by the Staff of the International Monetary Fund*, World Economic and Financial Surveys (Washington).

Karanassou, Marika, and Dennis J. Snower, 1993, "Explaining Disparities in Unemployment Dynamics," CEPR Discussion Paper No. 858 (London: Centre for Economic Policy Research).

Layard, Richard, and Stephen Nickell, 1991, "Unemployment in the OECD Countries," Applied Economics Discussion Paper No. 130 (Oxford, England: University of Oxford, Institute of Economics and Statistics).

———, and Richard Jackman, 1994, *The Unemployment Crisis* (Oxford, England; New York: Oxford University Press).

Lindbeck, Assar, and Dennis J. Snower, 1988, *The Insider-Outsider Theory of Employment and Unemployment* (Cambridge, Massachusetts: MIT Press).

Moghadam, Reza, 1995, "Why Is Unemployment in France So High?" in *France: Financial and Real Sector Issues*, ed. by Paul Masson (Washington: International Monetary Fund).

Schmitt, John, and Jonathan Wadsworth, 1993, "Unemployment Benefit Levels and Search Activity," *Oxford Bulletin of Economics and Statistics*, Vol. 55 (February), pp. 1–24.

4

Italian Unemployment, 1975–95: An Analysis of Macroeconomic Shocks and Policies

Charalambos A. Christofides

THE SUBSTANTIAL AND persistent rise in Italian unemployment since the mid-1970s has prompted attempts by academics and policymakers to characterize its causes and provide possible policy responses. The research approach followed in this paper relies on two insights that appear not to have been fully explored to date either in Italy or in any other European economy that has experienced persistent unemployment. The main insight is that lags in labor market behavior are important and may reinforce one another. Thus, the full effects of a labor market shock on unemployment may take much longer to appear than the length of any simple lag, and unemployment may even overshoot its long-run equilibrium in response to either temporary or permanent shocks.

The second insight is that labor market policies can affect the length of the lags and thereby influence the speed with which unemployment recovers from a recession. This feature of policy is significant, because an important aspect of the unemployment problem in Italy, as in other European countries, is not just that unemployment is high on average, but that it takes a long time to fall after adverse shocks have occured. A number of academic papers have pointed out potential sources of lagged

Note: The author wishes to thank Dimitrios Demekas, Jeffrey Franks, Karl Habermeier, Timothy Lane, Paolo Mauro, Thierry Pujol, Ramana Ramaswamy, Massimo Russo, Tessa van der Willigen, and, especially, Brian Henry, Marika Karanassou, Alessandro Leipold, Alessandro Prati, and Dennis Snower for many valuable discussions and insights. Gislene Jeffers and Valerie Pabst provided excellent publication support. Any remaining errors are the author's responsibility.

responses of unemployment, such as hiring and firing costs, labor force adjustment costs, and insider employment effects.[1] Thus, legislation on wage indexation, legal obstacles to firing and hiring, or even direct lagged responses to changes in policy variables, such as tax rates, can have an important impact on the speed with which unemployment adjusts to macroeconomic shocks. For time periods over which policymakers can have an impact (including not only on unemployment but also on inflation and other important macroeconomic aggregates), quantifying the sources and lengths of the various lags can be very important. The relevant lags can be quite long, but to the extent that they depend on policy, policies can to some degree reduce them: one can even argue that increasing labor market flexibility is synonymous with reducing the length of the lags. This is important in the present context, where the Italian authorities are adopting policies that are designed to increase labor market flexibility and ultimately reduce unemployment.

Overview of Macroeconomic, Labor Market, and Institutional Developments

Aggregate unemployment in Italy has followed a pattern similar to that in a number of other European economies. From relatively low levels of about 6 percent in the early 1970s, it began increasing after the first oil shock in 1974, reaching levels of 8 percent by 1980 (Chart 1). Unemployment accelerated after the second oil shock and continued to increase until about 1988, peaking at over 13 percent. It fell by about 2 percentage points following the economic recovery, but lost all gains during the most recent recession, which started at the end of 1991. From about 6 percent in 1971–72, inflation also increased significantly during 1973–80, indicating the presence of adverse macroeconomic supply shocks and accommodative aggregate demand policies by the authorities (Chart 2). Inflationary pressures have eased steadily since 1981, with inflation returning to 6 percent by 1986. Since 1986, inflation has tended to track the economic cycle.

That important adverse macroeconomic shocks contributed to the rise in Italian unemployment is not in dispute. Real business sector capital stock has been in continuous decline in percentage terms (albeit punctuated by short-lived periods of resurgence) since about 1970. From a rate of

---

[1]Karanassou and Snower (1994) provide a fuller explanation of these sources and how they are expected to affect the lagged responses of the labor market.

Chart 1. *Italy: Adjusted Versus Unadjusted Unemployment*
(In percent of adjusted/unadjusted labor force)

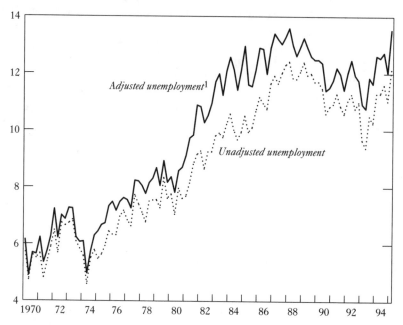

Sources: Italian authorities; and IMF staff estimates.
[1]Unemployment adjusted for the impact of the wage supplementation fund (WSF).

increase of more than 1.2 percent a year, capital accumulation has slowed to just over 0.5 percent (Chart 3). Real GDP growth has also fallen, although there is also some evidence that its variability declined during 1983–90. Competitiveness, defined as the ratio of the import price deflator over the GDP deflator, also turned sharply negative in 1974–83, reflecting movements in oil prices (Chart 4). In general, however, the Italian economy has benefited from movements in competitiveness, especially since 1985. At the same time, social security contributions have risen, punctuated by plateaus (Chart 5), increasing both the costs of employment to employers and the wedge between pre- and post-tax returns to work.

Over this period, the labor force participation rate has also varied over and above the change that would normally be expected as a result of movements in employment. During 1972–76, participation was relatively low at 56.5 percent of the working-age population, moderating the initial impact of the oil shock on unemployment (Chart 6). However, from 1976 to 1981, the participation rate rose in two steps, reaching more than 59 percent by 1980, substantially exacerbating unemployment. This rise was

Chart 2. *Italy: Unemployment Versus Inflation*
(In percent)

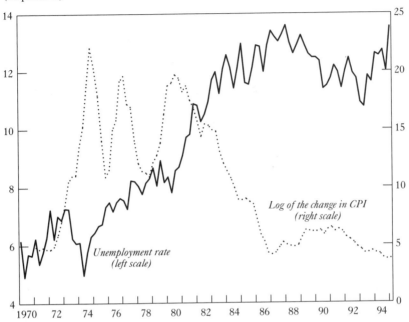

Sources: Italian authorities; and IMF staff estimates.
Note: Unemployment adjusted for the impact of the WSF.

entirely due to the increase in the female participation rate, which increased from 30 percent to 36.7 percent. The female employment rate jumped from 26.7 percent in 1972 to 31.4 percent in 1981, even as the female unemployment rate increased to 14.4 percent from 10.9 percent. The male participation rate, in contrast, fell to 75.1 percent from 78.2 percent. The male employment rate declined to 71.1 percent from 74.6 percent over this period, while the male unemployment rate increased marginally to 5.4 percent from 4.6 percent. (See de Luca and Bruni (1993), Table 8, p. 22.) By 1991, the female participation rate stabilized at 40.1 percent, and the female employment rate increased to 33.6 percent, while the male participation rate continued to fall, reaching 70.5 percent, as the male employment rate fell to 65.5 percent. Thus, aggregate unemployment at least partly reflected shocks arising from an increasing labor force participation rate for females; it will be seen later that this increase in the participation rate was partly caused by factors exogenous to the labor market.

Chart 3. *Italy: Real Capital Stock Versus GDP*
(In percent)

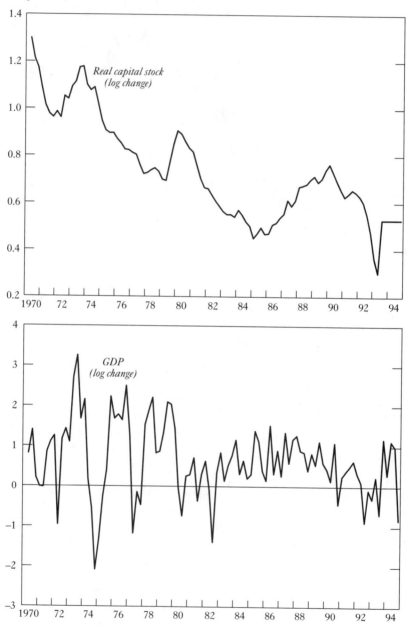

Sources: Italian authorities; and IMF staff estimates.

Chart 4. *Italy: Competitiveness*
(Import deflator over GDP deflator, index)

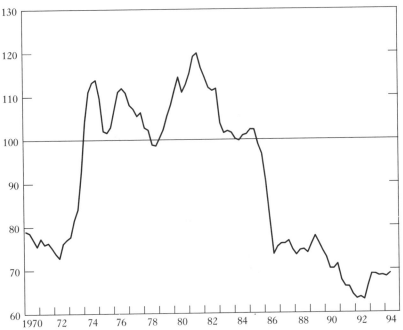

Sources: Italian authorities; and IMF staff estimates.

A comparison of unemployment in Italy and in other countries of the European Union (EU) reveals that, although the pattern of time variation is similar, Italian unemployment is higher than the average: in fact, Italy has the third highest rate of unemployment after Spain and Ireland. This is the result of a striking regional dualism that has taken root in Italy, where the north is more industrialized and has relatively low unemployment rates, while the central region and the south are relatively more agrarian, more dependent on public employment, and have substantially higher rates of unemployment. In 1995, for example, the unemployment rate (according to the national unemployment definition) in the south was over 20 percent, a rate almost three times higher than in the north and the central region.[2] An important explanation for the dual unemployment rate has

---

[2]The reasons for the regional disparities are complicated; they include historical developments, public policies, weaknesses in the political structures of the south, and proximity to the center of gravity of Europe. For a brief overview, see de Luca and Bruni (1993), pp. 28–32.

Chart 5. *Italy: Social Security Contribution Index*
(SSC divided by a wage bill index)

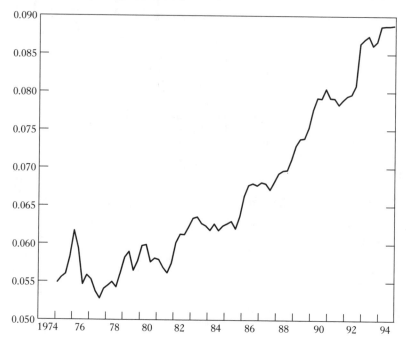

Sources: Italian authorities; and IMF staff estimates.

in fact to do with the relatively small wage differentials between north and south despite wide productivity differentials.[3]

Adverse macroeconomic shocks and the marked regional duality provide only one part of the explanation for Italy's higher unemployment rate. Another part has to do with the institutional framework in the labor market and various policies that determine the response of the labor market to macroeconomic shocks. Clearly, if the labor market were perfectly flexible—except perhaps for purely frictional unemployment—then one would expect unemployment to be less persistent than the macroeconomic shocks that are affecting it. But the institutional and policy framework of Italian labor markets is far from being perfectly flexible: according to the recent jobs study of the Organization for Economic Cooperation and Development (OECD) (1994) and Demekas (1994), the Italian labor mar-

---

[3]Studies quoted by de Luca and Bruni (1993) put the productivity gap in industry between north and south at 75–80 percent.

Chart 6. *Italy: Participation Rate*
(Labor force over working-age population)

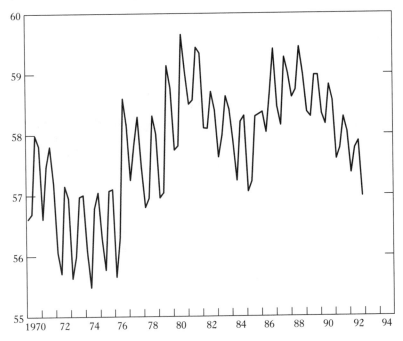

Sources: Italian authorities; and IMF staff estimates.

ket is one of the least flexible in Europe.[4] To facilitate discussion and later econometric work, Appendix I provides a table of labor market and institutional and policy events for Italy.

At the beginning of the 1970s, the Italian labor market already had an institutional and legal structure that significantly inhibited flexibility. Nonagricultural firms were required to hire from a "public list" maintained by public employment agencies with a monopoly on employment services. The rank order of employees to be hired was determined by the state, taking into account such criteria as status of employment, duration of unemployment, and social factors, including the number of dependents. Wage indexation, the *scala mobile*, had already evolved to a national system of uniform adjustments based on a specially calculated index (the *indice sindacale*). Worker unrest during the fall of 1969 (the "hot autumn") led to

[4]The OECD jobs study (1994) and Demekas (1994) provide a wealth of additional institutional detail on the Italian labor market.

legislation (Charter of Workers' Rights, or Statuto dei Lavoratori), which further expanded employment regulations, while Law No. 300/1970 gave special privileges to the three largest national trade unions. These reforms, together with the already significant dominance of the national trade unions, resulted in a centralized wage bargaining system whereby national wage agreements would be negotiated at three-year intervals: in general, longer contracts tend to result in more persistence and longer adjustment lags. The bargaining sessions of 1970 and 1973 resulted in wage increases that some observers characterized as "huge." Firing workers was costly not only because of strong legal protection accorded employees and the presence of implicit contracts with them, but also because of a system of severance pay whereby wage deductions from employees were used to finance a severance pay fund that entitled employees to automatic severance payments upon termination of employment. Another institution peculiar to Italy was the wage supplementation fund (WSF, or *cassa integrazione guadagni*). Industrial workers who would normally be laid off would instead receive 80 percent of their wages from the WSF, almost entirely paid for by the state. Since official Italian unemployment statistics exclude these workers, all data used in this paper (in text, charts, and model estimation/simulation, except where otherwise indicated) have been adjusted to include them.

Before the first oil shock, labor market restrictions were not especially detrimental, as unemployment remained low because of the favorable macroeconomic conditions. It began to rise, however, after the first oil shock, when macroeconomic conditions became less favorable (GDP growth and capital accumulation slowed, while import prices grew faster than domestic prices), suggesting that labor market inflexibility was indeed costly. Despite the persistent rise in unemployment, labor market participants continued to seek—and achieved—further changes in labor market institutions that resulted in even greater inflexibility. A 1975 agreement between trade unions and Confindustria (the main national employers' association) that was fully implemented by 1977 extended the coverage of the *scala mobile* to agricultural and service agreements (previously it had applied mainly to industrial northern regions); it also increased the frequency of indexation by adjusting wages on a quarterly basis. The increase in indexation implied by these changes was a reaction to the mounting inflation, yet it also contributed to a nominal inertia in wages, which raised the costs of disinflation. This would become apparent after 1981. Another important effect of the extension of the coverage of the *scala mobile* was to reduce wage differentials, both between industries and between regions, which tended to disproportionately penalize employment in the south, where productivity was relatively lower. Wage differentials, as measured by the coefficient of variation of interindustry wages, fell from about 23 percent in 1970 to about 16 percent in 1975 and 11 percent in 1977. Compared with other countries, Italy went from a position of relatively high wage differentials (above Germany, France, and the United States and below Japan) to a position of very low wage differentials (lower than all the aforementioned countries).

In 1977–83, unemployment continued to rise, and the authorities attempted without much success to introduce reforms in the labor market. Trade unions generally resisted, and the resulting reforms were piecemeal and contradictory. For example, the 1979 wage agreement indicated that more wage differentiation would be allowed in the next wage agreement: this might be taken as a sign of progress. However, the 1982 wage bargaining session failed to be concluded because of a stalemate on reform proposals for the *scala mobile* and wage increases, and wage differentials remained at the same low levels between 1981 and 1984. (See de Luca and Bruni (1994), Fig. 17, p. 77.) In 1980, the maximum payout from the WSF was increased in nominal terms for salaried employees, although average coverage fell to 76 percent from 80 percent. The severance pay system was relaxed somewhat by reducing the constant of proportionality for payments into the severance pay funds to less than 100 percent, but the *scala mobile* wage component was now included in the bases. In general, during this period there were complicated changes at the margin that were the result of compromise and did not address any of the fundamental institutional issues and policies.

In 1983–84, there was a more serious attempt to deal with the *scala mobile*. The 1983 wage bargaining agreement reduced the effective degree of indexation by 15 percent, while a once-off reform of incomes policy was introduced in 1984, which limited the *scala mobile* points that were allowed to be counted for wage indexation purposes. These reforms had some success in reducing overall wage indexation, as measured by the average degree of coverage in the manufacturing sector. This measure declined from over 70 percent in 1982 to about 60 percent (with some fluctuations) between 1983 and 1991. (See de Luca and Bruni (1994), Fig. 12, p. 63.) In 1984, hiring and firing regulations were changed to allow employers to hire a limited number of workers without regard to the rank order contained in the public list. Some improvement was also made regarding firms' internal flexibility—their ability to reorganize internally—by introducing "solidarity contracts" that would permit workers in firms with more than 1,000 employees to share the work. These contracts were apparently only lightly used, however.

Labor market reform did not begin in earnest until 1991–92, when continuing high unemployment finally resulted in a political consensus to put in place a number of reforms designed to remove some of the impediments to labor market flexibility. The long-standing system regulating the rank order of hires was abolished in 1991. Some exceptions remained for the disabled and the disadvantaged (that is, the long-term unemployed). In addition, firms were allowed to place workers who were unemployed because of mass layoffs on a "mobility" list rather than on the WSF. Although workers on the mobility list and the WSF receive approximately equivalent benefits, and workers on the mobility list are supposed to receive priority in hiring, the effective employment protection accorded workers on the mobility list was substantially reduced relative to the protection enjoyed under the WSF. The 1991 wage accord suspended wage indexation, and the 1992 *scala mobile* adjustment was suspended. By 1993, the *scala mobile* was also definitively abolished and the wage bargaining system was reformed. Two levels of wage bargaining were defined (national/sectoral, and regional/firm) to take into account national benchmarks based on targeted inflation. Labor contracts were extended to four years, although nominal wages would be renegotiated every two years.

The effect of these policies was to improve wage flexibility somewhat, but also, more important in the Italian context, to improve the ability of firms to hire and fire. The recession, which began at the end of 1991, also resulted in an unprecedented shakeout in services (including the public sector). Unlike in previous recessions, employment in the services sector declined. The result of these changes was an unprecedented decline in employment and an increase in unemployment by about 2 percent. Comparing the behavior of employment during the most recent recession with that of earlier recessions shows that employment was much more cyclical and responsive to output than before (Chart 7). Clearly, firms used the opportunity of lower firing restrictions to restructure, and productivity increased substantially as a result (which is atypical for an Italian recession). The difficult question is whether firms will prove equally flexible in hiring people during the upswing.

Finally, it is worth mentioning that a number of policies that are often important when considering the unemployment experience of other countries have not played an important role in Italy. Minimum wage legislation, for instance, does not exist at the national level. Unemployment benefits have also been relatively unimportant, with a replacement ratio of 10 percent throughout most of the period under review. However, the WSF in large part substituted for the absence of a more typical system of unem-

Chart 7. *Italy: Behavior of Employment During the Business Cycle, 1973–94*
(Index; trough = 100)

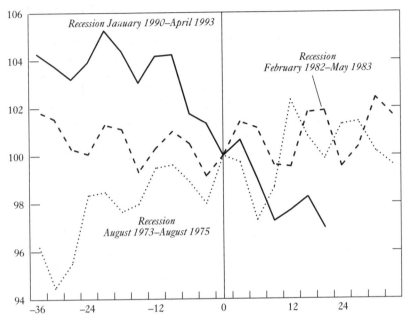

Sources: Bank of Italy; and IMF staff estimates.
Note: Employment series reconstructed before 1992 and spliced before 1981.

ployment benefits, which is why this paper uses labor market figures adjusted for the WSF.[5] In addition, the Italian authorities have recently increased the replacement ratio to 25 percent.

A Model-Based Analysis of Historical Developments

The analysis presented in the previous section was suggestive of the causes of unemployment in Italy, but, in the absence of a quantified framework, it is not possible to pinpoint the relative importance of the various factors or the time scale over which they operate. In this section, two structural vector autoregressive (VAR) models of the labor market in Italy

[5]The replacement rate applicable to the WSF has varied very little throughout the sample period.

are estimated for the period 1977–94 on the basis of quarterly data available as of April 1995. The first model will be referred to as the "basic" model. It will be used to calculate measures of persistence and imperfect responsiveness. The second model is an expanded, 11-equation version of the basic VAR model. The added equations are simple autoregressions for the exogenous variables in the basic VAR (so that the additional equations in the 11-equation VAR remain block-exogenous to the basic set of equations). The purpose of the expansion is to be able to perform a variance decomposition for unemployment (also for employment, real wages, and the labor force) that includes the exogenous variables.

The basic VAR consists of three behavioral equations, shown below:

$$n_t = f_n(t) + a_{nn}(L)n_{t-1} + a_{nw}wp_t + a_{nk}k_t + a_{nr}r_t + a_{ny}y_t + a_{ns}(L)SSC_t, \quad (1)$$

$$wc_t = f_w(t) + a_{wn}(L)n_{t-1} + a_{ww}wc_{t-1} + a_{wp}p_t + a_{ws}(L)SSC_t, \text{ and} \quad (2)$$

$$l_t = f_l(t) + a_{ln}(L)n_t + a_{ll}(L)l_{t-1} + a_{lw}wc_t + a_{la}WAP_t, \quad (3)$$

where n denotes employment, wc the consumption wage, wp the product wage, l the labor force, k business sector capital stock, r competitiveness, y real GDP, p productivity, WAP the working-age (14–64) population, and SSC the ratio of social security contributions to the wage bill (in index form). L denotes the lag operator (for any time series x_t, $Lx_t = x_{t-1}$), $a(L)$ a polynomial in the lag operator, and $f(t)$ a deterministic function that includes a constant, a time trend, and quarterly dummies, because all data are seasonally unadjusted. All variables, except SSC, are measured in logarithms. Appendix II provides further details on data sources and definitions.

Equation (1) is an employment equation (which may be interpreted as a labor demand equation), equation (2) a wage setting equation, and equation (3) a labor force (participation, or labor supply) equation. The unemployment rate is then determined as a log-linear approximation to the identity linking unemployment, employment, and the labor force ($u_t = l_t - n_t$). Because the appropriate wage concept for the labor demand equation is the product wage, but for the wage setting/labor supply equation it is the consumption wage, an additional equation is appended for the product wage (in effect, capturing the wedge, which is shown in Chart 8). For the work reported in this section, the product wage is computed as an identity that uses the within-sample wedge together with the simulated consumption wage.

In choosing the specifications included in equations (1)–(3), a number of alternatives were considered, especially regarding which explanatory variables to include and whether to use the unemployment rate directly rather

Chart 8. *Italy: Wedge*
(Log CPI-log PPI)

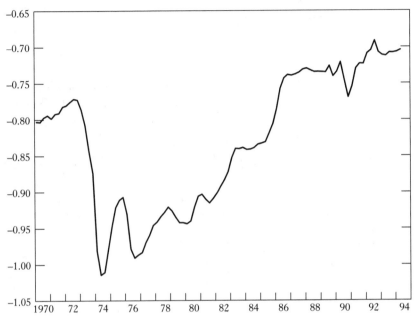

Sources: Italian authorities; and IMF staff estimates.
Note: CPI refers to the consumer price index, and PPI to the producer price index.

than employment or the labor force or both. The statistical significance of the coefficients as well as the overall fit of the system and its dynamic properties were considered for inclusion. Variables such as oil prices and direct tax rates were not statistically significant in the employment equation. The labor force participation equation also tended to have worse autocorrelation properties when unemployment was used instead of employment and lagged labor force.[6] Table 1 summarizes the best specification achieved for each equation.

[6]Appendix III provides more detail regarding the estimation methods used, as well as further diagnostic tests. The nonstationarity of the variables requires that the estimated relationships be tested for cointegration. This was done, and all the relationships reported here pass this test: this implies that the coefficients are estimated consistently. The nonstationarity of the variables could raise some concerns regarding the correctness of the estimated standard errors, however. A Monte Carlo simulation study was performed, the results of which are included in Appendix IV. The regression-based *t*-statistics were found to be close to the simulated *t*-statistics. Thus, the conclusions reported in the text were not significantly affected by the nonstationarity of the variables.

Table 1. *Regression Results, Basic VAR*

	Dependent Variable		
	n_t	wc_t	l_t
Summary statistics			
R^2	0.944	0.972	0.977
SE dependent variable	0.020	0.033	0.034
SE estimate	0.005	0.006	0.005
Durbin-Watson statistic	2.004	2.084	1.806
Q-statistic (significance)	0.626	0.568	0.512
Coefficients (*t*-statistics without regard to sign; in parentheses)			
Constant	−7.91 (4.4)	−1.96 (3.3)	0.45 (0.8)
Trend	−0.004 (3.9)	— (0.2)	−0.0003 (2.3)
Second-quarter dummy variable	0.007 (2.8)	−0.004 (1.8)	−0.006 (2.1)
Third-quarter dummy variable	0.016 (8.7)	−0.001 (0.6)	−0.011 (3.0)
Fourth-quarter dummy variable	0.009 (6.0)	−0.005 (2.7)	−0.006 (2.0)
n_t	. . .	. . .	0.952 (10.5)
n_{t-1}	0.556 (6.6)	. . .	−0.505 (3.1)
n_{t-2}	. . .	. . .	−0.434 (2.6)
n_{t-3}	0.145 (1.9)	0.187 (3.3)	0.217 (1.2)
n_{t-4}	. . .	. . .	−0.147 (1.0)
wc_t	. . .	. . .	0.007 (1.7)
wc_{t-1}	. . .	0.77 (17.7)	. . .
l_{t-1}	. . .	. . .	0.664 (5.8)
l_{t-2}	. . .	. . .	0.103 (0.7)
l_{t-3}	. . .	. . .	−0.183 (1.4)
l_{t-4}	. . .	. . .	0.272 (2.5)
wp_t	0.12 (3.2)	. . .	. . .
k_t	0.66 (4.0)	. . .	. . .
r_t	−0.07 (5.0)	. . .	. . .
y_t	0.158 (5.4)	. . .	. . .
p_t	. . .	0.05 (1.1)	. . .
WAP_t	. . .	. . .	0.00001 (1.8)
SSC_t	−4.49 (7.1)	−4.68 (6.5)	. . .
SSC_{t-1}	3.76 (5.1)	4.54 (5.0)	. . .
SSC_{t-3}	−1.44 (3.7)	0.03 (0.1)	. . .

Notes: n denotes employment, wc the consumption wage, wp the product wage, l the labor force, k business sector capital stock, r competitiveness, y real GDP, p productivity, WAP the working-age (14–64) population, and SSC the ratio of social security contributions to the wage bill (in index form). All variables, except SSC, are measured in logarithms. Appendix II provides further details on data sources and definitions.

In the employment equation, the coefficients on the explanatory variables have the expected signs. According to the results, increases in the product wage decrease employment, as do unfavorable competitiveness shocks and increases in social security contributions.[7] They show that faster capital stock accumulation and GDP growth increase employment. The inclusion of GDP in the employment equation requires some explanation because, according to the standard competitive model of the firm, output does not enter the factor demand equation (although it does enter the conditional factor demand equation, in which case capital does not enter; see Varian (1984), Section 1.7). One interpretation is that the model of the firm that implicitly underlies the employment equation considered here is one of imperfect competition. As in Layard and Nickell (1987), an activity variable (or, in their model, an expected activity variable, which could be proxied by contemporaneous or lagged GDP) plays a role in a firm that is not perfectly competitive and that chooses prices, output, and employment on the basis of its expectation of activity.

The phenomenon of labor hoarding (whereby the firm hoards labor in anticipation of increases in activity, which again is signaled by increases in contemporaneous activity) is an instance of this. The results show that employment appears strongly correlated with output and has an implicit coefficient of 1.9, a reasonable number.[8] In the short run, however, the estimated responsiveness of employment to output is very low, which also corresponds to conventional wisdom.

Interestingly, after the effects of the explanatory variables are accounted for, a statistically significant trend decline in employment remains. This could be the result of an omitted, and as yet unidentified, explanatory variable. Alternatively, it could indicate the effect of a continuous introduction of labor-saving technology. Significant lagged employment effects are estimated, which are normally interpreted as capturing employment adjustment costs. Overall, social security contributions also affect employment negatively with a lag pattern that is related to employment adjustment costs: not all of the adjustment to a change in social security contribution rates can take place immediately.

---

[7]Because data on social security contributions decomposed by employer and employee are not readily available, the *SSC* variable is an imperfect proxy. Nevertheless, it appears that *SSC* approximates the employer contribution portion of social security contributions closely enough to allow the negative coefficient on this variable to be adequately measured.

[8]Lindbeck and Snower (1994) explore the issue of the transmission of demand changes to the labor market in greater detail. Snower, especially, has argued that the effects of GDP on employment should be small, or that the model should be expanded to incorporate nominal effects. This suggestion is not pursued here.

For the wage equation, it proved difficult to obtain significant and plausible effects from a set of potential explanatory variables. Unemployment, either contemporaneously or with a lag, appears to affect consumption wages only weakly, and the results indicated that it could be dropped from the final specification. This points either to significant insider power (because insiders are able to insulate themselves from market forces in the wage setting process) or to a weak effect of the excess supply of labor on wage settlements (a Phillips curve effect). This effect is strong in Italy, but it operates through the participation rate rather than through wages. Productivity affects wages positively, but does not appear to be statistically significant. This may be partly because the productivity variable has been smoothed by applying a centered five-quarter moving-average filter, which may be too short to smooth out cyclical movements in productivity (a nonsmoothed productivity variable yielded similar results). However, other researchers have also noted the lack of a strong link between real wages and productivity. (See de Luca and Bruni (1994), pp. 69–71.) The social security contribution variable also does little, and there is no residual trend movement in wages. Direct taxes also proved insignificant.

Most of the important effects in the wage equation are lagged effects. There is a significant lagged real wage coefficient, which can be theoretically linked to wage staggering effects. Because of the operation of the *scala mobile* in Italy throughout most of the sample period, one would expect strong wage staggering effects, which indeed are shown to exist. The other interesting lag effect is the statistically and economically significant three-quarter lagged effect of employment on wages, which can be interpreted as the "insider employment" effect. Recalling the earlier discussion of hiring and firing rigidities, it can be inferred that insiders will have an unusually strong bargaining position in the Italian labor market. This means that as employment increases, so does the strength of insiders, perhaps after some lag, before the new insiders become fully entrenched. According to the estimated effect, a 10 percent increase in employment results in an almost 2 percent increase in real wages after three quarters. Overall, the results for the wage equation are consistent with the conventional description of wage bargaining in Italy; namely, centralized trade unions negotiated with centralized employers under conditions that have tended to favor insiders in the past and resulted in wage bargains that did not take market conditions into account.

The labor force equation is notable for the strength of the discouraged-worker effect. Variations in employment appear to cause significant variations in labor force participation; the long-run elasticity of the labor force with respect to employment is 0.576. These results suggest that a significant part of labor market clearing takes place through variations in labor supply. Consequently, the unemployment series underestimates the amount of excess capacity in the labor market in the aftermath of a recession. Considerable labor force adjustment effects are also evident in the equation, with significant lags for both employment and the labor force. The working-age population variable appears to be only marginally significant, perhaps because the relatively large shifts in labor participation caused by female entrants into the labor force—which are unrelated to the increase in working-age population—are masking its effect. Nevertheless, the coefficient has the correct sign. The consumption wage has the expected positive effect on labor participation, although its statistical significance is marginal. Finally, there remains a statistically significant residual trend reduction in the labor force, which may be related either to an omitted variable or to the reduction in the male participation rate noted earlier.

Perhaps more interesting than the individual equation results is the way in which the equations interact in the context of a system. VARs were in fact emphasized by Sims (1980), among other researchers, with a view to examining cross-equational effects and dynamic impulses. However, VARs also raise some difficult issues of interpretation. One is the identification problem, which stems from the fact that in general the VAR covariance matrix is nondiagonal (so that the shocks to the individual equations tend to be contemporaneously correlated) and a unique method for "diagonalizing" a general VAR is not available. Typically, researchers using VARs accept them either as "atheoretical," which means that they are meant to capture generic dynamic responses that may not correspond to easily understood economic shocks (for example, demand or supply), or as "structural"; that is, they identify the sources of shocks using restrictions. A good example is the analysis of demand and supply shocks by Blanchard and Quah (1989). These researchers were able to identify the demand and supply shocks by a priori imposing a restriction on the lag structure of the moving-average representation of the VAR. (They assumed that the demand shock had a purely temporary effect, so that the long-run response of the VAR to a demand shock was zero, while a supply shock had a permanent effect.) However, in this project, the aim is to estimate the lag structure directly.

The VAR estimated here is of the structural type. The case rests partly on theoretical grounds, which provide guidance as to which variables to include in a labor demand or supply equation (see Chapter 1 in this volume). However, because of data limitations or an unsuccessful specification, the estimated VAR may not possess the requisite properties. Two pieces of evidence support the structural interpretation of the estimated VAR for Italy. First, the estimated covariance matrix for the VAR is "near diagonal" (see Table 2 for the expanded version of the VAR), indicating

Table 2. *Correlation Matrix of Residuals, 11-Equation System*

Explanatory Variable	wc_t	l_t	u_t	wp_t	k_t	WAP_t	y_t	r_t	SSC_t	p_t
n_t	−0.20	−0.29	−0.16	0.11	−0.01	−0.00	−0.02	−0.11	−0.01	−0.02
wc_t		−0.15	0.06	0.35	−0.08	0.07	0.12	0.01	−0.01	0.19
l_t			0.11	0.28	−0.06	0.19	−0.13	−0.08	−0.57	0.19
u_t				−0.08	−0.72	0.06	−0.15	0.26	−0.18	−0.06
wp_t					−0.08	0.37	−0.08	−0.49	−0.49	0.05
k_t						−0.25	0.13	0.01	0.14	−0.02
WAP_t							0.16	−0.49	−0.21	−0.04
y_t								−0.09	0.01	0.13
r_t									−0.03	0.06
SSC_t										−0.22

Notes: For definitions, see Table 1; see also Appendix II.

Chart 9. *Italy: Persistence Versus Imperfect Responsiveness*

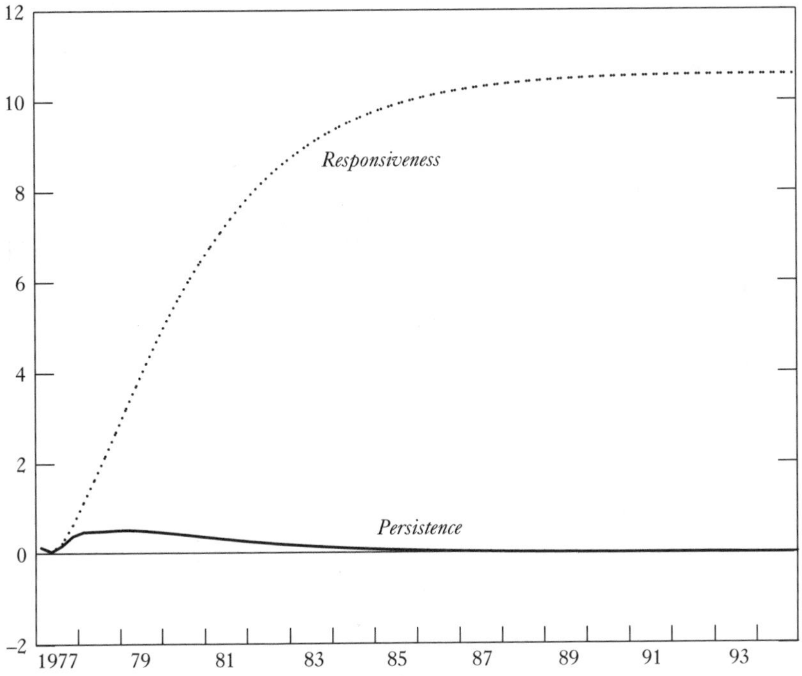

Sources: Italian authorities; and IMF staff estimates.

that contemporaneous covariances between the endogenous variables are successfully captured by the VAR specification and obviate the need for complicated—and possibly unfounded—identifying assumptions. Second, the impulse responses of shocks to the employment equation are damped, and the long-run response of employment to a temporary shock on employment is zero (see Charts 9–11), as would be expected if the employment equation corresponded to a demand equation.

The covariance matrix elements (in fact, reported as correlations) are fairly small in almost all cases, and a correlation of -0.49 between working-age population and competitiveness is not considered to signify substantial misspecification. A few exceptions may not represent sampling error; these include a negative residual correlation between the product wage and social security contributions and competitiveness, a negative correlation between the labor force and social security contributions, and an apparently strongly negative correlation of -0.72 between

Chart 10. *Italy: Impulse Responses and Labor Demand*
(Temporary shock)

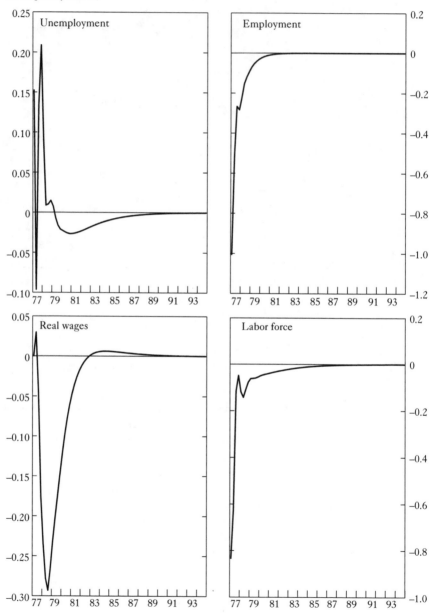

Sources: Italian authorities; and IMF staff estimates.

Chart 11. *Italy: Impulse Responses and Labor Demand*
(Permanent shock)

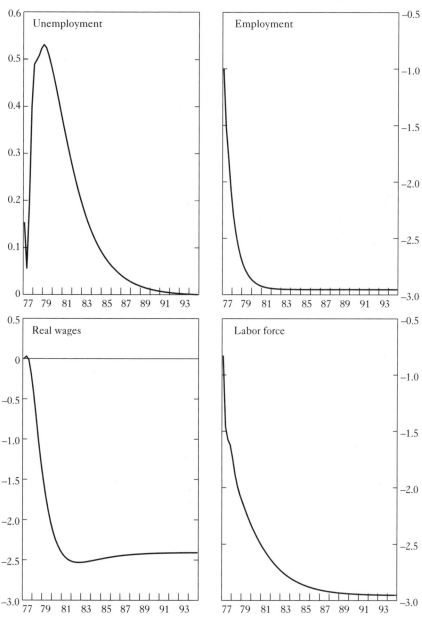

Sources: Italian authorities; and IMF staff estimates.

Table 3.   *Theil* U *Statistic*
(RMS error in parentheses)

Variable	1 Step Ahead	4 Steps Ahead	8 Steps Ahead	12 Steps Ahead
n_t	0.20 (0.003)	0.08 (0.002)	0.07 (0.004)	0.11 (0.008)
wc_t	0.65 (0.004)	0.55 (0.006)	0.01 (0.0001)	0.07 (0.001)
l_t	0.02 (0.0002)	0.41 (0.016)	0.12 (0.006)	0.12 (0.007)
u_t	0.17 (0.001)	1.11 (0.012)	0.25 (0.001)	0.10 (0.002)

Notes: n denotes employment, wc the consumption wage, l the labor force, and u the unemployment rate. The Theil U statistic computes the ratio of the forecast error to the forecast error obtained by a random walk model in each variable.

unemployment and capital stock. But, overall, most of the correlations reported appear small enough to justify the characterization of the covariance matrix as near diagonal.

To further check the result of the estimated VAR, its out-of-sample forecasting performance was examined and dynamic simulations were performed. The out-of-sample forecasting performance was examined systematically by calculating the root-mean-squared (RMS) error statistic and the Theil U statistic over different forecast steps. (See the results in Table 3.) The dynamic performance of the model can be seen in the simulations presented in Charts 12–15. Generally, the model has good out-of-sample forecasting properties, with RMS increasing only gradually as the forecasting horizon increases. The calculated Theil U statistics, which are well below 1, indicate that the basic model easily outperforms a "naive" random walk model. The dynamic simulations (which will be discussed more fully in a later section) also seem to indicate that the model tracks well within sample and forecasts reasonably well out of sample. Appendix III provides further tests of the statistical adequacy of the model.

Given that the model adequately captures some of the dynamic interrelationships that seem important for the Italian labor market, it is possible to use the model to gain a quantitative understanding of the sources of unemployment. The main tool will be a variance decomposition for unemployment that uses the extended version of the model. Although this method has the disadvantage (when compared with the direct measures of persistence and imperfect responsiveness to be provided below) of not disentangling the lagged effects from the effects of exogenous variables, it is nevertheless a convenient way to characterize the "gross" sources of unemployment. The variance decomposition is a way of determining the fraction of the innovations in employment, real wages, labor force, and unemployment explained by each endogenous

Chart 12. *Italy: Employment and Unemployment*

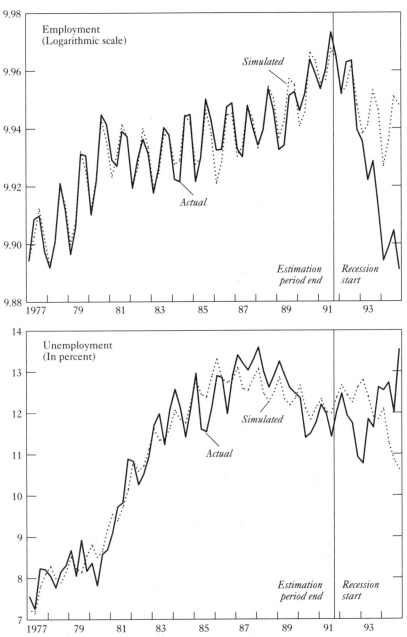

Sources: Italian authorities; and IMF staff estimates.

Chart 13. *Italy: Labor Force and Real Wages*

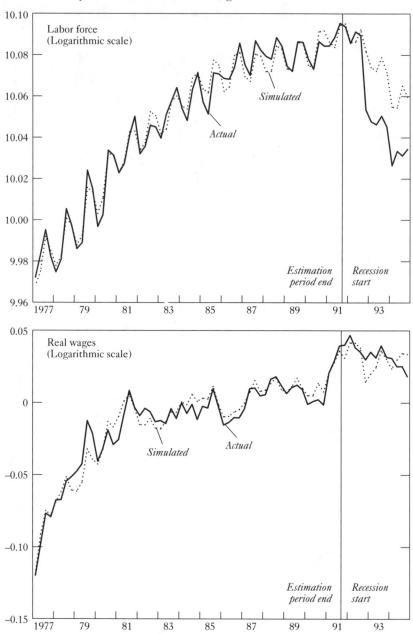

Sources: Italian authorities; and IMF staff estimates.

Chart 14. *Italy: Behavior of Industrial Production During the Business Cycle,*
1973–94
(Index; trough = 100)

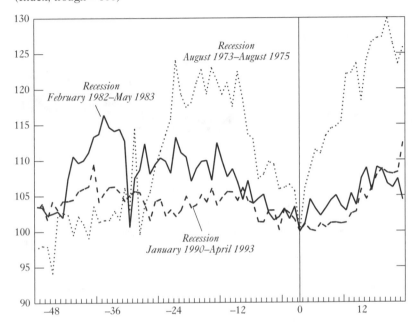

Sources: Bank of Italy; and IMF staff estimates.

variable in the model. To implement this, the variables that appeared as exogenous in the basic model must be endogenized. This is accomplished by appending autoregressions for the exogenous variables to the basic model and re-estimating the extended model (in effect, the additional variables are treated as being block-exogenous). The results of the variance decomposition in the short run (1 step ahead, or one quarter) and in the medium to long run (24 steps ahead, or six years) are collected in Table 4.

A number of results become apparent. Unemployment is significantly affected by changes in the labor force (in fact, labor force appears to dominate employment), a result that holds in both the short and the long run. This result seems plausible for Italy, given the large exogenous changes in the participation rate over the sample period; it may be less significant for

Chart 15. *Italy: Behavior of the Labor Force During the Business Cycle,
1973–94*
(Index; trough = 100)

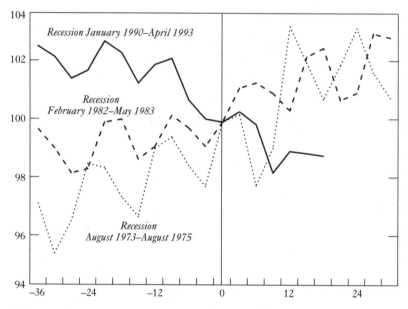

Sources: Bank of Italy; and IMF staff estimates.
Note: Labor force series reconstructed before 1992 and spliced before 1981.

other countries.[9] In the short run, all series are dominated by their own
innovations. However, in the long run, the labor force retains about 33 percent explanatory power, and the consumption wage about 20 percent,
while employment shocks become negligible. These findings are consistent with the interpretation that employment represents short-run
demand by firms, whereas wage setting and labor force participation represent supply-side effects, which are expected to persist in the long run—
as argued, for example, by Blanchard and Quah (1989). The product wage
seems to behave differently, retaining a 20 percent long-run effect from
the consumption wage, but a 60 percent effect from its own innovations.

[9]Layard and Nickell (1987), for example, report that labor force movements were
relatively unimportant in explaining U.K. unemployment.

Table 4.   *Variance Decomposition, 11-Equation Model*
(1 step ahead; 24 steps ahead in parentheses; in percent)

Explanatory Variable	n_t		wc_t		l_t		u_t		wp_t	
n_t	62	(8)	2	(2)	10	(2)	20	(13)	1	(1)
wc_t	1	(3)	65	(22)	3	(2)	1	(2)	16	(18)
l_t	8	(2)	13	(5)	73	(32)	73	(68)	19	(0)
u_t	0	(0)	0	(0)	0	(0)	2	(0)	0	(0)
wp_t	1	(1)	2	(1)	1	(1)	0	(1)	64	(58)
k_t	1	(23)	0	(16)	0	(14)	3	(5)	0	(1)
WAP_t	2	(10)	0	(8)	2	(13)	0	(4)	0	(0)
y_t	8	(32)	0	(24)	4	(22)	0	(4)	0	(1)
r_t	0	(9)	3	(12)	0	(5)	0	(2)	0	(1)
SSC_t	16	(12)	13	(9)	8	(9)	0	(1)	0	(0)
p_t	0	(0)	0	(2)	0	(0)	0	(0)	0	(0)

Notes: For definitions, see Table 1; see also Appendix II.

This surprising result is probably related to the rather persistent behavior of the wedge over the sample period (Chart 8).

One result with far-reaching implications, however, is that variables treated as exogenous in the extended model (capital, GDP, working-age population, and competitiveness) ultimately become predominant, explaining 64 percent of employment, 60 percent of the consumption wage, and 54 percent of the labor force variance in the long run. This result is consistent with a view that attributes much of the rise in unemployment to the weak macroeconomic performance of the Italian economy together with unfavorable external shocks. However, it must be kept in mind that the impact of the unfavorable macroeconomic environment was magnified and sustained by the inflexibility of Italian labor market institutions, which kept real wages high and made it difficult for new entrants into the labor force to find jobs.

Another significant result is the effect of the increases of the social security contributions over the sample period. This variable alone explained 16 percent of the variance of employment and 13 percent of the variance in the consumption wage. Perhaps more important, this effect largely persists into the long run. This finding is important, however, not only because it indicates that policy had a significant detrimental effect, but also because of the implied statistical properties of a policy variable. Social security contribution is a persistent variable—it is I(1). Thus, to the extent that the statistical properties of social security contributions are representative for other policy variables, the effects of policy (both detrimental and favorable) can be more powerful and long lasting.

Evidence on Labor Market Policies and Lagged Effects

In the framework adopted in this paper, policy can have three distinct roles. One, it can affect unemployment directly (for example, social security contributions were shown to reduce employment in both the short and the long run). Two, it can affect unemployment indirectly, by influencing variables that were considered exogenous from the point of view of the model (for example, GDP growth, capital formation, and competitiveness). Three, it can affect the lags with which both policy and nonpolicy variables affect unemployment, an area of particular importance under the framework of Karanassou and Snower (1994). For example, social security contributions affect employment both contemporaneously and with a lag; the *scala mobile* resulted in more rigid wages and a longer wage adjustment lag; and firing costs resulted in longer employment adjustment lags. Each will be discussed in turn.

The direct effects of policy on unemployment are the simplest to describe. As already shown, social security contributions increased the cost of employment to employers and introduced a wedge between the value of work to employees. The overall impact on employment and wages was significant and persistent, as shown by the variance decomposition. The reason for the continuous rise in social security contributions is probably related to two factors: demographics (Italy has one of the highest old-age dependency ratios in the OECD), and increasing spending on pensions, which have grown from some 5 percent of GDP in the 1960s to more than 15 percent in the 1990s. Compared with other countries, Italian spending on pensions in the 1960s was close to the average of the seven major industrial countries, but increased to the highest in the OECD (except Austria) by the 1990s. Although the increase in pensions is partly related to demographics, the generosity of the Italian pension system is also responsible: Italy's old-age pension benefits, when expressed as a ratio to per capita GDP, are the highest of the EU countries (see Canziani and Demekas (1995)).

The indirect effects of policy on unemployment, which operate through such variables as GDP, capital accumulation, and competitiveness, are harder to pin down because they touch upon a number of difficult macroeconomic issues that cannot be analytically resolved in the absence of a fully specified macroeconomic model.[10] However, a number of comments can be made. Demand-management policies were shown to be ineffective after the first oil shock. Academics and policymakers alike no longer believe that it is possible for the authorities to raise GDP (or capital accumulation) in a sustained fashion through demand-management policies.[11] However, structural policies can influence GDP and capital accumulation. Two such sets of policies that, overall, could be expected to have detrimental effects on GDP and capital accumulation in Italy can be mentioned. The first concerns regional policies vis-à-vis the south, while the second concerns the net effect of overall revenue and expenditure policies—the continuing accumulation of a large stock of public debt.

In the 1960s and 1970s, regional development in the south was predominantly attempted through the installation of capital-intensive industrial enterprises, which were at the time expected to contribute to employment through linkages with other sectors. (See de Luca and Bruni (1993), pp. 28–33.) This policy, by effectively subsidizing capital-intensive activities at the expense of relatively abundant labor, had precisely the opposite effect from what was intended. (Another way of describing the effect of the policy is that, for a given level of investment, fewer jobs were created.) In addition, the south was granted easy access to public sector employment, but wages were set in a centralized fashion without adjusting for local conditions, including cost of living, wages, and unemployment. As previously discussed, this was exacerbated by the effect of centralized bargaining and wage setting. The overall effect was to raise wages for the whole region well above market-clearing levels.

The other major policy influence on both GDP and capital accumulation is the continuing accumulation of public debt, which raised long-term real interest rates. Although academics tended to challenge this point, recent evidence suggests that the levels of public debt have risen throughout the industrial world, with statistically and economically significant effects on real interest rates (see Ford and Laxton (1995)). In addition, Italian public debt has risen faster than in the rest of the EU, and real inter-

---

[10]The adverse movements in competitiveness for Italy were reversed after 1984, so they no longer represent an important impediment to employment creation.

[11]Modigliani and Padoa Schioppa (1986) argue that unemployment in Italy can be traced to two primary factors: real wage rigidity and an inability to raise aggregate demand on account of leakages—in effect, an external constraint. They argue that what is required is a coordinated increase in aggregate demand by industrial countries. Of course, this begs the question of whether demand policies can affect output in a sustained fashion, which is valid regardless of the presence or absence of coordination (although the presence of an external constraint does tend to make the deficiencies of demand-management policies obvious faster).

est rate differentials between Italy and Germany are wider. Clearly, these phenomena will continue to depress capital formation in Italy until the level of public debt is brought down.

The third way in which policy in Italy has affected unemployment is through its influence on the delay with which both policy and nonpolicy variables affect unemployment. These lags have received special attention in this study. Italy appears to exhibit a full complement of these effects: an employment adjustment effect (lagged employment in the employment equation), a wage staggering effect (lagged real wages in the wage setting equation), an insider membership effect (lagged employment in the wage setting equation), and a labor force adjustment effect (lagged labor force in the labor force equation). A fifth effect, arising from the fact that the long-term unemployed discourage employment, seems important for Italy, although a similar effect appears to operate through lagged employment terms in the labor force equation rather than through lagged unemployment terms in the wage setting equation. In other words, the long-term unemployed tend to leave the labor force altogether, with little effect on wages; in contrast, insiders appear to have an effect on wages.

Policy in Italy has tended overall to act in a way that would be expected to magnify these lags. The main policies were described in greater detail in an earlier section. To recapitulate, wage indexation in the form of the *scala mobile* would be expected to result in more rigid wages and a longer wage adjustment lag (a stronger wage staggering effect); firing costs and employment protection would be expected to result in a stronger insider membership effect as well as longer employment adjustment lags; hiring costs (the requirement that hiring be done through public employment agencies in the order determined by the state) would be expected to increase employment adjustment lags, strengthen the insider membership effect, and perhaps increase the discouraged-worker effect.

Not all of these effects are necessarily expected to affect the average level of unemployment. The employment adjustment effect, the wage staggering effect, and the labor force adjustment effect would tend to increase the lag with which unemployment adjusted after being subjected to shocks, but would not in themselves increase unemployment. On the other hand, the insider membership effect and the discouraged-worker effect can affect average unemployment by, respectively, increasing real wages and lowering the labor force. There is some theoretical controversy about whether employment protection legislation (hiring and firing costs) would be expected to affect average unemployment. Bertola (1990) constructs models that imply that the variance of employment would tend to be reduced, but average unemployment remain largely unchanged. Snower and Lindbeck (1990), on the other hand, argue that because the bargaining power of insiders would increase in the presence of hiring and firing costs, and because the presence of insiders would tend to increase wages, average unemployment would also be expected to increase.

Estimating the quantitative impact of policy on the various lag effects for Italy is complicated by a number of factors. First, it is generally impossible to measure policy directly: policy changes tended to be of a complicated, legal nature that is not amenable to direct measurement. Second, not all policies changed in a discrete manner over the sample period. Finally, when policy did change discretely, it tended to happen in a number of areas simultaneously, which complicates the interpretation of the results. Nevertheless, the effect (or the absence thereof) was estimated through the construction of dummy variables that captured the effect of policy changes that occurred at known times; Appendix I lists known policy changes and their timing. Two potentially significant break points were found in the sample when policy changed: 1985, when the *scala mobile* was somewhat weakened and internal labor flexibility increased; and 1992, when the *scala mobile* was abolished, the national wage bargaining system was revised, the public list system of hiring was abolished, and firing costs were generally reduced.

A statistical investigation of coefficient stability before and after 1984 was carried out to see whether policies (or, indeed, other factors) had significant effects on labor market behavior. Given preliminary results for other countries,[12] and some existing research results for Italy,[13] it was expected that a structural break would be found. Surprisingly, the evidence points instead to a rather impressive degree of parameter stability and a relative lack of policy-induced changes. First, F-tests of overall parameter stability were performed for each of the three equations (employment, wage setting, and labor participation). For all three equations, the hypothesis of joint parameter stability failed to be rejected at conventional significance levels.[14] A visual examination of the residuals of each equation also failed to reveal large outliers or any other evidence of misspecification (such as heteroscedasticity, or lack of stationarity of the residuals). Then, the equations were re-estimated, allowing the major policy-related coefficients to differ across the two subsamples.[15] The relevant results are reported in Table 5.

---

[12]For example, estimates of coefficients for France are generally thought to contain significant breaks in the early to mid-1980s.

[13]Fachin (1991) found that an employment equation for Italy during 1970–84 exhibited structurally unstable coefficients, while Jaramillo, Schiantarelli, and Sembenelli (1991) found evidence consistent with nonconstant adjustment cost parameters. However, because of different samples and sample periods, these studies are not directly comparable to the results contained here.

[14]For the employment equation, $F(14,44) = 1.79$; for the wage equation, $F(11,50) = 1.61$, and for the labor force equation, $F(16,40) = 0.92$. The 95 percent critical value for the tests was 1.90 or higher.

[15]The sensitivity of employment to output was also allowed to vary.

Table 5. *Parameter Stability, 1977–84 Versus 1985–94*

	Dependent Variable		
	n_t	wc_t	l_t
Coefficients (*t*-statistics without regard to sign; in parentheses)			
Constant	−10.91 (2.7)	−2.17 (2.9)	−1.02 (0.9)
Trend	−0.005 (2.6)	— (0.4)	−0.0006 (2.3)
Second-quarter dummy variable	0.007 (2.5)	−0.004 (1.7)	−0.004 (1.1)
Third-quarter dummy variable	0.017 (8.0)	−0.001 (0.5)	−0.006 (1.5)
Fourth-quarter dummy variable	0.009 (5.0)	−0.005 (2.3)	−0.003 (1.0)
n_t (1977–84)	...	...	0.913 (7.3)
n_t (1985–94)	...	...	0.730 (6.3)
n_{t-1} (1977–84)	0.534 (4.6)	...	−0.266 (1.3)
n_{t-1} (1985–94)	0.535 (4.6)	...	−0.267 (1.3)
n_{t-2} (1977–84)	...	...	−0.510 (2.4)
n_{t-2} (1985–94)	...	...	−0.510 (2.4)
n_{t-3} (1977–84)	0.116 (1.2)	0.203 (3.0)	0.347 (1.6)
n_{t-3} (1985–94)	0.115 (1.2)	0.202 (3.0)	0.348 (1.6)
n_{t-4} (1977–84)	...	...	−0.210 (1.2)
n_{t-4} (1985–94)	...	...	−0.210 (1.2)
wc_t	...	...	0.063 (1.0)
wc_{t-1} (1977–84)	...	0.75 (9.6)	...
wc_{t-1} (1985–94)	...	0.82 (8.5)	...
l_{t-1}	...	...	0.562 (3.1)
l_{t-2}	...	...	0.210 (1.2)
l_{t-3}	...	...	−0.227 (1.4)
l_{t-4}	...	...	0.262 (2.0)
wp_t (1977–84)	−0.12 (1.8)	...	...
wp_t (1985–94)	−0.14 (2.9)	...	...
k_t	0.86 (2.6)	...	...
r_t	−0.08 (3.8)	...	...
y_t (1977–84)	0.148 (3.4)	...	...
y_t (1985–94)	0.139 (2.8)	...	...
p_t	...	0.08 (1.3)	...
WAP_t	...	...	0.00001 (1.9)
SSC_t	−3.93 (4.9)	−4.35 (5.2)	...
SSC_{t-1}	3.36 (3.8)	4.33 (4.0)	...
SSC_{t-3}	−1.21 (2.1)	−0.18 (0.3)	...

Notes: For definitions, see Table 1; see also Appendix II.

Most coefficients change remarkably little from one subsample to the next. The main exception is a weakening of the discouraged-worker effect in the labor force equation, a change that is relatively large and approaches statistical significance.[16] The only statistically significant change was in the first employment lag in the employment equation, but the economic significance of the magnitude of the difference was negligible. In all other cases, statistical tests failed to reject the hypothesis of individual coefficient equality across subsamples. The principal conclusion then is that policy changes after 1984 were largely ineffective, failing to reduce labor market rigidities.

Finally, the model was simulated to investigate the degree of inertia and the sources of lags. To conduct the simulations, the three basic labor market equations were augmented by the unemployment and product wage identities, and by an estimated production function to capture the fact that output would be expected to change from the actual path because the simulation resulted in employment paths that differed from actual.[17] The model was subjected to a 1 percent transitory negative labor demand shock. The model exhibited persistence in the sense that the path of the variables settled down to equilibrium after a considerable lag (approximately seven to eight years; see Charts 9–11). The long-run effect, however, was negligible, as would be expected for a stable system. Equally, when the model was subjected to a 1 percent permanent negative shock, it exhibited imperfect responsiveness in that the endogenous variables reached their new equilibrium level after a considerable lag (also approximately seven to eight years; see Chart 9). The impulse responses of the system are shown in Charts 10 and 11. Measures of these effects, and their sources, are contained in Table 6.

The model exhibits positive persistence, as unemployment is driven up for up to two years following a temporary shock. However, the discouraged-worker effect eventually drives so many workers out of the labor force that measured unemployment undershoots its long-run path (Chart 10).[18] In fact, the sum of deviations is approximately zero, as is shown by the aggregate persistence measure. The absolute persistence measure is strictly positive, reflecting the undershooting. Employment also exhibits overshooting, although the effect of a temporary shock lasts longer. Some overshooting occurs because of output effects. The inclusion of a production function magnifies swings in employment, because as employment comes down,

---

[16]The t-statistic on the test is 1.74 (without regard to sign).

[17]The production function coefficients were constrained to preserve constant returns to scale.

[18]Of course, to the extent that measured unemployment is reduced by the discouraged-worker effect, the social welfare effects may be worse than they appear.

Table 6.   *Measures of Persistence and Imperfect Responsiveness*

	Persistence	Absolute Persistence	Imperfect Responsiveness
Aggregate	—	1.30	9.94
Employment lags, employment equation	−0.21	−2.38	6.91
Employment lags, wage equation	−2.02	−0.90	37.56
Wage lags, wage equation	0.07	0.31	43.96
Labor supply lags plus interaction effects	2.16	4.27	−78.49

Note: Persistence is defined as the sum of deviations from the base path when unemployment is subjected to a temporary shock. Absolute persistence sums absolute deviations. Imperfect responsiveness sums deviations from the base path after subtracting the change in the long-run equilibrium resulting from subjecting unemployment to a permanent shock. Both measures are standardized by the size of the shock, which is a 1 percent reduction in labor demand. The sources of persistence and imperfect responsiveness are calculated by leading all lagged terms (setting $L^{-k}x_{t-k}$) of the source variable while leaving all other lags intact.

output is also reduced, which further reduces employment; the opposite occurs as employment increases. In terms of both persistence measures, employment lags in the employment equation contribute negatively. This can be explained by the fact that lags in the employment equation delay the initial fall in employment, hastening the reversal of employment to its eventual equilibrium level. Similarly, the wage staggering effect contributes to persistence positively, albeit by extending the time period over which wages adjust; in addition, wages also overshoot slightly, and the absolute persistence measure is higher.

In contrast, the insider employment effect tends to moderate persistence. An intuitive explanation is that wages fall as the stock of insider employees is reduced, which tends to moderate the fall in employment, which therefore adjusts faster back to its initial equilibrium level. The lag effects stemming from the labor supply equation are both more complicated and difficult to separate into their constituent parts, because they tend to interact intimately with lag effects from the employment equation. More intuitive results are obtained by considering these effects together. Clearly, although the labor force adjusts temporarily downward, as does employment, the net effect on unemployment remains positive. Hence, the net effect of the lagged terms plus their interaction is to contribute significantly to both persistence and absolute persistence.

The model also exhibits positive imperfect responsiveness, to which all but one term contribute. Clearly, employment lags cause employment to fall sluggishly to its new equilibrium level, contributing to imperfect responsiveness. The wage lags also cause wages to adjust downward toward their new equilibrium level with a lag. The two most interesting reactions to permanent shocks come from the insider employment and labor supply effects. The employment lags in the wage equation contribute positively to imperfect responsiveness because, by reducing wages, they tend to increase employment and hence delay its reduction to the new, lower equilibrium level. The discouraged-worker effect, together with employment interactions, tends by contrast to speed adjustment strongly because in Italy labor force participation effects are especially strong.[19] Some workers are so discouraged as to leave the labor supply permanently: this causes equilibrium unemployment to shrink, which makes the transition to the new equilibrium level occur faster.

The Recent Recession and Increased Labor Market Flexibility

Whereas the labor market policies of the mid-1980s failed to have much of an impact, the same cannot be said for the reforms after 1991. Employment appeared much more flexible, although evidence of this exists only for the downward direction. This section will attempt to interpret events, although the short sample and some data uncertainties mean that the conclusions reached here should be treated with caution.

To gain an understanding of changes in labor market behavior after 1991, the model was estimated only up to 1991 and was used to produce forecasts up to 1994 (see Charts 12 and 13). Employment fell much more than would be expected based on the historical relationship between output and employment during a recession (see also Charts 7, 14, and 15). A formal statistical test of parameter change along the lines pursued earlier is not possible, because there are not enough degrees of freedom. However, it is possible to perform Chow's predictive test, which compares the forecasting performance of the model with actual developments. When this test was performed, the hypothesis of parameter constancy in the employment and labor force participation coefficients was decisively rejected, whereas for the wage setting equation it was

---

[19]In the early part of the twentieth century, the discouraged-worker effect was also very strong, resulting in significant outward migration flows.

accepted.[20] The results for the wage setting equation are somewhat surprising, because wage behavior was thought to have changed markedly after the recent reforms. The results suggest that wage setting behavior has not changed very much, although labor demand could have become much more sensitive to wage variation. It should also be kept in mind that the model is couched in terms of real wages and that nominal wages could have improved substantially.

Although we do not have sufficient degrees of freedom to test for parameter inconstancy in general, it is possible to get a sense of the sources of the changes by imposing some prior conditions. This is accomplished by re-estimating the equations for two subsamples, 1977–91 and 1992–94, but allowing only a small number of the most policy-relevant coefficients to change. The employment equation had difficulty distinguishing between changes in the relationship between employment and output, changes in the effect of wages on employment, and changes in the effect of a level shift, which is not surprising given the shortness of the sample. When all three were allowed to change, the effect of wages on employment increased from –0.11 to –0.87. The change was not statistically significant at conventional levels of confidence (the t-statistic was 1.3), but, if held over a longer period, this result would be a very important development. The employment adjustment effect was lower than it was when the equation was estimated over the full sample, with lagged employment coefficients at 0.41 and 0.08, at the first and third lags, respectively. Moreover, a statistically significant reduction in the third lag was observed after the reforms. In addition, a statistically significant upward level shift seemed to take place, while the sensitivity of employment to output appeared to weaken.[21] The wage setting equation showed a decline in the wage staggering effect: the coefficient on lagged wages fell from 0.75 to 0.52. Again, the change was not statistically significant at conventional levels of confidence, but, with a t-statistic of 1.5, could prove more significant in the future. Finally, the labor force equation showed both economically and statistically significant reductions in the discouraged-worker effect, with lower coefficients on lagged employment.

---

[20]Chow's predictive test is an F-test: for the employment equation, $F(12,58) = 3.12$ and for the labor force equation, $F(12,56) = 4.11$, compared with a critical value of about 1.9. For the wage equation, however, $F(12,61) = 1.47$.

[21]This last result is surprising, because a number of observers interpreted developments during the last recession as implying an increase in the sensitivity of output to employment. The regressions seem to indicate instead that firms continued to shed labor even as output rebounded.

In summary, preliminary results suggest that labor market behavior changed markedly after the reforms. Employment was much more flexible, with a weaker employment adjustment effect and a weaker discouraged-worker effect. Firms became much more sensitive to wages and the wage staggering effect became less pronounced. It was not possible to detect statistically significant changes in real wage setting behavior, but this could change as more data become available (reforms on wage bargaining have been in place only since 1994). These results accord well with the nature of the reforms, which eliminated the *scala mobile* and concentrated on removing impediments to hiring and firing.

The Future

To investigate further the possible future effects of a more flexible labor market, the model (estimated on the basis of the full sample) was simulated to produce forecasts for employment, unemployment, wages, and the labor force (see Charts 16 and 17). The underlying assumptions, including output and capital formation projections, were consistent with the assumptions contained in the most recent version of the IMF's *World Economic Outlook*.[22] The simulation shows that, although employment is projected to increase substantially and real wages are projected to decrease somewhat before they rebound, unemployment falls by less than 1 percent over the forecast period. This result is consistent with the average behavior of unemployment over the whole sample, but does not take into account the possibility of continuing shedding of employment by firms. The previous section presented evidence of a regime shift as a result of the labor market reforms. Future developments will therefore hinge on which of these two forces predominates and on whether the labor market reforms are maintained or, better yet, strengthened.

It is important to attempt to investigate the potential positive impact of making the labor market more flexible and reducing the various adjustment lags. This will provide some indication of the "upside" potential of labor market reforms. To investigate this, an additional simulation was performed that assumed that labor shedding did not continue.[23] The equations were simulated with lagged coefficients on employment and wages consistent with the reductions suggested by the preliminary estimates reported earlier. The lagged employment terms in the employment equation

---

[22]The forecasts reported here use information available as of April 1995.

[23]It is not yet possible to judge whether productivity gains have run their course. One can conceive of a realistic scenario whereby firms continue to shed labor, which would weaken output growth through the production function.

Chart 16. *Italy: Employment and Unemployment*

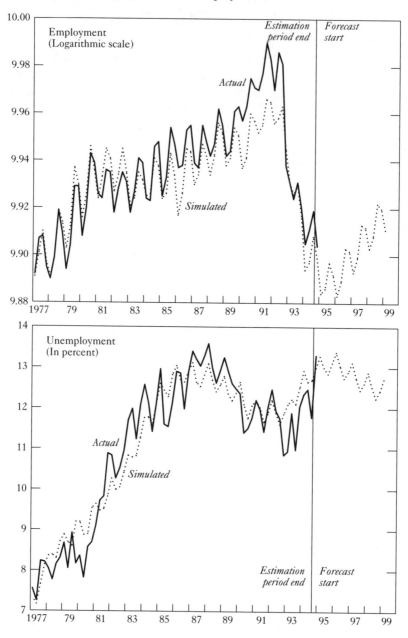

Sources: Italian authorities; and IMF staff estimates.

Chart 17. *Italy: Labor Force and Real Wages*

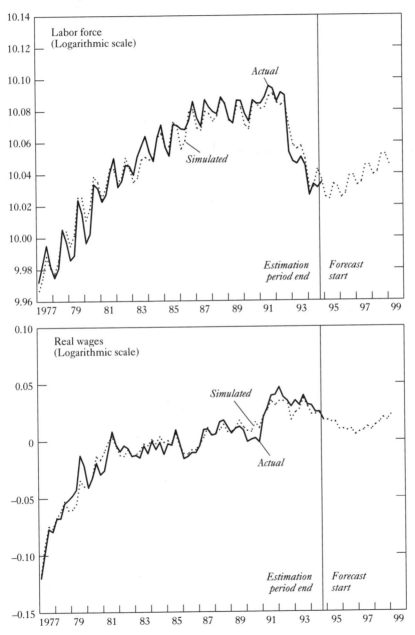

Sources: Italian authorities; and IMF staff estimates.

were reduced by 0.20, the wage elasticity of employment increased by –0.76, the lagged wage coefficient in the wage equation was reduced by 0.25, and the lagged employment terms in the labor force equation were reduced by 0.02.[24] (See Charts 18 and 19.) With the aforementioned caveats in mind, they indicate that impressive gains in employment, wages, and the labor force are possible and that unemployment could fall to less than 10 percent—translating the results of the WSF-adjusted unemployment figures to the national definition—by 1999.

Conclusions

The structural VAR model that was estimated in this paper appears to capture well a number of important dynamic and structural relationships in the Italian labor market. It was used to investigate Italian unemployment from different points of view. Over the long run, it was found that increasing Italian unemployment resulted from the interaction between adverse macroeconomic shocks and an inflexible wage setting mechanism. Over the short to medium run, substantial lags were found to exist that were linked to a number of policies and that interacted in significant ways. When subjected to a temporary shock, unemployment tended to settle down to equilibrium after a considerable lag (seven to eight years). Employment adjustment costs and the wage staggering effect tended to increase unemployment persistence, while the insider employment effect tended to reduce it. Unemployment also responded sluggishly to permanent shocks, owing to lags from all effects except the discouraged-worker effect.

The labor market reforms that were introduced after 1984 were found, as a result of statistical tests, to have been largely ineffective in reducing labor market rigidities. However, the reforms after 1991 appear to have resulted in a labor market that exhibits substantially more flexibility on the employment and labor-supply sides, although wage setting remains a question mark. There is, however, some evidence of a reduction in wage staggering, which is the expected result of the abolition of the *scala mobile*. Provided that the labor shedding witnessed since the last recession is discontinued and that the labor market flexibility that seems to have increased after 1991 persists or is strengthened, significant gains against unemployment could well take place.

---

[24]Tinkering with a dynamic model by changing only a few parameters will in general result in outcomes that do not make economic sense. The simulation reported here also required level shifts in the employment and labor force equations that were, however, much smaller than the estimated changes.

Chart 18. *Italy: Employment and Unemployment*
(Post-1994 scenarios)

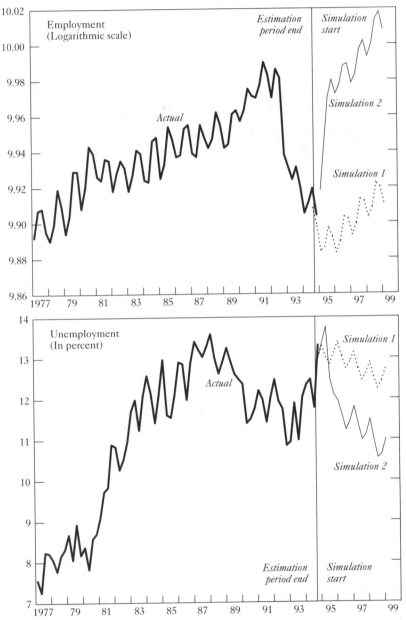

Sources: Italian authorities; and IMF staff estimates.

Chart 19. *Italy: Labor Force and Real Wages*
(Post-1994 scenarios)

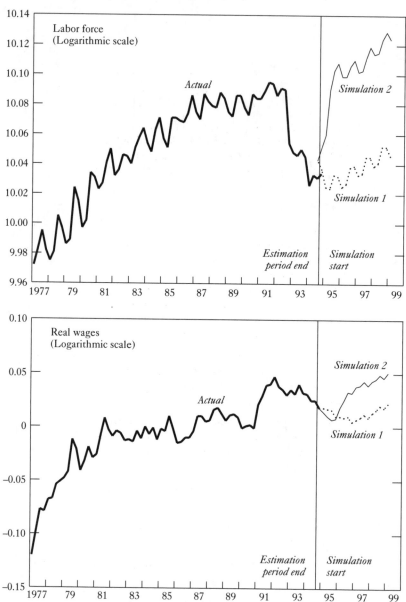

Sources: Italian authorities; and IMF staff estimates.

Appendix I: Labor Market Institutional and Policy Events

Date	Event	Main Affected Areas
Post–WWII	SM introduced; allowed for region-specific adjustments based on regional retail price indices.	SM
1952	SM evolved to national scheme of uniform adjustments based on a specially calculated index (*indice sindacale*), which put more weight on consumables such as food but excluded petrol while putting less weight on other energy products.	SM
1957	SM adjustments done on a quarterly basis.	SM
1950–60s	Initial system on hiring rules emerged. Nonagricultural companies required to hire employees from a public list in the order in which they appeared. In determining rank order, the state took into account criteria such as status of employment, duration of unemployment (if unemployed), and social factors, such as the number of dependents. Private employment agencies were banned.	Hire/Fire
Fall 1969	"Hot autumn" of worker unrest that led to the Charter of Workers' Rights (Statuto dei Lavoratori) that provided the basis for restrictive employment regulations.	Hire/Fire
1970	Law No. 300/1970 gave special privileges (rights to hold meetings at the place of work; work time could be used by union officials for union business) to the three largest national unions.	WB
	Three-year wage agreement concluded. Granted "huge" increases.	WB
1973	Three-year wage agreement concluded. Granted "huge" increases.	WB
1975	SM agreement between the social partners established the new system (put into effect fully in 1977).	SM
1976	Three-year wage agreement concluded. Granted "lower" increases.	WB

Appendix I (*continued*)

Date	Event	Main Affected Areas
1977	Severance pay system reformed. Wage withholdings put in a special severance fund, but SM component excluded from wage basis (1973–76 system included). Amount awarded proportional to average monthly wage (100 percent for salaried, less for workers) and adjusted to reflect level of last wage payment.	Hire/Fire
End-1977	1975 reforms of SM put into effect. Now, SM standardized and extended from industrial sector to all the workforce. Employees accorded compensation of set amount, Lit 2,389 increase a month, in the *indice sindacale* for each increase of 1 percent.	SM
Summer 1979	Three-year wage agreement concluded; granted "lower" increases; equal increases granted to all workers except in industry; agreed that next round would allow more differentiation.	SM
End-1979	Public sector workers (2.3 million) agreed to put the SM on a quarterly rather than a semiannual basis.	SM
1980	Monthly maximum paid from WSF raised to Lit 600,000 from Lit 200,000 for salaried employees; it remained at Lit 200,000 for workers although they received partial adjustment for inflation (average cover fell to 76 percent from 80 percent).	WSF
June 1, 1982	Severance pay system reformed. Constant of proportionality reduced from 100 percent, but SM component included in basis. Also, enterprise contributions were raised.	Hire/Fire
June 2, 1982	Three-year wage agreement failed to be concluded (except for public transport and bank employees). Discussions about reforming the SM coincided with wage negotiations, resulting in stalemate. Confindustria led the way; others followed in the second half of 1983.	WB
Jan. 22, 1983	SM revised; sliding scale index rebased from August–October 1974 to August–October 1982. Monthly value of each point raised to Lit 6,800 from Lit 2,389. Degree of indexation fell 15 percent, because a 1 percent increase under the new index corresponded to a 3.35 percent increase under the old index.	SM

Appendix I (*continued*)

Date	Event	Main Affected Areas
Jan. 22, 1983	Wage negotiation stalemate broken. Overall wage growth of 13 percent in 1983 and 10 percent in 1984 agreed to. Contractual changes in wages to be limited to Lit 25,000 (1983), Lit 35,000 (1984), and Lit 40,000 (1985). Also agreed to reduce hours worked by 20 hours in the second half of 1984, and by another 20 hours in the first half of 1985 (~1 hour/week, to 40 hours/week).	WB
1982, second half	Three-year wage agreement concluded. "Moderate" but retroactive wage increase granted.	WB
Feb. 16, 1984	Once-off reform to incomes policy introduced: limited SM points allowable to 4 points in each half of 1984. It proved a binding constraint only during the first half of 1984 (which would have seen an 8-point increase).	SM
1984	Hiring system reformed, so employers could hire employees without regard to their rank order, provided the proportion of such workers was small. The system was not strictly adhered to.	Hire/Fire
	"Solidarity contracts" introduced, whereby firms with more than 1,000 employees could allow workers to share the work. Were not much used, however.	Hire/Fire
1985	Three-year wage agreement failed to be concluded.	WB
Jan. 1986	SM reformed: from quarterly to semiannual adjustments (May–November). Coverage reduced, with 100 percent coverage only applying up to monthly wages of Lit 580,000 and 25 percent thereafter. The Lit 580,000 threshold was indexed to the *indice sindacale*. Bonuses and overtime pay were not indexed. End of flat adjustment-based system, move to proportional system.	SM
Jan. 1987	Three-year wage agreement finally concluded. Most contracts had expired in 1985, and wage growth during 1986 was moderate despite the absence of contracts.	WB
1988	Employers required to contribute 4.5 percent of the WSF benefits accruing to workers as a social security contribution. Until now, the WSF was free to employers.	WSF

Appendix I (*continued*)

Date	Event	Main Affected Areas
Sep. 1988	Employee guarantees in cases of dismissal on disciplinary grounds extended to firms with fewer than 16 employees.	Hire/Fire
1990	Three-year wage agreements concluded for public sector and most of the private sector. Some agreements contained forward-looking provisions based on targeted inflation for the first time (given that actual targeted inflation was less than 0.75 percent). Certain contracts froze the wage drift component.	WB
1991	"Mobility list" created, which grants special benefits to redundant workers arising from collective redundancies. Workers receive 80 percent of last wage up to a maximum of Lit 1.2 million/month, for a maximum of 12 months. It is renewable once for workers over 40 years old and twice for workers over 50 (but 20 percent fewer benefits).	UnB
	Hiring system regulating the rank order of hires finally abolished. Some rules remained, mandating a 15 percent quota for the disabled for firms with more than 35 employees and a 12 percent quota for the "disadvantaged" (long-term unemployed) workers on the mobility list for firms with more than 10 employees. The 12 percent can be increased to 20 percent by regional employment agencies, provided the Ministry of Labor concurs.	Hire/Fire
July 1991	WSF reformed: "ordinary" wage supplementation (WS) extended to cover white-collar workers, who would also become subject to wage withholding. WS limited to industrial firms with at least 15 dependent employees and extended to trade sector enterprises with at least 200 dependent employees. Maximum length for "extraordinary" intervention set at 36 months in five years (subject to exceptions). Same benefits as WSF now apply to workers on mobility list.	WSF
Dec. 1991	Accord suspended wage indexation.	SM
May 1992	SM indexation adjustment suspended (did not take place).	SM
July 1992	Accord formally ended SM system of wage indexation. Stipulated suspension of all bargaining rounds at the	SM/WB

Appendix I (*concluded*)

Date	Event	Main Affected Areas
	plant level during 1992–93. Instead, employees would get 13 monthly payments of Lit 20,000 during 1993, partly compensating for likely indexation-related wage increases in that period.	SM/WB
Jan. 1993	Labor force survey definitions made more internationally comparable, but a break in the relevant time series was introduced.	Data
July 1993	Wage bargaining system reformed: SM definitively abolished; two levels of wage bargaining defined (national/sectoral and regional/firm); timetable and procedures set for wage bargaining and conflict resolution; benchmarks set to be taken into account during negotiations (notably targeted inflation at the national level). Four-year national labor contracts while nominal wages to be renegotiated at two-year intervals.	WB

Notes: SM = *scala mobile* (sliding scale)
WB = wage bargaining
WSF = wage supplementation fund (*cassa integrazione guadagni*)
UnB = unemployment benefits; WSF is a form of UnB

Appendix II: Data Sources and Definitions

Most of the raw quarterly data used in this paper were provided by the Bank of Italy, and were available as of April 1995. Exceptions include the capital stock and the fiscal variables (social security contributions and direct taxes), which were provided by the OECD, and exchange rate and oil price data, which were provided by the IMF. As mentioned in the text, the main labor market aggregates (labor force, employment, and unemployment) for Italy do not include those workers placed on the wage supplementation fund (WSF). Hence, all figures used in the paper have been adjusted to include them, except where otherwise indicated.

The Italian authorities recently revised the main labor market aggregates from 1992Q4 onward. This created a problem of interpretation, since the dramatic changes evident in labor market data after 1991 could possibly be attributed to the data revisions. The Bank of Italy has produced revised figures for labor force, employment, and unemployment going back to 1981, and these figures are used in the paper (further revised to include the impact of the WSF).[25] The revised figures indicated that the evident break in the series after 1991 was not caused by the data revisions themselves. However, in 1992Q4 there is also an evident break in population data, and further revisions of the labor force statistics are likely as new census data are processed. Hence, the post-1991 results should be treated with caution.

The wage series used in this paper is wages in the manufacturing sector. Although an economywide aggregate would have been preferable, the manufacturing wage series goes back further in time and appears to track the economywide aggregate closely where the two overlap. The consumption wage is defined as the manufacturing wage deflated by the consumer price index (CPI), and the product wage is defined as the manufacturing wage deflated by the producer price index (PPI). Although these definitions are at best proxies for the theoretically indicated concepts, corrections were provided for any definitional imprecisions by including tax variables in the regressions—both social security contributions and direct taxes. Owing to data limitations, it was not possible to decompose social security contributions into employer and employee components (at least at a quarterly frequency for the time period under consideration).

Appendix III: Estimation and Testing of the Labor Market Model

All the series used in this paper were tested for stationarity using Augmented Dickey-Fuller (ADF) tests. Results indicated that all variables were integrated of order one, denoted as I(1). This result held even for the product wage. The null hypothesis assumed the existence of a deterministic linear trend. Given these results, the equations finally selected for inclusion in the main model (the employment, wage setting, and labor force equations) were tested for cointegration. For each equation, the hypothesis of cointegration among the included variables failed to be rejected, and the residuals were found to be stationary using ADF tests. The cointegrating vectors were also estimated using the Johansen procedure, and were found to have the same signs as those estimated for the main model. When the full set of variables was tested for the existence of cointegrating vectors using the Johansen procedure, the hypothesis that there existed six to seven cointegrating vectors failed to be rejected.

The main model was estimated using three different procedures: equation-by-equation using ordinary least squares (OLS); a seemingly unrelated regressions (SUR) technique; and a three-stage least squares technique (3SLS), which took into account estimated contemporaneous correlations between the errors (3SLS + SUR). OLS estimates are known

---

[25]The Bank of Italy's revised series were spliced with the earlier series so as to obtain consistent time series back to 1975.

to be at least consistent when variables are I(1) and cointegrated (see Chapter 1 in this volume for further discussion of these and related topics). Interestingly, for the final specification of the main model, different estimation methods yielded very similar results, provided that a full set of instruments was used in the 3SLS case.[26] This result is probably related to the near diagonal nature of the residual variance-covariance matrix (which is reported in the main text). The results reported in the paper were obtained using the SUR procedure, which seemed somewhat advantageous from the computational point of view.

Finally, the individual equations of the main model were subjected to a series of tests additional to those reported in the main text, including further tests of serial correlation (LM tests with four lags), tests of normality (Jarque-Bera), and heteroscedasticity (ARCH tests with four lags). For each equation, the usual assumptions (no serial correlation, normality, and homoscedasticity) failed to be rejected.

Appendix IV: Inference Reliability in the Presence of Nonstationarity

Although it is clear that estimating relationships involving nonstationary variables is technically correct in the presence of cointegration—in the sense that the estimated coefficients converge to the correct value—it is less obvious that this is also true for the standard errors of these coefficient estimates. The literature on this topic provides some support that this will be so for many, but not necessarily all, of the coefficients. In addition, almost all distributional results from the cointegration literature rely on large sample approximations, which may or may not be applicable to the actual sample lengths available.

To address some of these concerns, a Monte Carlo simulation technique was employed to empirically calculate the distribution of the estimated coefficients. This included the mean and associated t-statistics, the minimum, median, and maximum, as well as various fractiles of the distribution. The specific technique used is known as the "bootstrap," and works by resampling the estimated residuals a large number of times, shocking the model with the resampled residuals, and recomputing the variables of interest. This method is known to generate good approximations to the empirical distribution function of the estimated coefficients (or, indeed, to other statistical functions of interest).

The results of applying this technique are included in Table 7. The first entry, for example, indicates that the coefficient of the first employment

---

[26]And variables such as wages and output were instrumented using lagged wages and output, respectively. This procedure should successfully purge the biasing effects of endogeneity, provided the error terms were serially uncorrelated. Tests failed to reject the hypothesis of no residual serial correlation.

Table 7. *Bootstrapped Coefficient Estimates versus Regression (SUR) Estimates*

	Regression Estimates		Bootstrapped Estimates								
	Mean	t-stat.	Mean	t-stat.	Minimum	5 per-cent fractile	10 per-cent fractile	Median	90 per-cent fractile	95 per-cent fractile	Maximum
Employment											
n(1)	0.5560	6.60	0.4757	5.63	0.2180	0.3309	0.3617	0.4779	0.5807	0.6014	0.7013
n(3)	0.1450	1.90	0.1452	1.87	−0.0970	0.0170	0.0466	0.1461	0.2419	0.2711	0.4355
wp	−0.1200	−3.20	−0.1351	−3.13	−0.2601	−0.2080	−0.1889	−0.1353	−0.0818	−0.0630	−0.0127
Constant	−7.9100	−4.40	−9.3882	−4.37	−17.1641	−13.1284	−12.1857	−9.2565	−6.6996	−6.0105	−4.3732
Time trend	−0.0040	−3.90	−0.0047	−3.86	−0.0084	−0.0068	−0.0062	−0.0046	−0.0032	−0.0028	−0.0016
Q4(−2)	0.0070	2.80	0.0054	2.36	−0.0024	0.0019	0.0025	0.0054	0.0084	0.0091	0.0116
Q4(−1)	0.0160	8.70	0.0155	7.93	0.0087	0.0123	0.0130	0.0156	0.0179	0.0189	0.0206
Q4	0.0090	6.00	0.0098	6.06	0.0046	0.0072	0.0077	0.0099	0.0118	0.0122	0.0147
k	0.6600	4.00	0.8015	4.33	0.3210	0.5149	0.5755	0.7903	1.0496	1.1542	1.4077
r	−0.0700	−5.00	−0.0795	−5.90	−0.1200	−0.1024	−0.0962	−0.0786	−0.0632	−0.0577	−0.0327
SSC	−4.4900	−7.10	−4.6979	−6.86	−6.6648	−5.8667	−5.6037	−4.6548	−3.8610	−3.6682	−2.9161
SSC(1)	3.7600	5.10	3.7491	5.16	1.5911	2.5045	2.7463	3.7499	4.6548	4.9973	5.6525
SSC(3)	−1.4400	−3.70	−1.5284	−3.76	−2.4691	−2.1753	−2.0473	−1.5257	−1.0167	−0.8577	−0.1208
y	0.1580	5.40	0.1833	4.99	0.0801	0.1258	0.1372	0.1815	0.2308	0.2474	0.3026
Wage setting											
n(3)	0.1870	3.30	0.2171	3.16	0.0264	0.1089	0.1301	0.2114	0.3078	0.3434	0.4378
wc(1)	0.7700	17.70	0.6938	8.47	0.3310	0.5576	0.5865	0.7001	0.7938	0.8150	0.8743
Constant	−1.9600	−3.30	−2.2599	−3.25	−4.6152	−3.5108	−3.1762	−2.2088	−1.3814	−1.1654	−0.3917

Time trend	0.0000	0.20	0.0001	0.26	-0.0008	-0.0004	-0.0003	0.0001	0.0006	0.0008	0.0016
Q4(-2)	-0.0040	1.80	-0.0035	-1.79	-0.0097	-0.0069	-0.0062	-0.0034	-0.0011	-0.0004	0.0019
Q4(-1)	-0.0010	-0.60	-0.0012	-0.54	-0.0083	-0.0048	-0.0040	-0.0011	0.0015	0.0021	0.0040
Q4	-0.0050	-2.70	-0.0042	-2.42	-0.0095	-0.0071	-0.0065	-0.0041	-0.0020	-0.0014	0.0007
ρ	0.0500	1.10	0.0512	0.84	-0.1763	-0.0458	-0.0284	0.0508	0.1281	0.1517	0.2315
t1	-4.6800	-6.50	-4.7633	-6.33	-7.1614	-5.9331	-5.7098	-4.7679	-3.7987	-3.6038	-2.5141
t1(1)	4.5400	5.00	4.2664	4.52	1.5413	2.6643	3.1089	4.2378	5.4658	5.7939	7.6832
t1(3)	0.3000	0.10	0.2533	0.47	-1.7311	-0.6342	-0.3991	0.2580	0.9429	1.1110	1.7683
Labor force											
n	0.9520	10.50	0.8396	8.29	0.5457	0.6620	0.7015	0.8390	0.9724	1.0021	1.1361
n(1)	-0.5050	-3.10	-0.3440	-2.21	-0.7839	-0.6069	-0.5429	-0.3467	-0.1418	-0.0898	0.1951
n(2)	-0.4340	-2.60	-0.4012	-2.64	-0.7922	-0.6516	-0.6022	-0.3990	-0.2091	-0.1611	0.1068
n(3)	0.2170	1.20	0.2107	1.33	-0.2702	-0.0385	0.0166	0.2070	0.4091	0.4714	0.7727
n(4)	-0.1470	-1.00	-0.1376	-1.00	-0.5877	-0.3610	-0.3086	-0.1446	0.0401	0.0932	0.2476
wc	0.0070	1.70	0.0718	1.14	-0.1265	-0.0361	-0.0112	0.0762	0.1537	0.1685	0.2397
l(1)	0.6640	5.80	0.6184	5.01	0.2642	0.4051	0.4606	0.6243	0.7726	0.8183	1.0381
l(2)	0.1030	0.70	0.0624	0.44	-0.5422	-0.1856	-0.1072	0.0654	0.2397	0.2915	0.4107
l(3)	-0.1830	-1.40	-0.1532	-1.21	-0.5687	-0.3636	-0.3207	-0.1545	0.0111	0.0430	0.4762
l(4)	0.2720	2.50	0.2424	2.24	-0.0962	0.0586	0.1045	0.2470	0.3756	0.4095	0.5582
Constant	0.4500	0.80	0.3937	0.57	-1.7574	-0.7336	-0.5038	0.4225	1.2577	1.5070	2.5579
Time trend	-0.0003	-2.30	-0.0004	-2.34	-0.0010	-0.0007	-0.0006	-0.0004	-0.0002	-0.0002	0.0002
Q4(-2)	-0.0060	-2.10	-0.0040	-1.49	-0.0121	-0.0085	-0.0075	-0.0040	-0.0003	0.0004	0.0041
Q4(-1)	-0.0110	-3.00	-0.0081	-2.11	-0.0195	-0.0147	-0.0129	-0.0082	-0.0031	-0.0016	0.0030
Q4	-0.0060	-2.00	-0.0048	-1.71	-0.0140	-0.0093	-0.0082	-0.0048	-0.0010	-0.0001	0.0045
popw	0.000010	1.80	0.000007	2.30	-0.000001	0.000003	0.000004	0.000007	0.000011	0.000013	0.000020

Notes: Five hundred replications. For definitions, see Table 1; see also Appendix II.

lag in the employment equation was estimated as 0.556 using standard regression methods (in this case, the SUR technique), which also reported a *t*-statistic of 6.6. Using the bootstrap, the mean of the estimated coefficient is seen to be somewhat lower, at 0.4757, as is the corresponding *t*-statistic. However, the coefficient remains highly statistically significant, and in fact there is not a single replication among the 500 attempted that produced a coefficient estimate lower than 0.218.

Overall, the bootstrapped *t*-statistics tend to be somewhat lower, but the correction is in no case so large as to overturn a conclusion of statistical significance reached using the regression-based estimates, except for some quarterly dummy coefficients, which have no policy significance. The one exception has to do with the effect of the real consumption wage on the labor force, whose statistical significance deteriorates to the point where the coefficient becomes suspect.

References

Bertola, Giuseppe, 1990, "Job Security, Employment, and Wages," *European Economic Review*, Vol. 3 (June), pp. 851–86.

Blanchard, Olivier, and Danny Quah, 1989, "Dynamic Effects of Aggregate Demand and Supply Disturbances," *American Economic Review*, Vol. 79 (September), pp. 655–73.

Canziani, Patrizia, and Dimitri G. Demekas, 1995, "The Italian Public Pension System: Current Prospects and Reform Options," IMF Working Paper 95/33 (Washington: International Monetary Fund).

de Luca, Loretta, and Michele Bruni, 1993, *Unemployment and Labour Market Flexibility: Italy* (Geneva: International Labor Office).

Demekas, Dimitri G., 1994, "Labor Market Institutions and Flexibility in Italy: A Critical Evaluation and Some International Comparisons," IMF Working Paper 94/30 (Washington: International Monetary Fund).

Fachin, Stefano, 1991, "Is the Employment Function Structurally Unstable? An Empirical Test: Italian Manufacturing Industry, 1970–1984," *Labor*, Vol. 5 (Spring), pp. 175–214.

Ford, Robert, and Douglas Laxton, 1995, "World Public Debt and Real Interest Rates," IMF Working Paper 95/30 (Washington: International Monetary Fund).

Jaramillo, Fidel, Fabio Schiantarelli, and Alessandro Sembenelli, 1991, "Are Adjustment Costs for Labor Asymmetric? An Econometric Test of Panel Data for Italy," *Review of Economics and Statistics*, Vol. 75 (November), pp. 640–48.

Karanassou, M., and D.J. Snower, 1994, The Sources of Unemployment Persistence and Responsiveness (unpublished; London: University of London, Birkbeck College).

Layard, P.R.G., and S.J. Nickell, 1987, "Unemployment in Britain," in *The Rise in Unemployment*, ed. by C.R. Bean, P.R.G. Layard, and S.J. Nickell (New York: B. Blackwell).

Lindbeck, Assar, and Dennis J. Snower, 1994, "How Are Product Demand Changes Transmitted to the Labour Market?" *Economic Journal*, Vol. 104 (March), pp. 386–98.

Modigliani, F., and F. Padoa Schioppa, 1986, "Aggregate Unemployment in Italy, 1960–1983," *Economica*, Vol. 53 (Supplement), pp. S245–S273.

Organization for Economic Cooperation and Development, 1994, *The OECD Jobs Study: Evidence and Explanations, Part I: Labour Market Trends and Underlying Forces of Change* (Paris).

Sims, Christopher A., 1980, "Macroeconomics and Reality," *Econometrica*, Vol. 48 (January), pp. 1–49.

Snower, D.J., and Assar Lindbeck, 1990, "Demand- and Supply-Side Policies and Unemployment: Policy Implications of the Insider-Outsider Approach," *Scandinavian Journal of Economics*, Vol. 92 (No. 2), pp. 279–305.

Varian, Hal R., 1984, *Microeconomic Analysis* (New York: Norton, 2nd ed.).

5

The U.K. Labor Market: Analysis of Recent Reforms

S.G.B. Henry and M. Karanassou

THE UNITED KINGDOM adopted far-reaching labor market reforms in the 1980s. The aim of the reforms was not just to raise the employment level and reduce the unemployment rate; they were intended primarily to change the nature of industrial relations prevailing in the United Kingdom, decentralize wage bargaining, and make the labor market more flexible and more resilient in the aftermath of adverse shocks. This paper evaluates the dynamic behavior of the U.K. labor market and the extent to which it was altered by the policy changes of the 1980s, using the methods described in Chapter 1 of this volume. The U.K. labor market is particularly suited for an analysis of policy change.

A number of policy changes were proposed in the 1980s as part of the labor market reforms launched by the Conservative Government led by Mrs. Thatcher. An important policy shift related to legislation that would reduce the incidence of industrial disputes by raising the costs to unions of going on strike. The legislative changes in this period also banned "secondary action," so that workers could not participate in the industrial disputes of enterprises to which they were not directly connected. Furthermore, secret balloting of employees was made mandatory before the employees could go on strike. The strengthening of the prerogative of employers through legislation was perceived as an important way of enhancing flexibility in the labor market. In addition, the Employment Acts of 1980 and 1982 and the Trade Union Act of 1984 decentralized the level at which wage bargaining was conducted.[1] Decentralization of wage

Note: Grateful thanks are extended to Ramana Ramaswamy for his help in producing this paper. We would also like to thank Professors W. Buiter, R. Smith, and D. Snower for comments.

[1]A detailed analysis of the legislative changes in the labor market in the 1980s can be found in Brown and Wadhwani (1990) and Ramaswamy and Prasad (1994).

bargaining was conceived as the appropriate strategy for moderating the United Kingdom's traditionally high wage inflation.

The reforms of the 1980s also aimed to remove a number of other restrictions that hampered flexibility in the labor market. Restrictions on hiring and firing were eased significantly. There are currently no restrictions on the dismissal of workers who have worked fewer than two years for an employer, and the United Kingdom does not practice affirmative action programs for hiring except in the case of handicapped persons. In addition, the labor market reforms made significant changes to the benefits system. The maximum duration of unemployment benefits was reduced to one year, and the replacement ratio was reduced to one of the lowest in Europe.[2] The reforms of the early 1980s also considerably reduced the scope of wage councils, which were instrumental in setting minimum wages; the wage councils were completely abolished in 1993, and there are currently no minimum wages in the United Kingdom except those for agricultural workers.[3] The removal of minimum wage laws was expected to improve the employment prospects of unskilled labor.

This paper explores the effect of these market reforms on the lag structures determining employment, wage, and labor force participation behavior. This topic is important because the U.K. unemployment problem—like that of most continental European countries—has entailed not only a high average rate of unemployment, but also a slow decline of unemployment after recessions in the product market are over. The reaction of unemployment to both temporary and permanent shocks (unemployment persistence and imperfect unemployment responsiveness in the terminology of Chapter 1) is estimated with a view to determining if the reforms made a significant difference to the dynamic behavior of the labor market.

One finding of this paper is that the responsiveness of employment to changes in output may have increased after the reforms were instituted. The increased flexibility has been associated with a decline in the time it takes unemployment to respond to shocks. Surprisingly perhaps, in light of the reforms of the 1980s, this analysis does not reveal evidence of significant changes in the wage formation process.

In comparing the recession of the early 1980s with that of the early 1990s, it is striking that the lag in the response of unemployment to changes in national output has quickened much more than the response of

---

[2]Also, unemployment benefits have been replaced by the Jobseekers' Allowance, which has reduced the duration of benefits to six months for most applicants.

[3]See Organization for Economic Cooperation and Development (1993 and 1994) for further details on labor market legislation.

employment to changes in output. (See the OECD Economic Survey for the United Kingdom (1995).) However, this observation suggests that, over the past decade, U.K. employment behavior may have changed less than labor force participation behavior. But, because the U.K. labor market reforms were designed to alter employment and wage setting behavior, not to reduce labor force participation in the aftermath of recessions, it is difficult to interpret changes in participation as evidence of improved labor market flexibility as envisaged in the policy reforms.

Some Stylized Facts About the Labor Market

One of the striking features of the U.K. labor market is the dramatic increase in unemployment in the early 1980s (Chart 1). The unemployment rate increased from just over 4 percent in 1979 to about 11 percent by the mid-1980s. This increase was also associated with a substantial increase in the long-term unemployed, who, in 1980, constituted just about 23 percent of the total unemployed. By the mid-1980s, long-term unemployment had doubled to almost 45 percent of the total unemployed, raising concerns about hysteresis in the labor market.

However, unlike in the other European countries,[4] the unemployment rate in the United Kingdom came down sharply following the consumption-led boom associated with financial liberalization in the mid-1980s. In fact, the unemployment rate had fallen to less than 6 percent by the end of 1989 (Chart 1). One question that is analyzed in this paper is whether the fall in the unemployment rate in the late 1980s was also associated with a better trade-off between wage inflation and unemployment. This trade-off is generally considered to be worse for European countries than for the United States. However, because the record of employment creation over this period was significantly better in the United Kingdom than in continental Europe, it is not wise to assume that its trade-off between wage inflation and unemployment necessarily follows the European pattern.

Another notable feature of the U.K. labor market is the significant increase in the participation rates for women (Chart 2), which increased steadily from just over 50 percent in 1970 to 65 percent in 1994. However, this phenomenon was associated with a gradually declining participation rate for men, so that there has not been a significant change in overall participation rates.

---

[4]See Bean (1994) and other chapters in this book.

Chart 1. *United Kingdom: Unemployment*

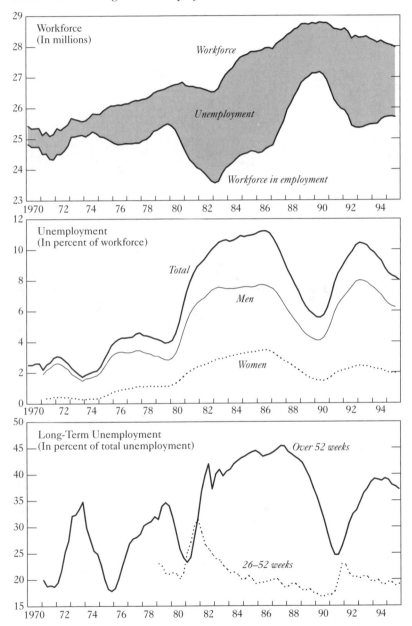

Sources: Central Statistical Office, *Monthly Digest of Statistics;* and Employment Department, *Employment Gazette.*

Chart 2. *United Kingdom: Labor Force Participation and Part-Time Employment*

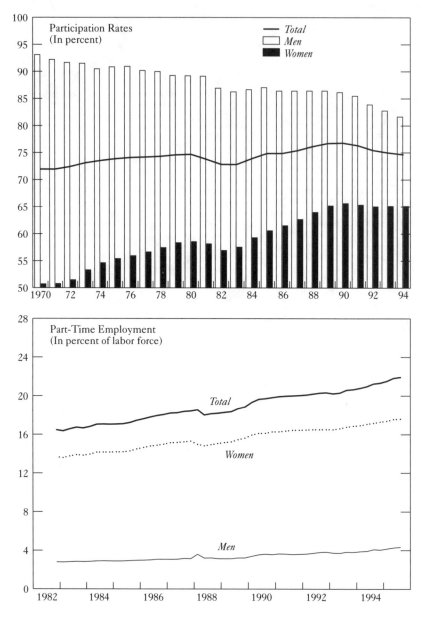

Sources: Central Statistical Office, *Monthly Digest of Statistics;* Employment Department, *Employment Gazette;* and OECD, *Quarterly Labor Force Statistics.*

The increased participation of women in the labor force has also been associated with a rise in part-time employment for women (Chart 2) and a rapid growth of employment in the services sector (Chart 3). Labor force surveys in the United Kingdom indicate that an increasing proportion of part-time job choices are becoming voluntary.[5] Both employers and employees have the option of "trying out" jobs on part-time or temporary contracts before entering into permanent contracts, so that there is a greater possibility of matching labor supply more closely to labor demand. These developments indicate a greater degree of flexibility in the types of labor contracts that are being offered in the United Kingdom, but not, as argued later in this paper, an improvement in the wage formation process.

Accounting for the Rise in U.K. Unemployment

The methodological approach focuses on major lags in the labor market in order to identify prominent dynamic processes at work. This approach helps overcome some important limitations of the standard model of the nonaccelerating inflation rate of unemployment (NAIRU), which devotes little attention to the dynamics of change. NAIRU models are particularly unconvincing in explaining the unemployment trend in the United Kingdom in the 1980s. The NAIRU, as is well known, is influenced by such factors as the degree of union power, the generosity of the benefits system, and the degree of mismatch in the labor market. The 1980s in the United Kingdom were characterized by declining union power and a tightening of social welfare in general. One would expect the NAIRU to decline on these counts. However, most estimates of the NAIRU show it rising in the 1980s, although it is generally estimated to have fallen more recently.

Quite apart from the general lack of conformity of movements in the NAIRU with a priori expectations, there is also a disturbingly wide range of estimates for it depending on which model of the labor market is used and on precise assumptions made about the behavior of variables, such as the real exchange rate. A recent paper provides a comprehensive survey (Coulton and Cromb (1994)). Table 1, taken from one of the tables in the

---

[5]See Robinson (1994) for a discussion of the long-term trends in participation rates and part-time employment. The proportion of part-time workers who say they are working part time because they are unable to find full-time work (involuntary part-time working) was found to be just 6 percent of the total in 1990, having declined from 10 percent in 1987. Robinson's study shows that the extent of involuntary part-time work in the United Kingdom is below the average for most other industrial countries—a particularly favorable finding, given that the country has an above-average share of part-time workers.

Chart 3. *United Kingdom: Employment by Sector*
(In percent of labor force)

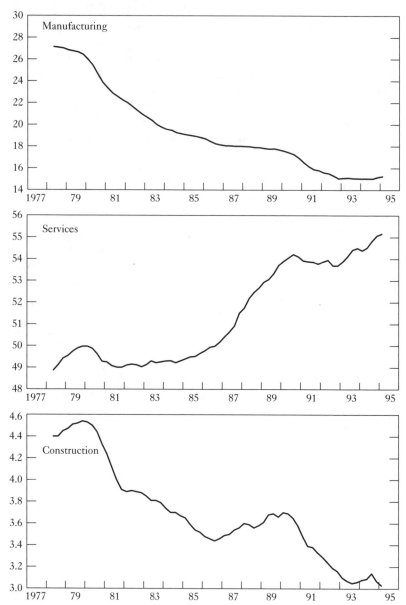

Sources: Central Statistical Office, *Monthly Digest of Statistics;* and Employment Department, *Employment Gazette.*

Table 1.   NAIRU Estimates
(In percent standardized on current definition)

	1974–80	1981–87	1988–90
Liverpool (1990)	7.3	7.0	3.5
Layard and Nickell (1986)	4.5	5.4	n.a.
Layard, Jackman, and Nickell (1991)	5.3	7.9	8.1
Wren-Lewis and others (1990)	n.a.	9.0	7.0
Joyce and Wren-Lewis (1991)	7.0	6.0	4.0

Source: Coulton and Cromb (1994), p. 39.

paper, illustrates the variation in estimates both over time and between modelers. Not surprisingly, the authors conclude that estimates of the NAIRU for the United Kingdom are not reliable enough to serve as a firm basis for economic policymaking or forecasting (Coulton and Cromb (1994), p. 50).

Instead of emphasizing long-run behavior, the present paper tests the extent to which the employment, wage setting, and labor force equations exhibit persistence and imperfect responsiveness. The reason for the emphasis on the effects of lags is that it is difficult to identify a sequence of negative shocks that can fully explain the rising NAIRU in the 1980s in the absence of long-lasting dynamic responses to these shocks within the economy. So, it is necessary to look for potential explanations when temporary shocks have possibly long-lasting effects on the labor market, as well as when permanent shocks hit the labor market.[6]

There is, in linear models at least, no incompatibility between the dynamic characteristics of the labor market and its long-run behavior, and analysis of one does not preclude the other. Generally, the long run is simply the steady-state part of a dynamic model. However, an important question of emphasis is involved. Many theories of labor market behavior—of wage setting, employment, and participation—suggest that there are considerable time delays in the evolution of wage changes, in the adjustment of employment to shocks, and in labor force responses to higher unemployment. Each of these mechanisms implies that the labor market will show considerable inertia when hit by shocks—a widely recognized phenomenon. In their recent book (summarizing the arguments of their earlier,

---

[6]Some of the conceptual issues relating to this theme are explored in Bean (1994). See also, in this context, Blanchard and Summers (1986).

more extensive, study), Layard, Nickell, and Jackman (1994) emphasize the role of persistence in accounting for the sluggish improvement in unemployment in the member countries of the European Union (EU) after 1982, as contrasted with that in the United States, where it fell rapidly (Layard, Nickell, and Jackman (1994)). They further suggest that this persistence is due exclusively to the duration of benefits and the coordination of wage bargaining. However, this view of the sources of persistence seems narrow and does not emphasize the role of other important lags operating in the labor market.

It is clear that other persistence mechanisms may be at work, ensuring that the long-lasting effects of temporary shocks are an important feature of the labor market. A temporary negative shock that increases unemployment, for instance, also has long-lasting effects. The unemployed miss the opportunity of augmenting human capital through firm-specific training and also tend to lose the habit of working, thereby reducing their probabilities of finding future employment. Unemployment thus has a tendency to perpetuate itself. "Insider-outsider" mechanisms act further to reinforce the persistence of unemployment, as the "insiders," or the employed workers, collude to prevent real wages from falling. (See Lindbeck and Snower (1988) for a discussion of the insider-outsider theories of unemployment persistence.[7]) In turn, there is considerable evidence that wage staggering effects are long lasting in the United Kingdom. (See Wadhwani (1985), for example.) Finally, there is substantial evidence of significant employment inertia, owing in turn to sizable adjustment costs faced by firms both in recruiting for and in reducing their workforce. (See Henry (1981) and Nickell (1984), for example.) All this suggests that the evolution of unemployment may be highly "path dependent," in that the trend in unemployment depends crucially on the starting point and on the nature of the shocks that the labor market is initially subject to.

From the modeling point of view, to capture the sources of inertia in the labor market, it is preferable to focus on the interaction of all the lags in the employment, wage, and labor force equations—as is done here—rather than simply using a single equation for unemployment and testing whether it shows path dependency. (An influential example of the latter used to test for persistence appears in Blanchard and Summers (1986).)

---

[7]Insider-outsider theories are based on the assumption that there are large transactions costs in replacing existing workers with the unemployed. Such costs include not only hiring and firing costs, but also more subtle mechanisms whereby insiders as a group refuse to cooperate with outsiders, thus increasing the effective costs of employing the latter.

Labor Market Model and Estimation Methods

The model and estimation methods are briefly described below. Further detail on estimation methods is to be found in Chapter 1 of this volume.

Model Equations

The model is one of labor demand, wages, and the labor force. Equations for each are given next, together with a short motivation.

Labor Demand Equations

It has been recognized for some time that employment behavior in the United Kingdom is characterized by a distinct lag pattern, with employment depending upon its first and second lagged values. Employment should depend on past employment in this way for a number of reasons. The reason most favored by economists is that it is costly to change employment, either when hiring or when firing employees. Among these costs are search (by the employer) and training costs when the firm is expanding its workforce, but there are also costs associated with decreasing the workforce, including institutional restrictions on firing and redundancy payments. To allow for such costs, a dynamic model of the following form is used:

$$e_t = \alpha_0 + \alpha_1 e_{t-1} + \alpha_2 e_{t-2} + \alpha_3 y_t + \alpha_4 rw + \alpha_5 t, \tag{1}$$

where e is employment, y is output, rw is the real wage (all in logs), and the equation assumes that exogenous technical change is taking place, represented by the time trend (t) in the equation. An equation of this form may be derived from the first-order maximizing condition for the profit-maximizing imperfectly competitive firm. Barrell, Morgan, and Pain (1994), for example, derive such an equation, assuming a constant elasticity of substitution (CES) production function. They include materials in the production function, implying that the prices of material inputs affect employment in addition to the terms included in equation (1). The evidence for this is briefly discussed below. The choice of two lagged values of employment reflects the assumption that adjustment costs are quadratic. (See Hall and Henry (1988) for a fuller discussion of adjustment cost models.) Although it is clear that this assumption could be violated by, for example, asymmetric costs (such as when the costs of expanding the work-force exceed those of an equivalent decrease, as described in Burgess (1993)), the assumption of quadratic costs is nonetheless both plausible and convenient.

Wage Equations

The wage equation used here is based on a "competing claims" model of union-firm behavior, as is the labor demand equation above. The wage (and price or, alternatively, labor demand) is then the outcome of a bargain between the firm and the union, where—in the "right to manage" ver-sion—once the wage has been determined, the firm sets the level of employment according to an equation like (1) above. Underlying the union's behavior is a utility function that depends on employment, the real wage, and earnings elsewhere—the reservation wage, which depends, in turn, on unemployment benefits. Models of this sort produce an equation for the real wage dependant upon real unemployment benefits, productiv-ity (or real profits per head), unemployment, and indices of union strength (see Layard, Nickell, and Jackman (1991)). One addition emphasized here is given by the phenomenon of wage staggering, which occurs when there are overlapping contracts in different sectors (or unions) in the economy. As emphasized in the seminal article by Taylor (1980), wage staggering is one reason why aggregate wages will then depend on past wages, and, if unions and firms are forward looking, on future expected wage settlements also. Although forward-looking expectations are not explicitly incorpo-rated, lags in real wages are allowed for with a dynamic equation for the real wage of the following form:

$$W_t = \beta_0 + \beta_1 W_{t-1} + \beta_2 W_{t-2} + \beta_3 Z_t, \qquad (2)$$

where Z is a set of variables affecting real wage bargaining outcomes, such as unemployment, union strength, and productivity. In equation (2), two lags are proposed, but, as shown, the lag length will be determined by sta-tistical criteria because, although theory suggests there may be lags, it does not indicate what the lengths of the lags are likely to be.

Labor Force Equation

The labor force equation is taken to be a simple equation where the labor force depends on the working population and unemployment, which depends on the discouragement effect—whereby higher levels of unemployment discourage workers from participating in the workforce—and the added-worker effect—which entails higher participation as unemployment increases. Hence, a priori, the sign of γ_3 is ambiguous. Lagged effects can be expected to operate through the lagged effects of unemployment on the cumulative experience of would-be labor market participants. Such dynamic possibilities are allowed for in the labor force equation (3) below, which is the basis of the empirical models reported subsequently:

$$l_t = \gamma_0 + \gamma_1 l_{t-1} + \gamma_2 l_{t-2} + \gamma_3 U_t. \tag{3}$$

Estimation Methods

Each of the equations described above is in the form of an autoregressive distributed lag (ARDL) model, which in its simplest form has only one lag on each variable (that is, it is of the order (1.1)) and may be written:

$$Y_t = \alpha_0 + \alpha_1 Y_{t-1} + \beta_0 X_t + \beta_1 X_{t-1} + \epsilon_t, \tag{4}$$

where $|\alpha_1| < 1$, and ϵ_t is assumed to be white noise.

In this equation, Y and X are assumed to be nonstationary variables. In current parlance, this means that they are at least I(1) variables, and they need to be differenced once to make them stationary. The following steps are taken to estimate this equation:

(1) Test for the presence of cointegration between all the I(1) variables using Johansen's maximum likelihood procedure.

(2) Estimate the long-run relationship between the variables using the method of identifying a cointegrating relation from an ARDL equation as recently proposed by Pesaran and Shin (1995).

(3) Using this relationship as the long-run equilibrium term, estimate the short-run parameters of the model using its equivalent error correction model (ECM) representation, comprising stationary variables throughout, thus ensuring that the short-run parameters are estimated consistently. Where there are current values of other endogenous variables on the right-hand side of an equation, they are taken into account by using instrumental variable (IV) estimation.

Estimation Results

This section describes first the time-series characteristics of the data and then the estimated model equations.

Time-Series Properties of Variables

The orders of integrations of the variables are first tested using Dickey-Fuller (DF) and Augmented Dickey-Fuller (ADF) (of order 4, ADF (4)) tests. The results are shown in Table 2. Unless otherwise stated, the sample period is 1968Q3–1994Q3.

The variables are all in logs, except U, REP, $WEDGE$, and RR, and are employment *(LE)*, output *(LY)*, the real product wage *(LRWP)*, the capital stock *(LK)*, the real consumption wage *(LRWC)*, the unemployment rate *(U)*, labor productivity *(LPROD)*, the working population *(LPOP)*, the labor force *(LL)*, the real interest rate *(RR)*, the replacement ratio *(REP)*, the tax wedge *(WEDGE)*, competitiveness *(LCOMP)*, and the real oil price *(LROILP)*.

While most of these statistics are unambiguous, the results in a couple of cases are rather more difficult to interpret. For example, the capital stock has a low ADF when tested for integration in differences. This appears to be due to a pronounced long cycle in the data, attributable in part to the effects of premature scrapping of capital equipment in the first half of the 1980s. Nonetheless, the variable is treated as I(1). Similarly, the evidence that the unemployment rate may be integrated at an order greater than unity is discounted. Even treating it as I(1) raises familiar problems: in principle, the unemployment rate cannot be I(1) because it is bounded between 0 and 1. However, it can clearly appear I(1) in short samples, as here.

Table 2.   *Tests of Integration*

Variable	Level		Differences	
	DF	ADF(4)	DF	ADF(4)
LE	−1.77	−3.17	−4.93	−3.07
LGDP	−2.04	−2.71	−11.85	−4.44
LRWP	−2.24	−1.68	−15.85	−5.54
LK	−1.74	−1.85	−4.55	−2.29
LRWC	−2.24	−1.73	−14.03	−5.13
U	−0.90	−2.37	−3.52	−3.52
LPROD	−2.18	−2.30	−13.3	−4.86
LPOD	−1.02	−0.14	−8.15	−2.79
LL	−1.3	−0.89	−9.07	−2.91
RR	−5.07	−2.97	−	−
REP	−6.03	−3.49	−	−
WEDGE	−3.36	−3.72	−	−
LCOMP	−1.4	−2.1	−8.9	−5.4
LROILP	−1.6	−1.2	−11.46	−6.36

Note: Critical values at 95 percent: DF = −3.4; ADF(4) = −3.4.

But one clear and important result is that the replacement ratio and the tax wedge are both stationary. The importance of this result is that neither of these variables is expected to be part of the explanation of the real wage in the long run, because the real wage is nonstationary, and stationary variables cannot statistically "account" for nonstationary ones. Hence, they do not figure in the tests reported later on the long-run real wage equation.

Labor Demand Equation

Tests for cointegration among the set of relevant variables (in logs) showed that a set involving employment *(LE)*, output *(LY)*, the real product wage *(LRWP)*, the real oil price *(LROILP)*, and a deterministic time trend (treated as a strongly exogenous variable) cointegrates. As noted earlier, inclusion of *real oil prices* implies a production function that includes energy as an input (and this is not assumed to be separable from other inputs). This version was estimated by IV owing to the presence of the current value of output and the real wage as independent variables in the employment equation. The IV estimates are shown in Table 3, which are used in the subsequent discussion.

Table 3. *Employment Equations*

Dependent Variable			Independent Variables				
	Constant	LY	LRW	$ROILP$	T	(p,q)	LR
LE	0.13	0.81	−0.25	−0.001	−0.002	(2,0,00)	22.4 (20.9)
	(0.90)	(3.43)	(1.3)	(2.9)	(2.7)		
	Constant	$\Delta LE(-1)$	ΔY	ΔLRW	$\Delta ROILP$	ECM	
ΔLE	0.13	0.55	0.05	−0.02	0.0	−0.06	
	(2.7)	(7.4)	(3.0)	(1.3)	(2.95)	(4.45)	

$R^2 = 0.56$,
  $\chi_1^2(4) = 3.9$, $\chi_2^2(1) = 0.9$, $\chi_3^2(2) = 8.6$, $\chi_4^2(1) = 1.2$, $\chi_5^2(1) = 9.9$

Notes: (p,q) refers to the orders of lag selected for the dependent and independent variables, respectively. In determining the dimension of the ARDL (p,q), the *Schwartz Bayesian* (SB) information criterion is used throughout. $\chi_1^2(.)$ is a Lagrange multiplier test of residual correlation; $\chi_2^2(.)$ is the Ramsey RESET test; $\chi_3^2(.)$ is a test for normality of residuals; $\chi_4^2(.)$ is a test for heteroscedasticity; and $\chi_5^2(.)$ is Sargan's test that the instruments are valid. $LR(.)$ is the likelihood ratio given by Johansen's trace statistic, that $r = 0$, where r is the number of co-integrating vectors, and where the value shown as the second number in parentheses is the 95 percent critical value.

Wage Equation

Cointegration appears to exist between the real consumption wage, unemployment, productivity, and competitiveness, which apparently gives a statistical explanation of the real wage in the long run. On estimating the long-run equation from an ARDL as described earlier, two extra refinements were included. The first was to impose the productivity effect at unity. This restriction was easily accepted and is plausible. The second was to include a dummy variable taking the value 1,1, −1 for 1974Q3 to 1975Q1. This was necessary to deal with outlining observations attributable to the effects of the three-day week. The equation estimated by instrumental variables is shown in Table 4.

The wage levels equation is fairly satisfactory and includes a well-determined unemployment effect. Competitiveness also appears to be a significant influence on the level of wages according to this result. This term can be interpreted as arising from external effects when the wage bargaining model is extended to the open economy—see Layard, Nickell, and Jackman (1991).

The model thus suggests a well-determined effect from unemployment on the level of the real wage, and the effect for changes in unemployment is significant. A change effect from unemployment in the wage equation is often interpreted as showing hysteresis in wage behavior, but, as emphasized already, other persistence mechanisms are working in the model as a whole.

Table 4. *Wage Equation*

Dependent Variable	Independent Variables		
	Constant	*UR*	*LCOMP*	(p,q)
WageProd	3.5	−0.95	−0.11	(1,0,1)
	(14.1)	(5.54)	(2.27)	
LR (69.4; 27.1)				
Δ(*WageProd*)	Constant	ΔUR	$\Delta LCOMP$	*ECM*(−1)
	0.58	−0.16	0.07	−0.16
	(4.9)	(3.9)	(2.1)	(4.6)

$R^2 = 0.33$,
$\chi_1^2(4) = 12.3$, $\chi_2^2(1) = 0.5$, $\chi_3^2(2) = 0.5$, $\chi_4^2(1) = 0.0$, $\chi_5^2(1) = 0.03$

Note: For definitions see Table 3.

Labor Force Equation

General evidence of cointegration was found among the key variables—the working population, unemployment, and the labor force—although this effect was not strong.

The best results were obtained using the participation ratio (labor force/working population), and in what follows this is used as the dependant variable (defined as *LPART*). Again, the long-run and dynamic (ECM) version of the distributed lag model estimated by IV is provided (see Table 5).

Although this is clearly a simplified equation, it has certain interesting features. The effects of unemployment on participation show some disparity between short- and long-run effects. In the short run, higher unemployment appears to encourage participation, suggesting an added-worker effect, although in the long run, this effect appears to go the other way, implying that a discouraged-worker effect dominates. However, this long-run effect is less well determined.

Evaluating the Effects of the Reforms

Subsample Estimates: Evidence for Structural Change

There has been considerable debate about the possible effects on labor market behavior of the reforms of the 1980s. That substantial changes in

Table 5. *Participation Equation*

Dependent Variable	Independent Variables		
	UR	Constant	*(p,q)*
LPART	−0.28	0.31	(2,2)
	(1.1)	(14.7)	
LR (29.7; 29.7)			

$\Delta PART$	Constant	*LPART*(−1)	ΔUR	ΔUR(−1)	*ECM*(−1)
	0.008	0.21	0.1	0.13	−0.021
	(1.6)	(2.48)	(1.65)	(2.2)	(1.68)

$R^2 = 0.18$,

$\chi_1^2(4) = 2.7$, $\chi_2^2(1) = 0.19$, $\chi_3^2(2) = 0.06$, $\chi_4^2(1) = 0.01$, $\chi_5^2(3) = 1.46$

Note: See Table 3.

some key features of the labor market occurred over the 1980s is apparent: employment grew rapidly in the late 1980s, fueled in part by increases in part-time and self-employment. It also fell both more rapidly and earlier in the 1990s recession than in previous recessions. As noted earlier, policy initiatives in trade union reform, redundancy legislation, and the introduction of tighter unemployment legislation could be expected to produce greater labor market flexibility. The attendant movement toward more decentralized wage bargaining may, however, have neutralized this improved flexibility—as it is generally believed that more centralized wage bargaining can produce a better trade-off between unemployment and wage inflation. A seminal article on this issue is that by Calmfors and Driffill (1988), who found that the relation between centralization and labor market performance was hump-shaped, but their, and subsequent, discussion has suggested that the United Kingdom may be near the top of this hump, implying that either more or less centralization might improve the country's performance.

On the macroeconomic effects of the reforms, opinions appear to differ. Anderton and Mayhew (1994) are skeptical that a major improvement has occurred. In their view, the pattern of real wage growth has been difficult to alter, and they suggest that, in consequence of continued real wage resilience (and the failure of substantial measures to improve skills and training given the large structural changes in the economy away from manufacturing to service industries), excessively high levels of unemployment are needed to maintain downward pressure on wage inflation. (Similar skepticism on the effects of the 1980s policies on wage developments is found in Metcalf (1994).) Others have pointed to the existence of positive signs of improved flexibility attributable to policy, including decreasing costs of laying off workers as demand falls, without commensurately increasing the costs of taking workers on when demand increases, and reducing union power and increasing work incentives. The OECD Economic Survey for the United Kingdom notes possible improvements in labor market flexibility in the country's recent behavior, including the faster response of unemployment (OECD (1995)).

The evidence for improved flexibility is considered using the estimated model presented earlier. The strategy adopted is to establish whether the model shows changes when estimated over subsamples and whether these changes could be interpreted as the effect of policy changes on employment, wage setting, and participation. Some caution must be applied to any such interpretation of the evidence. An apparent change in the adjustment of employment to changes in output may, for example, be prima facie evidence that employment decisions have become more flexible. There may, however, be an alternative explanation for it, such as labor-saving technical change. That said, this discussion focuses on evidence for changes in the adjustment of employment, as shown by the output effect on employment and the estimated lag structure in the labor demand equation; and on alterations in the degree of real wage rigidity as estimated by changes in the unemployment effect on real wages.

We look for evidence of parameter change in the equations we estimated earlier when these are re-estimated over data samples that end in 1990, and, separately, in 1991. These dates are taken because they allow time for the effects of the policy reforms, if there are any, to be felt. We have also initiated the tests long enough after the onset of recession to prevent the tests from being contaminated by the model's failure to predict the downturn. Although statistical methods exist for selecting dates when changes in underlying models occur, these are rather technical (see, for example, Banerjee and Urga (1995)), and the method employed here—although less refined—has the merit of being likely to capture significant changes in behavior if they have occurred.

The first test entailed re-estimating the employment equation over two periods beginning in the early 1990s, that is, dropping the observations from 1990Q1 from the data sample in one case and then redoing the test starting one year later (that is, dropping sample data from 1991Q2 onward, inclusive). The summary tests of model parameter stability were obtained (see Table 6). For the wage equation, only the first test was done, for reasons that are outlined below. In all cases, the model was used to predict the level of the variable (employment and the real wage, respectively).

According to the tests, there is no significant evidence that the parameters of the employment equation have changed in the 1990s compared with the experience of the 1960s and 1980s. The tests are not powerful ones, however, and it is arguable from inspection of the predictions this model makes that a change in employment behavior has occurred, which is largely one of a stronger and more rapid response of employment to output.

Table 6. *Summary Tests of Parameter Stability*

	Estimation Sample Ending	*PRED*	*CHOW*
Employment	1990Q1	18.67 (28.9)	15.3 (16.9)
	1991Q1	13.4 (23.7)	11.7 (16.9)
Wages	1990Q1	18.79 (28.9)	n.a. (. . .)

Note: Figures in parentheses are 95 percent critical values. Both are χ^2 statistics.

Charts 4 and 5 show two ex ante predictions made by the employment model over the two periods—from 1990Q2 and from 1991Q2, respectively, until 1994Q3. These indicate that the model does indeed overpredict employment when its forecast is initiated from 1990Q2 (Chart 4). By 1994Q3, this overprediction amounts to almost 5 percent (of the employed labor force). As Chart 5 shows, however, if the model is initiated a year later (1991Q2), then its cumulative forecast error over the next 3½ years is negligible, amounting to just over 100,000 by the end of the period (less than ½ of 1 percent). Although the second forecast is begun well after the recession started, the first test encounters the well-known problem of the inability of time-series models to capture a cyclical downturn. But the discrepancy in the forecast performance of the model over these two periods is suggestive, if nothing more, of a break in the behavior of employment and its main determinants in the early part of the recession. Employment appears to have declined rapidly and by substantial amounts in the early 1990s compared with its previous behavior. It is too early to say whether this changed behavior will be repeated in the upturn, with increases in employment becoming more rapid and so matching the more rapid decreases in employment that occurred in the downturn. The evidence provided by the forecast performance of this employment model is consis-

Chart 4. *United Kingdom: Employment Equation: Dynamic Forecast for 1990Q2–1994Q3*

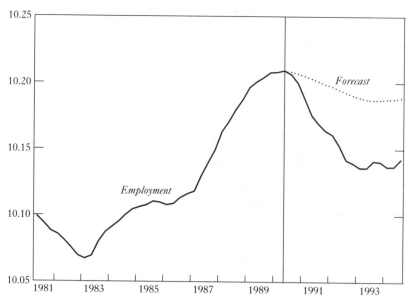

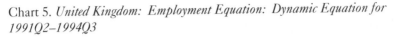

Chart 5. *United Kingdom: Employment Equation: Dynamic Equation for
1991Q2–1994Q3*

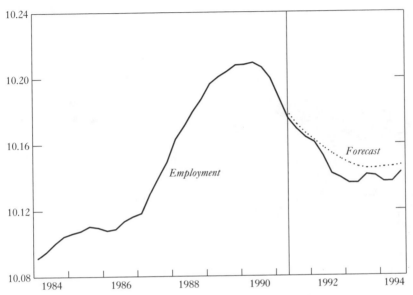

tent with the analysis that the change in employment is more of a step
down, or onetime "shakeout," of employees (which the first forecast suggests), but that once this change occurred, the previous pattern of behavior
was re-established (that is, as the second forecast suggests).

There is a further complication, which this exercise unfortunately does
not shed light on, and that is whether the behavior of employment in this
recession is different from that in previous ones. There is now increasing
evidence that U.K. employment behavior is asymmetric. During recessions, in particular, decreases in employment are sharper and continue for
shorter periods than increases in employment. In a recent study, Acemoglu
and Scott (1994) estimate that the rate of job losses in a cyclical downturn
may be as much as four times greater than job creation in an upturn. The
more precise question raised by such evidence is whether the sharp rate of
job losses in the 1990s recession is "normal" recessionary behavior or
whether it marks a significant change from normal, with employment
declining even more rapidly than in other recessions. The evidence is too
limited to answer this question yet.

Turning to the wage equation, according to the test in Table 6, there is
little evidence of any change in the relationship between real wages, productivity, and unemployment. The relationship seems stable. Indeed,

Chart 6. *United Kingdom: Wage Equation: Dynamic Forecast for 1990Q1–1994Q3*

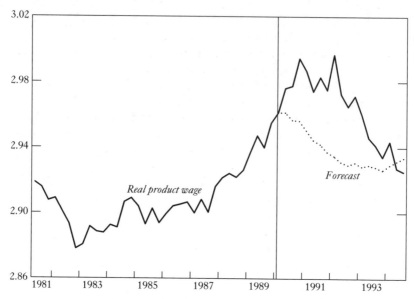

there is evidence that, over much of the 1990s, the model actually under-predicts the real wage (see Chart 6); the real wage in much of the 1990s has actually been higher than might have been expected from the relation-ships fitted to earlier data. But overall, and more precisely, the result indi-cates that there is little significant change in wage setting in the 1990s compared with earlier periods.[8]

Simulations of Dynamic Responses

To obtain an overall quantitative measure of the dynamic behavior of the labor market, the complete model described earlier is used. As described in Chapter 1 of this volume, the method involves administering simple shocks to the model and calculating the response of wage employ-ment and unemployment to the shocks using the estimated model. In each

---

[8]This uses the model with productivity constrained to have a unit effect. Relaxing the con-straint, however, gave a result similar to that described in the text, and the formal test still rejects parameter instability $[\chi^2(18) = 20.6]$.

case, the solution is conducted over a long period of time to give the model time to settle down. Both a temporary and a permanent shock are applied, and their effects calculated, to estimate how the labor market responds to shocks that disturb it temporarily, such as a temporary productivity shock, but also to establish how the market moves from one equilibrium to another when one of the determinants of long-run behavior, such as a permanent change in competitiveness, changes.

Summary indicators of the dynamic behavior of the U.K. labor market, which our earlier statistical modeling implies, are shown in Table 7. These show the single-equation results for employment, wages, and participation. Whole model indicators of persistence, whereby for the whole model the mean lag following a temporary shock is cited—estimated using full model simulations—are given for unemployment.

The values in the table show that, on our estimates, there is evidence of substantial sluggishness in each part of the labor market except in wages. Our estimates tend to be higher than some others, although Alogoskoufis and Manning (1988) have higher estimates of persistence in real wages and in unemployment than we report. As we have made some effort both to identify behavioral models of the key labor market variables involved and to estimate these allowing for long-run equilibrium behavior, there are reasons for thinking our estimates are to be preferred. It is striking, however, that even after allowing for the presence of long-run equilibrium in employment, wages, and the participation rate, the evidence we find of considerable persistence in some single equations is strong.

Table 7 illustrates the diversity of views on the overall measure, that of unemployment persistence. The estimates by Alogoskoufis and Manning (1988) are flawed because they do not allow for the possible existence of cointegrating (or long-term equilibrium) relations in the labor market. In turn, Layard, Nickell, and Jackman (1991) suggest that persistence is relatively unimportant, although they use very simple specifications for the dynamics in their model and do not investigate the possibility of cointegration. According to our estimates of persistence, based on a simulation of the complete macro model, unemployment takes about five years to reach halfway to its equilibrium once the model is hit by either a temporary or a permanent shock. This estimate falls roughly halfway between the two estimates quoted in Table 7, but, for reasons already mentioned, we think it is a more refined and plausible estimate.

Following a permanent adverse shock to productivity, in our model, unemployment again approaches a higher equilibrium rate monotonically but slowly, as is to be expected. Again, it takes about five years to get halfway to the new equilibrium rate (see appendix to Chapter 1 in this volume).

Table 7. *Labor Market Dynamics*
(Persistence in years)

	Henry and Karanassou (1996)[1]	Alogoskoufis and Manning (1988)	Barrell, Morgan, and Pain (1994)	Layard, Nickell, and Jackman (1991)
Employment	6	...	...	3
Wages	1.5	4.3	2.8	...
Participation	12	...	...	...
Unemployment	5	12.5	...	2.2

[1] Reference is to the present study.

Conclusions

The principal conclusion emerging from this paper is that the U.K. labor market is strongly subject to inertia. There is some evidence that the behavior of the labor market may have changed following the reforms of the 1980s, although the tests applied here are not able to pinpoint precisely what this change represents. However, it appears that employment decreased faster in the 1990s recession than would be predicted on the basis of previous behavior, at least initially. From 1991 onward, behavior consistent with previous relationships may have resumed. Thus, although there is some evidence of an improvement in employment flexibility, it is too early to rule out the possibility that it is an employment response to recession similar to that which occurred in the 1980s recession. While the analysis of the paper does not find evidence that the wage formation process changed significantly following the implementation of the labor market reforms, recent wage behavior suggests that this area merits further study.

Finally, the response of unemployment to the changes in output is very different from those in the last recession. The main reason for this difference is a large change in participation rates (as the OECD points out in its comments on the apparent shortening of the lag between output and unemployment). There is still little evidence that employment has changed its adjustment to output in the upturn. Furthermore, although there have been substantial changes in participation, it is difficult to regard these as the objective of, or indeed the result of, the labor market reforms of the 1980s.

References

Acemoglu, Daron, and Andrew Scott, 1994, "Asymmetries in the Cyclical Behavior of U.K. Labor Markets," *Economic Journal*, Vol. 104 (November), pp. 1303–23.

Alogoskoufis, George, and Alan Manning, 1988, "On the Persistence of Unemployment," *Economic Policy: A European Forum*, Vol. 3 (October), pp. 428–69.

Anderton, R., and K. Mayhew, 1994, "A Comparative Analysis of the U.K. Labour Market," in *The U.K. Labour Market*, ed. by R. Barrell (Cambridge, England: Cambridge University Press).

Banerjee, A., and G. Urga, 1995, "Modelling U.K. Trade: An Exercise in Sequential Structural Break Procedures," Discussion Paper No. 24-95 (London: London Business School).

Barrell, R., J. Morgan, and N. Pain, 1994, "Employment Inequality and Flexibility" (unpublished; London: National Institute for Economic and Social Research).

Bean, Charles, 1994, "European Unemployment: A Survey," *Journal of Economic Literature*, Vol. 32 (June), pp. 573–619.

Blanchard, Oliver, and Laurence Summers, 1986, "Hysteresis and the European Unemployment Problem," *NBER Macroeconomics Annual 1986*, Vol. 1 (Cambridge, Massachusetts: MIT Press).

Brown, William, and Sushil Wadhwani, 1990, "The Economic Effects of Industrial Relations Legislation Since 1979," *National Institute Economic Review*, No. 131 (February), pp. 57–70.

Burgess, S., 1993, "Nonlinear Dynamics in a Structural Model of Employment," in *Nonlinear Dynamics, Chaos, and Econometrics*, ed. by M. Pesaran and Simon Potter (Chichester, England; New York: Wiley).

Calmfors, Lars, and John Driffill, 1988, "Centralization of Wage Bargaining," *Economic Policy: A European Forum*, Vol. 3 (April), p. 13.

Coulton, B., and R. Cromb, 1994, "The U.K. NAIRU," Government Economic Service Working Paper No. 124 (London: H.M. Treasury).

Hall, S.G., and S.G.B. Henry, 1988, *Macroeconomic Modelling* (Amsterdam: North-Holland).

Henry, S.G.B., 1981, "Forecasting Employment and Unemployment," in *The Economics of the Labour Market*, ed. by Z. Hornstein, J. Grice, and A. Webb (London: HMSO).

Layard, R., S. Nickell, and R. Jackman, 1991, *Unemployment: Macroeconomic Performance and the Labor Market* (Oxford, England; New York: Oxford University Press).

———, 1994, *The Unemployment Crisis* (Oxford, England; New York: Oxford University Press, rev. ed.).

Lindbeck, Assar, and Dennis Snower, 1988, *The Insider-Outsider Theory of Employment and Unemployment* (Cambridge, Massachusetts: MIT Press).

Metcalf, D., 1994, "Transformation of British Industrial Relations? Institutions, Conduct and Outcomes, 1980–1990," in *The U.K. Labour Market*, ed. by R. Barrell (Cambridge, England; New York: Cambridge University Press).

Nickell, S., 1984, "The Modelling of Wages and Employment," in *Econometrics and Quantitative Economics*, ed. by D. Hendry and K. Wallis (Oxford, England; New York: Blackwell).

Organization for Economic Cooperation and Development, 1993, *Employment Outlook* (Paris: OECD).

———, 1994, *The OECD Jobs Study—Evidence and Explanations, Part 2, The Adjustment Potential of the Labor Market* (Paris).

———, 1995, *OECD Economic Surveys: United Kingdom* (Paris).

Pesaran, H., and Y. Shin, 1995, "An Autoregressive Distributed Lag Modelling Approach to Cointegration Analysis," DAE Discussion Paper No. 9514 (Cambridge, England: University of Cambridge, Department of Applied Economics).

Ramaswamy, R., and E. Prasad, 1994, "Shocks and Structural Breaks: Labor Market Reforms in the United Kingdom," IMF Working Paper 94/152 (Washington: International Monetary Fund).

Robinson, Peter, 1994, "British Labour Market in Historical Perspective: Changes in the Structure of Employment and Unemployment," Centre for Economic Performance Discussion Paper No. 202 (London: London School of Economics and Political Science).

Taylor, John B., 1980, "Aggregate Dynamics and Staggered Contracts," *Journal of Political Economy*, Vol. 88 (February), pp. 1–23.

Wadhwani, S. B., 1985, "Wage Inflation in the United Kingdom," *Economica*, Vol. 52 (May), pp. 195–207.

6

Labor Market Policies and Unemployment Dynamics in Spain

Jeffrey R. Franks

NO COUNTRY IN Europe has as great an unemployment problem as Spain. From less than 5 percent in the mid-1970s, the unemployment rate has peaked at more than 20 percent in each of the last two economic slowdowns, without dropping below 15 percent in times of strong growth. From an analytical standpoint, the Spanish case is a fascinating, extreme example of the pan-European unemployment problem. From the policy perspective, it is essential to understand and attack labor market problems successfully in Spain if the unemployment crisis of the European Union (EU) is to be tackled, especially since the number of jobless in Spain in 1995 was higher than in the much larger EU countries of France, Italy, and the United Kingdom, and nearly as high as in Germany.

Broadly speaking, two competing schools of thought have existed in analyses of European unemployment over the last twenty years. One approach is to focus primarily on cyclical factors in generating unemployment, the implication being that macroeconomic shocks have caused unemployment to deviate from a (low) "natural" or nonaccelerating inflation rate of unemployment (NAIRU).[1] Studies in this vein look to a series of adverse macroeconomic shocks to explain the high and persistent unemployment rates in Europe since the 1970s. The oil crises of the 1970s

Note: The author wishes to thank Brian Henry for helpful comments throughout the development of the paper. Discussions with the other participants in the unemployment project—Charalambos Cristofides, Karl Habermeier, Paolo Mauro, Ramana Ramaswamy, and Tessa van der Willigen—were also of great help. Marika Karanassou assisted with the policy simulations. All errors are my own.

[1]Friedman (1968) coined the term "natural rate of unemployment," which was subsequently used extensively in the so-called New Classical Economics school of thought.

and the recession of the early 1990s are seen as triggers for increased European unemployment, exacerbated by high real interest rates that reduced investment (Bianchi and Zoega (1994)). At the other extreme is the hysteresis theory invoked by Blanchard and Summers (1986) and others, which argues that most of the unemployment increase is due to an increase in the NAIRU rather than in deviations therefrom. Indeed, in its most extreme form, hysteresis implies that every change in unemployment becomes an equilibrium, as structural features of the labor market translate temporary shocks into permanent changes in the natural rate of unemployment.

In Spain, where unemployment has not only shown large cyclical swings (rising nearly 9 percentage points during the last recession), but has also demonstrated remarkable persistence at very high levels, the traditional NAIRU concept loses much of its usefulness. Can one really argue that an estimated NAIRU of 18–20 percent (as some economists have recently calculated) is a meaningful indication of what unemployment rate is "natural" for Spain? At the same time, however, the full hysteresis argument ignores the undeniably large cyclical movements in unemployment while implicitly arguing for an even higher (albeit path-dependent) natural rate of unemployment.

For these reasons, the analytical approach taken in this chapter is something of an intermediate position between the extreme NAIRU view that unemployment has a clearly defined (relatively low) equilibrium rate to which it returns after macroeconomic shocks, and the extreme hysteresis view that unemployment is a random walk, with the equilibrium rate equal to the current unemployment rate in each period. A simple three-equation model of the labor market—a labor force equation, a wage determination equation, and an employment equation—is presented. By permitting several lags in the system of equations—and by allowing full interaction among the lags in the different equations—the model permits an examination of the degree to which unemployment is persistent, while allowing the identification of the sources of persistence in the different equations. This model structure implicitly assumes that the true nature of unemployment dynamics is a subtle combination of factors generating persistence and forces pushing toward equilibrium.

On the one hand, the structural nature of the system implies that there is indeed some underlying "equilibrium" level of unemployment in the economy, thus rejecting the extreme hysteresis view. On the other hand, by allowing for long and interactive lags, the issue of what the precise equilibrium rate is becomes less crucial than the structural features of the economy that produce the pattern of lags (Karanassou and Snower (1993)). Long lags have profound implications for the actual rate of unemployment; once the period of adjustment exceeds the average time between shocks (or the length of the average economic cycle), shocks can compound their effects and feed back on each other, generating unemployment persistence far beyond what one would expect from a simplistic analysis of the natural rate of unemployment vis-à-vis the country's position in the economic cycle. Before one shock has worked its way through the labor market another has already arrived, producing a complex, dynamic evolution that may have little correlation with the underlying NAIRU. Indeed, the emphasis of the impact of labor market institutions on unemployment behavior focuses more on how structure affects the adjustment process (that is, the nature of the lags) than on structure as a determinant of some underlying natural unemployment rate.

Spanish Labor Market Since the Mid-1970s

The structure of the labor market has changed more profoundly in Spain than in any other Western European country in the past twenty years. No other country has seen its unemployment rate rise as dramatically and stay so persistently high. These two facts do not represent mere coincidence—in the profound transformation in the structure of employment relations (and the transformation of the Spanish economy more generally) lies much of the explanation for Spain's dismal unemployment rate. Although Spain was buffeted by the same macroeconomic shocks as the remainder of Europe in the 1970s, these shocks alone do not provide a satisfactory causal explanation of the rise in unemployment from less than 5 percent in 1975 to 24 percent in 1994.

Employment, Unemployment, and the Labor Force

The performance of the labor market in Spain from 1975 through 1994 can be divided into three cyclical periods. During the first period, in the late 1970s and early 1980s, the second oil crisis produced several years of weak economic growth that in turn led to a sharp decline in employment. The unemployment rate rose sharply, rising from 7 percent in 1978 to over 20 percent in 1984, while the size of the labor force was relatively stagnant, growing at an average rate of only 0.5 percent a year. Despite the increase in unemployment, real wages continued to rise at nearly 1 percent a year.

The second period began in 1985, with Spain's preparations to enter the European Community (EC). Spanish accession to the EC (in 1986) sparked a major economic recovery, with growth averaging 4.5 percent a year during 1986–90. This expansion, plus the Government's introduction of flexible temporary labor contracts in 1984 (see next section), fueled an increase in employment averaging 3 percent a year. The unemployment rate fell from over 21 percent in 1985 to 16 percent in 1990. This drop in unemployment was smaller than might be expected from such strong employment growth as the result of a sharp acceleration in the growth of the labor force to 2.1 percent a year, primarily because of a significant increase in the participation rate for women. Real wage growth continued, albeit at the slower pace of 0.6 percent a year.

The overall changes in employment and unemployment do not do justice to the depth of the changes in the labor market, because they mask a profound shift in the nature of employment. The progressive opening of the economy accelerated a major transformation in the economic structure that had already begun in the 1970s. The role of agriculture and basic industry (for example, coal, steel, and shipbuilding) declined sharply, while modern industry and the services sector (particularly tourism and financial services) surged.[2]

The economy slowed in 1991 and entered into recession in the second half of 1992. The unemployment rate climbed rapidly to 24.6 percent by the third quarter of 1994—a peak-to-trough variation of more then 8 percentage points in less than three years. While labor force growth decelerated (to an average of 0.7 percent), most of the increase in unemployment came from a sharp drop in labor demand. Employment fell by 7 percent between 1991 and 1994. Until labor market reforms began to bite in 1994, real wages continued an unabated rise despite the enormous slack in the labor market.

Structure of the Labor Market

During the Franco period, Spain had a rigidly controlled labor market. Trade union activism was prohibited and the social security benefits of the modern welfare state were largely nonexistent. In their place was a set of labor regulations that rigidly defined working conditions and provided social protection by making it difficult to fire workers and providing generous severance pay for dismissals.

---

[2]See Franks (1994) for a detailed discussion of the effects of these structural changes on the labor market in Spain.

After General Franco's death in 1975, the country underwent a major economic transformation that paralleled the political transition to democracy. The economy modernized rapidly, with sharp declines in traditional agricultural and basic industrial activity and the rise of modern manufacturing and services. The economy also opened to further international competition, culminating in accession to the EC in 1986.

Similarly profound changes occurred in the labor market, affecting every aspect of labor relations. The tight regulations on working conditions with their attendant restrictions on geographical and functional mobility were continued, but they were combined with the labor relations systems and the social protection of a modern welfare state. Trade unions became both legal and extremely active. Although union membership remains relatively low, the coverage of union-negotiated agreements was well in excess of 80 percent of all salaried workers by the late 1980s. After a series of national wage pacts in the late 1970s that kept industrial action and wage increases under control, collective bargaining moved largely to the sectoral level. Union activism surged, with Spain consistently among the European countries with the largest number of days lost to strike activity.

While the legal structure of dismissals did not change radically from the Franco era, the effective real costs of dismissals rose owing to the unions' ability to negotiate collectively for better severance payments and owing to government-supported schemes to support workers on temporary redundancies and to help pay severance costs of those permanently dismissed. Average severance payments grew from just over 4.5 months of pay in 1981 to over 12 months of pay by 1993.

To this severance system was added an increasingly complete social protection system providing relatively generous unemployment benefits for dismissed workers and pensions for those injured, disabled, or retiring. Whereas in 1983–84 fewer than 30 percent of nonagricultural workers were eligible for unemployment compensation, by 1993 over 60 percent were receiving compensation. The size of unemployment benefits also grew substantially. Benefits per unemployed person grew by 30 percent in real terms between 1984 and 1993. These high benefit levels reflected a system under which workers were entitled to unemployment compensation with a generous replacement ratio of the previous salary, particularly during the first year of joblessness. The period of work required to become eligible for benefits was also quite short—six months of work entitled one to three months of benefits, with the same 2:1 ratio holding for longer periods on the job.

Not all developments in the 1980s increased the rigidity of the labor market. Whereas during the 1970s the minimum wage grew by 55 percent in real terms (an average real growth rate of 4.5 percent a year), that growth leveled off in the early 1980s, and there was actually a 6 percent real decline in the level of the minimum wage by 1990. In 1984, in response to the sharply rising unemployment rate, the Government liberalized the use of temporary contracts, permitting temporary workers (on contracts of up to three years) to do essentially the same work as permanent workers. Because temporary workers were not subject to the same hiring and firing conditions and their contracts effectively granted the firms greater functional and geographical mobility, this step significantly reduced rigidities for those firms using temporary workers. The growing number of temporary workers increased the dualism of the labor market, as the labor force became increasingly segregated into permanent and temporary "castes."

As the Spanish economy slowed in 1991 and 1992 and unemployment again soared above 20 percent, it became increasingly clear that the labor market was in need of more profound reforms. In 1993 and 1994, the Government undertook a series of reforms designed to reduce unemployment compensation, facilitate workplace mobility, and reduce firing costs. Early results of these reforms appear to be favorable, but given the long response time in the labor market, it is premature to evaluate whether they will make a major contribution to the reduction of unemployment over the medium and long term.

In summary, the analysis of the causes of high and persistent unemployment in Spain must look to the interaction of two sets of factors. First, at the macroeconomic level, profound changes in the structure of the economy as a whole (opening to international trade, accession to the EC, the decline of agriculture and basic industry, and the rise of modern manufacturing and services) as well as sociodemographic changes in the size of the working-age population and the rise of female participation in the labor force have affected the labor market at least as profoundly as the macroeconomic shocks of the oil crises and the rise in real interest rates that are often cited as the source of European unemployment.[3] Second, at the level of the labor market itself, Spain has experienced profound changes in the structure of labor market institutions that could have a major impact on the level and persistence of unemployment. During the past twenty years, Spain has seen the resurgence of trade union activism and the rise of the protection of a modern social welfare state and has reformed the legal framework for the labor market.

---

[3]See Bean (1994) for a review of explanations of European unemployment.

Basic Model

In this section, a basic three-equation labor market model is constructed and estimated for 1971–93. It contains variables designed to measure the interactions between labor supply, labor demand, and real wages. In keeping with the focus on examining not just the equilibrium relationship, but also the adjustment process, each equation uses a set of lags on both the dependent and independent variables to capture the dynamics of the labor market. This model will be used to determine the basic relationships among the key variables, as well as to pinpoint structural breaks that could be identified with known changes in labor market institutions. Unfortunately, good time-series data on many important policy variables over the entire sample period are lacking, so the estimations over this period are conducted using a simple specification. Making virtue out of necessity, however, these results provided interesting contrasts with those of the policy model estimated over the 1980s and 1990s as described in the next section.

Structure

The empirical specifications used here are based on an underlying right-to-manage type of wage and employment setting process.[4] Potential workers decide unilaterally whether or not to enter the labor market based on the wage they can get if employed, the probability of employment, and sociodemographic factors exogenous to the model. To incorporate adjustment lags, lagged values on both the endogenous and the exogenous variables are permitted. Thus, the labor supply equation is as follows:

$$\ln LF_t = \alpha + \sum_{i=0}^{n} \beta_i UR_{t-i} + \sum_{i=0}^{n} \gamma_i \ln W_{t-i} + \sum_{i=1}^{n} \delta_i \ln LF_{t-i} + \Theta_i X_t + \epsilon, \quad (1)$$

where LF is the labor force, W is the real wage, UR is the unemployment rate, and X is a vector of variables exogenous to the model that could affect the labor supply. For the basic version of the model estimated in this section, the only exogenous variable included is the working-age population.

The real wage is a variable jointly determined by bargaining between employers and trade unions. This bargain is affected by past real wages, by

---

[4]See Booth (1995), pp. 124–28 for an exposition of the right-to-manage model. Oswald and Turnbull (1985) provide empirical evidence in support of the right-to-manage assumption for the United Kingdom.

the unemployment rate, by labor productivity, and by a vector of exogenous variables (such as the reservation wage determined by unemployment benefits). The empirical specification of the real wage equation is as follows:

$$\ln W_t = \alpha + \sum_{i=0}^{n} \beta_i UR_{t-i} + \sum_{i=1}^{n} \delta_i \ln W_{t-i} + \sum_{i=0}^{n} \rho_i \ln PROD_{t-i} + \Theta_i X_t + \epsilon, \qquad (2)$$

where PROD is labor productivity. For the basic version of the model estimated in this section, the only exogenous variable included is the minimum wage, under the assumption that minimum wage increases may have played a role in setting expectations for wage increases in the private sector.[5]

In accordance with the right-to-manage literature, once wages are determined in collective bargaining, employers are assumed to be free to set employment levels so as to maximize profits subject to the legal and institutional constraints of the Spanish labor market. Employment thus depends on past employment, real product wages (that is, the real wage of the worker plus social contributions paid by the employer), and a vector of exogenous variables as follows:

$$\ln E_t = \alpha + \sum_{i=0}^{n} \beta_i \ln W_{emp_{t-i}} + \sum_{i=1}^{n} \delta_i \ln E_{t-i} \, \Theta_i X_t + \epsilon, \qquad (3)$$

where E represents employment, and W_{emp} is the wage paid by the employer.[6] For the empirical specification in this section, the only "exogenous" variable included is GDP.

The model is closed by the following identities:

$$W_{emp} = W + TSS, \qquad (4)$$

---

[5]Minimum wages may not be a completely exogenous variable, because there is often an implicit or explicit linkage between average wages and the setting of the minimum wage. In Spain, there appears to have been some effort to maintain the minimum wage as a share of the average wage in the mid-1970s, but not since then. Nevertheless, in the estimation of the model, the minimum wage variable was included with a lag to avoid a possible simultaneity problem. See Dolado and others (1996) for an in-depth discussion of the effect of minimum wages on employment.

[6]This employer wage is not a fully fledged product wage because for simplicity it is deflated by the consumer price index (CPI) rather than by some producer price index. Nevertheless, because the CPI and producer prices are highly correlated, the results differ little if a pure product wage is used.

$$UR = 1 - \frac{E}{LF},\tag{5}$$

and

$$\ln PROD = \frac{\ln E}{GDP},\tag{6}$$

where *TSS* are social security taxes paid by the employer.[7] As shown in equation (5), the unemployment rate term in the labor force and real wage equations indirectly incorporates the effects of employment on labor supply and of employment and labor supply on real wages. Although GDP is not explicitly modeled, it is treated as an endogenous variable and a simple GDP equation is included in the simulations in the section Structural Change and Unemployment: Persistence and Responsiveness.

Characteristics of the Data

The empirical analysis was conducted using quarterly data from 1971 through 1993. The data were obtained from the databases of the Bank of Spain, the Ministry of Economy, and the Organization for Economic Cooperation and Development (OECD). For GDP data, for which quarterly information was not available for the entire period, interpolations developed by the OECD were used. The data are not seasonally adjusted; rather, seasonal dummies are included in all of the regressions. All variables, except for the unemployment rate, are in logs.

The most important feature of the variables under consideration is their stationarity (or lack thereof). Hysteresis theories of unemployment imply that unemployment is a nonstationary variable, raising the issue of nonstationarity of both employment and unemployment. An essential first step was to examine the variables to be used for the existence of unit roots. The results of Augmented Dickey-Fuller (ADF) tests on the variables to be included in the model in levels suggested that essentially all should be treated as nonstationary. From the unit root tests on the differenced variables, it appears that they may be treated as I(1).

---

[7]While for the basic model in this section the model results are reported for the employers' wage as a whole, in the policy model in the following section, the wage and security contribution variables are included separately, allowing their coefficients to differ.

Estimation Results

After initial exploratory regressions in ordinary least squares (OLS), the model was estimated as an autoregressive distributed lag (ARDL) model in levels using instrumental variables (IV) in order to find a cointegrating long-run relationship (Pesaran and Shin (1995)). The model was then estimated in error correction formulation in differences using instrumental variables when necessary to control for endogeneity.[8] In estimation, a strictly empirical approach was taken to the structure of the lags. Up to eight lags of each endogenous variable were included in initial specifications, with only lags with robust significance being retained in the chosen specifications. In this respect, the model differs from a structural vector autoregression (VAR) model—where all variables would contain the same number of lags—because only significant lags were retained in the final specifications. Chow tests were undertaken to test for structural breaks in the model, and in preparation for estimating the policy model in this section, the basic model was estimated separately for the two subperiods of 1971–80 and 1981–93.

In addition to an examination of the regression coefficients of the error correction model, diagnostics are presented to analyze the dynamic response of each estimated equation to changes in explanatory variables and to shocks. A series of diagnostic statistics on the dynamics is also calculated. First, the "cross-persistence" of temporary shocks and the "cross-responsiveness" to permanent shocks of each equation are examined, building on the measures of persistence and responsiveness for unemployment developed by Snower and Karanassou (1995). These indicators basically measure the sum of the deviations of the dependent variable from its equilibrium; in other words, they are a normalized version of the integral of the impulse response curve. The measures used, and how they differ from those developed by Snower and Karanassou, are discussed in detail in the appendix. Second, information on the "half-life" of impulse responses is presented. The half-life of a permanent change is defined as the time required for one-half the change to be transmitted through to the dependent variable. For a temporary shock, the half-life is the time required for the dependent variable to reach one-half its maximum deviation from its original (and final) value.

---

[8]The preferred specification was also estimated simultaneously using full information maximum likelihood (FIML) techniques to compare with the instrumental variables results. The FIML results did not differ substantially from those of the IV error correction model (ECM) specification reported below.

Labor Force Equation

Economic models of the labor force are notoriously difficult, because many noneconomic factors affect labor force participation. The results presented here are no exception. Table 1 shows the long-run cointegrating

Table 1. *Long-Run Cointegrating Regressions for the Basic Model*

Labor Force Equation

$\ln LF = 1.137 - 0.1727 \ln W + 1.149 \ln WorkPop - 0.09056$ Seasonal
(SE) (0.2336) (0.04182)   (0.133)   (0.0351)

WALD test $\chi^2(3) = 147.08$ [0.0000] **

Tests on the significance of each variable

Variable	F(num,denom)		Value	Probability	Unit root t-test
$\ln LF$	F(1, 80)	=	1316.2	[0.0000] **	−3.8009*
$\ln LW$	F(2, 80)	=	8.069	[0.0006] **	−3.1943
$\ln WorkPop$	F(2, 80)	=	11.332	[0.0000] **	3.7608
Constant	F(1, 80)	=	11.473	[0.0011] **	3.3872
Seasonal	F(3, 80)	=	14.518	[0.0000] **	−2.6918

Real Wage Equation

$\ln W = -2.713 - 0.003419\ UR + 0.7195 \ln PROD + 0.9247 \ln WMIN - 0.3595$ Seasonal
(SE) (0.5385)(0.001998)   (0.06656)   (0.05897)   (0.03558)

WALD test $\chi^2(4) = 1229.5$ [0.0000] **

Tests on the significance of each variable

Variable	F(num,denom)		Value	Probability	Unit root t-test
$\ln W$	F(2, 83)	=	19.74	[0.0000] **	−6.0076**
UR	F(1, 83)	=	3.802	[0.0546]	−1.9499
$\ln PROD$	F(1, 83)	=	30.207	[0.0000] **	5.4961
$\ln WMIN$	F(2, 83)	=	14.74	[0.0000] **	5.4275
Constant	F(1, 83)	=	13.743	[0.0004] **	−3.7071
Seasonal	F(3, 83)	=	17.304	[0.0000] **	−6.1764

Employment Equation

$\ln E = -7.366 - 0.333 \ln W_{prod} + 1.316 \ln GDP + 0.3234$ Seasonal
(SE) (1.723) (0.2191)   (0.171)   (0.06799)

WALD test $\chi^2(4) = 77.384$ [0.0000] **

Table 1   (*concluded*)

Tests on the significance of each variable

Variable	F(num,denom)		Value	Probability	Unit root t-test
ln E	F(4, 73)	=	709.45	[0.0000] **	−5.4854**
Constant	F(1, 73)	=	24.3	[0.0000] **	−4.9295
ln W_{prod}[1]	F(2, 73)	=	−16.685	[0.0000] **	−5.3147
ln GDP	F(2, 73)	=	21.05	[0.0000] **	6.0038
Seasonal	F(3, 73)	=	17.343	[0.0000] **	5.8042

Notes: One asterisk means significant at the 5 percent level and two asterisks mean significant at the 1 percent level.

Both the significance tests and the t-statistics should be taken as only rough guides to significance, since they do not make the adjustments necessary for Phillips-Hansen (1990) fully modified estimation of cointegrating relationships.

[1]Calculated by combining the estimates for social security contributions and real wages.

relationships of the model, while Table 2 presents the preferred specification for the labor force equation in error correction form. The long-run relationship shows a positive coefficient on the working-population variable, but a negative one on the real wage. While somewhat surprising, the negative relationship is not inconsistent with rational utility maximization in the decision to participate in the labor force, as higher wages among primary wage earners may lead secondary household members to participate less through an income effect.[9] The unemployment rate does not figure in the long-run relationship, because its coefficient was not robustly significant and the equation failed to cointegrate when it was included.

Turning to the error correction specification, several features of the regression results stand out. First, it is interesting that the coefficient on the error correction term, while significant and carrying the correct sign, is quite small, implying relatively slow adjustment to the long-run relationship. Second, unemployment, which did not participate in the long-run relationship, plays a dynamic role. Lagged changes in unemployment on

[9]Interestingly, when the sample is split and the same regression is run separately over 1972–80 and 1981–93, the negative relationship between wages and labor force participation disappears, particularly for the second half of the sample, implying that there may have been an exogenous change in the social attitudes regarding households' work-leisure trade-off. Indeed, exogenous shifts in the labor force participation of women would have precisely the effect of shifting the quantity of labor offered by the household at a given income level. Thus, while in the early period, households may have been at or close to the backward-bending section of their labor supply curves, exogenous changes in female participation made the elasticity of the labor supply to the real wage highly positive in the 1980s and 1990s.

Table 2. *Basic Model Results for the Labor Force Equation, 1972–93*
(Lags shown in parentheses)

Variable	Coefficient	Standard Error	t-Value	t-Prob	PartR^2
Constant	−0.0046171	0.0029604	−1.560	0.1230	0.0310
$D \ln W(1)$	0.025603	0.0094077	2.721	0.0081	0.0888
$D \ln W(3)$	−0.026833	0.010219	−2.626	0.0104	0.0832
$D \ln W(4)$	−0.027768	0.010260	−2.706	0.0084	0.0879
DUR (5)	−0.0027475	0.00080911	−3.396	0.0011	0.1317
DUR (8)	0.0029098	0.00098402	2.957	0.0041	0.1032
$D \ln WorkPop(4)$	−1.1142	0.52383	−2.127	0.0367	0.0562
$D \ln WorkPop(6)$	−1.0661	0.48717	−2.188	0.0317	0.0593
Seasonal	0.0017203	0.0021740	0.791	0.4312	0.0082
Seasonal(1)	0.016041	0.0039911	4.019	0.0001	0.1753
Seasonal(2)	0.011635	0.0025946	4.484	0.0000	0.2092
$LFECM$ (1)	−0.054273	0.025020	−2.169	0.0332	0.0583

$R^2 = 0.589644$ $F(11, 76) = 9.9277 \ (0.0000)$ $\sigma = 0.00260946$ $DW = 1.83$
$RSS = 0.00051750381$ for 12 variables and 88 observations

$AR\ 1–5\ F(5, 71)$ =   0.56186   [0.7288]
$ARCH\ 4\ F(4, 68)$ =   0.25429   [0.9061]
Normality $\chi^2(2)$ =   2.857   [0.2397]
$\chi^2\ F(19, 56)$ =   0.46904   [0.9647]
$RESET\ F(1, 75)$ =   0.053158   [0.8183]

Note: Dependent variable is $D \ln LF$, estimated by OLS. None of the endogenous variables was significant in contemporaneous variables, so the estimation was done with OLS rather than IV.

balance have a slightly negative effect on labor force participation growth, as do lagged changes in the rate of labor force growth. Although these results are not as strong as one would like, both the ARDL regressions producing the long-run cointegrating relationships and the error correction model regressions pass standard tests for misspecification, autocorrelation, normality of the errors, and heteroscedasticity.[10]

A clearer idea of the overall impact of the different explanatory variables on the labor force can be obtained by examination of the indicators of equa-

---

[10]The following tests were performed in PC-Give on both the ARDL specification and on the error correction equation: the Lagrange multiplier test for nth order autocorrelation; the Autoregressive Conditional Heteroscedastic (ARCH) test; the χ^2 test for normality of the residuals; the χ^2 test for heteroscedasticity and correct functional form; and the Ramsey regression specification (RESET) test.

tion dynamics presented in Table 3. As can be seen, permanent wage and population shocks take a long time to manifest their full effects on the equilibrium labor force. For a real wage shock, after 8 quarters only one-half of the final effect has been transmitted, while for a population shock, it takes 35 quarters. A onetime shock to the labor force itself will be reversed over time as the long-run equilibrium relationship reasserts itself, but this process is a long one. It takes 13 quarters for one-half of the adjustment to occur. The data on responsiveness show that the accumulated deviations from long-run equilibrium from permanent changes are quite significant in the case of real wages, where the difference between the long-run equilibrium labor force and the sum of the actual values is 2.6 percent.

Temporary shocks to wages and unemployment have relatively small maximum effects on the labor force, while a (totally unrealistic) temporary jump in the working-age population has a large temporary effect on the labor force. Of course, because the unemployment rate is not in the long-run relationship, it has only temporary effects. In all of these cases, it takes one to two years for the effects of these temporary shocks to dampen down to half their maximum level. A temporary shock to the labor force itself has a half-life of 14 quarters.

Chow tests on the labor force equation show clear evidence of structural breaks, so the model was re-estimated for the sample divided at 1981. Both halves of the sample now show a negative relationship between wages and labor force participation, as well as a negative link between unemployment

Table 3. *Indicators of Labor Force Equation Dynamics, Basic Model*

	Response of a 1 Percent Shock to			
	Wages	Unemploy-ment rate	Working population	Labor force
Permanent shock				
Long-run elasticity	−0.1727	0	1.149	0
Half-life				
(quarters)	8	—	35	13
Responsiveness				
(percent)	−2.62	0	−1.059	−0.02
Temporary shock				
Maximum deviation	−0.037	−0.0028	−1.075	1
Half-life				
(quarters)	5	8	7	14
Persistence				
(percent)	−0.1744	0	1.149	−1.009

and labor force participation. There was also an important drop in the coefficient on the error correction term between the first and second half of the sample, suggesting a lengthening of the time required for the labor force to adjust to shocks.

Real Wage Equation

The long-run cointegrating relationship for real wages (Table 1) shows a strongly positive relationship between real wages and labor productivity, as one would expect. Unemployment has a small negative impact on wages that is only marginally significant statistically, suggesting that wages are largely insensitive to labor market conditions. There is a strong correlation between minimum wages and average wages in the long run, which, although it may be a statistical artifact, may also indicate that general wage increases follow trends set in increases in the minimum wage.

The error correction specification (Table 4) also shows a significantly positive relationship between productivity growth and wage growth. The relationship with the minimum wage also remains positive in differences.

Table 4. *Basic Model Results for the Real Wage Equation, 1972–93*
(Lags shown in parentheses)

Variable	Coefficient	Standard Error	t-Value	t-Prob
Constant	−0.0084830	0.019519	−0.435	0.6650
$D \ln W(1)$	−0.30033	0.099220	−3.027	0.0033
$D \ln W(2)$	−0.34003	0.10596	−3.209	0.0019
$D \ln W(3)$	−0.34639	0.083345	−4.156	0.0001
$D \ln PROD$	1.7841	0.88210	2.023	0.0463
$D \ln PROD(2)$	−1.3308	0.51530	−2.583	0.0116
$D \ln WMIN(3)$	0.17398	0.063875	2.724	0.0079
$WECM(1)$	−0.30078	0.057241	−5.255	0.0000
Seasonal	−0.10570	0.020184	−5.237	0.0000
Seasonal(1)	0.093051	0.036693	2.536	0.0131
Seasonal(2)	0.037127	0.031524	1.178	0.2423

$\sigma = 0.0221772 \ DW = 1.99$
$RSS = 0.04082159323$ for 11 variables and 94 observations
2 endogenous and 10 exogenous variables with 12 instruments

Reduced form σ	=	0.0203942	
Specification $\chi^2(1)$	=	3.317	[0.0686]
Testing $\beta = 0$: $\chi^2(10)$	=	610.9	[0.0000] **

Note: Dependent variable is $D \ln W$, estimated by IV. Two asterisks mean significant at the 1 percent level.

Changes in the unemployment rate fail to be significant and are excluded from the preferred specification. Lagged changes in the real wage exert a strongly negative effect on wage growth in the current period, reflecting a strong tendency to revert to trend after variations in wage growth rates. The coefficient on the error correction term is highly significant and relatively large. As was the case with the labor force variable, there is clear evidence of structural breaks in the equation, but other specification tests are passed.

Table 5 indicates that, as expected from the higher coefficient on the error correction term, the adjustment to a permanent shock is faster in the wage equation than in the labor force equation. Productivity shocks are the slowest in transmission into wages, with a half-life of more than three years. This lag is also reflected in the large negative responsiveness number, which indicates a cumulative deviation of −21 percent in wages after a productivity shock from the new equilibrium wage. Temporary shocks in the wage equation work themselves out relatively quickly, with half-lives of five quarters or less from shocks in all of the variables.

Employment Equation

The long-run employment equation is presented in Table 1. As expected, it shows a strongly positive relationship between GDP and em-

Table 5. *Indicators of Real Wage Equation Dynamics, Basic Model*

	Response of a 1 Percent Shock to			
	Product	Minimum wage	Unemployment rate	Wages
Permanent shock				
Long-run elasticity	0.7185	0.9247	0.003	1
Half-life				
(quarters)	13	5	6	6
Responsiveness				
(percent)	−20.95	−6.133	−6.605	−6.623
Temporary shock				
Maximum deviation	−1.76	0.277	−0.001	1
Half-life				
(quarters)	5	5	3	2
Persistence				
(percent)	−0.74	−0.92	−0.034	−3.315

ployment (although the fact that the coefficient is larger than 1 is surprising). The product wage has the expected negative effect on employment, with a relatively large coefficient of –0.33.

The preferred specification for the error correction form of the model is presented in Table 6. Changes in GDP growth have a positive impact on employment growth. On balance, the evolution of the real product wage has a positive impact as well, in contrast to the long-run relationship. On balance, lagged values of the dependent variable have a slightly negative impact, with a long adjustment process implied (the sixth lag proves to be significant). The error correction term is significant and correctly signed, but the coefficient is quite small (only 0.1), which means that the adjustment to long-term equilibrium is quite weak. As with the other two equations, there is strong evidence of structural breaks in the model, but other statistical tests are passed, indicating no major problems with autocorrelation, heteroscedasticity, or misspecification of the equations.

Table 6.   *Basic Model Results for the Employment Equation, 1972–93*
(Lags shown in parentheses)

Variable	Coefficient	Standard Error	t-Value	t-Prob
Constant	0.00061231	0.0012243	0.500	0.6185
$D \ln E(1)$	0.27658	0.088304	3.132	0.0025
$D \ln E(6)$	–0.37990	0.082863	–4.585	0.0000
$D \ln W_{prod}{}^1$	–0.12430	0.040882	3.040	0.0026
$D \ln W_{prod}(1)^1$	0.15814	0.038609	4.096	0.0001
$D \ln W_{prod}(3)^1$	0.13946	0.034501	4.042	0.0001
$D \ln GDP$	0.36081	0.086105	4.190	0.0001
$EmpECM(1)$	–0.10588	0.013703	–7.726	0.0000
Seasonal	0.0081766	0.0035076	2.331	0.0224
Seasonal(1)	–0.016746	0.0031162	–5.374	0.0000
Seasonal(2)	0.0093842	0.0019501	4.812	0.0000

$\sigma = 0.0032641$ $DW = 1.72$
$RSS = 0.0007990785297$ for 12 variables and 87 observations
3 endogenous and 10 exogenous variables with 19 instruments

Reduced form σ = 0.00344761
Specification $\chi^2 (7)$ = 12.083   [0.0979]
Testing $\beta = 0$: $\chi^2 (11) = 355.71$ [0.0000] **

Note: Dependent variable is $D \ln E$, estimated by IV. Two asterisks mean significant at the 1 percent level.
[1]Calculated by combining the estimates for social security contributions and real wages.

The dynamic of the employment equation is intermediate between the relatively quick adjustment displayed by the real wage equation and the slow adjustment of the labor force equation. As can be seen from Table 7, half-life adjustments to shocks generally take one and a half to two and a half years, with the adjustment to output shocks somewhat quicker. Of particular interest is the dynamic of an adjustment in the product wage, which, despite its large long-term effect, demonstrates relatively slow adjustment to shocks. The responsiveness to permanent shocks is particularly poor.

Results of the Basic Model

The evidence of structural breaks in the equations, together with the unexpected negative relationship between wage and labor force participation, suggests that the exact results of this preliminary analysis should be interpreted with caution. Nevertheless, the results are strong enough to warrant several interesting qualitative conclusions. The most telling of these is the evidence that long lags in the adjustment of the labor market to shocks play a crucial role in sustaining high unemployment. The half-life numbers presented suggest that it takes between 3 and 35 quarters

Table 7. *Indicators of Employment Equation Dynamics, Basic Model*

		Response of a 1 Percent Shock to			
	GDP	Real wages	Social security taxes	Product wage	Employ-ment
Permanent shock					
Long-run elasticity	1.316	1.078	−1.411	−0.333	1
Half-life (quarters)	3	6	8	10	6
Responsiveness (percent)	−7.85	−9.81	1.411	−15.29	−9.43
Temporary shock					
Maximum deviation	0.35	0.128	−0.194	−0.124	1.172
Half-life (quarters)	3	7	7	11	7
Persistence (percent)	1.31	1.073	−1.403	−0.331	9.43

for one-half of the final effect of a permanent shock in an explanatory variable to be felt in the corresponding dependent variable. The numbers are even more striking as regards the time taken for 90 percent adjustment. For example, a permanent output shock takes over six years to manifest 90 percent of its final effect on employment; a permanent working-population shock (for example, the Spanish baby boom) takes 63 quarters (15.75 years) to manifest 90 percent of its final effect on the labor force; a permanent wage shock takes four years to show 90 percent of its final effect on the wages themselves, over eight years to show 90 percent of its final effect on employment, and nearly ten years for the labor force equation. While the exact values of these lags should not be relied upon, they are broadly consistent with other recent work on adjustment lags in Spain[11] and clearly justify the conclusion that adjustment is extremely slow. Chart 1 shows graphically the adjustment process for some of these key permanent shocks to give an idea of the full dynamics of adjustment in each equation.

The second interesting insight from the basic model is the striking lack of sensitivity of the labor market to the unemployment rate. Unemployment has no long-run and little short-run impact on the labor force and has a minuscule effect on real wages, suggesting that the labor market does not contain a strong self-correcting tendency in the face of high unemployment.

Even in this basic model, sociodemographic factors and policies and institutions of the labor market itself play a very important role in labor market outcomes. The increase in the working-age population coupled with changes in attitudes toward female labor force participation, which produce a coefficient on the population variable that is larger than unity, have clearly contributed to the rise in unemployment. In the two policy variables included in the basic model (the minimum wage and the tax wedge of social security contributions), there is strong evidence that institutional factors have also played an important role in pushing up product wages and reducing employment.

Finally, the instability of the coefficients of the basic model highlights the importance of structural changes in the labor market in Spain. This phenomenon will be explored in more detail in the next section.

---

[11]Dolado and López-Salido (1996) use a conventional VAR approach to look at the response of output, unemployment, and wages to different types of macroeconomic shocks. Their results indicate that the half-life adjustment of these variables is on the order of three to five years. As with the results obtained here, the adjustment to labor supply shocks tends to be even slower.

Chart 1. *Spain: Basic Model: Impulse Response Graphs for Permanent Shocks to Key Variables*
(Index, initial position = 100)

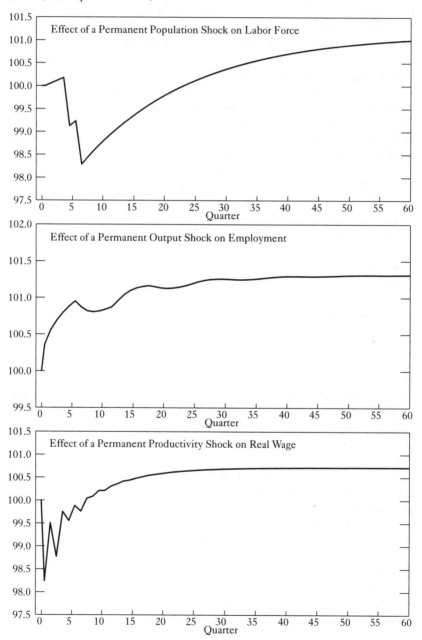

Policy Model

The results of the basic model, while providing some general information about the behavior of the Spanish labor market, are unsatisfactory for several reasons. First, the model is econometrically deficient owing to clear structural breaks (undoubtedly produced by the changes in the structure of the labor market since the early 1970s). Second, from a more conceptual standpoint, the basic model does not explain well the causes of Spanish unemployment. The institutional features of the labor market discussed as potential factors in generating high unemployment are not really modeled. These weaknesses motivate the development of another version of the model, where the structural problems and unanswered causal questions of the basic model can be addressed.

Additional Variables

The "policy" model has the same general form as the basic model but with the addition of a series of variables designed to capture explicitly some of the institutional features of the labor market that could have played a role in generating persistent unemployment in Spain. Including these aspects of the labor market structure makes the model less susceptible to structural breaks in the coefficients. The model is estimated only for 1981–93; this shorter time series also makes it less likely to suffer from structural breaks than the 1971–93 period used in the basic model because it excluded the Franco era and democratic transition in the 1970s. However, this restricted sample has the disadvantage of excluding the initial rise in unemployment in the wake of the oil shocks of 1973–74 and 1979–80, but the data for most of the key policy variables included do not reach back into the 1970s.

The basic labor force equation in the policy model includes two variables in addition to those in the basic model—the average level of disability pensions and the replacement ratio of unemployment compensation. Disability pensions would be expected to decrease the labor force directly because people granted disability benefits leave the labor force, but, in addition, a negative relationship is to be expected between the level of benefits and the labor force because some firms in Spain have used pensions as an alternative to redundancies. The disability pension variable may also capture some of the effect of retirement pensions on the labor force.[12] The inclu-

---

[12]Controls on disability pensions were fairly weak until the 1990s; there is substantial anecdotal evidence of firms using temporary disability classifications of workers as an alternative to redundancies for younger workers. For older workers, early retirements were often used with official acquiescence. This effect may also be captured by the disability pension variable.

sion of the replacement ratio variable reflects the incentives a person may have to remain in (or enter) the labor force despite high unemployment. High unemployment benefits could prevent discouraged workers from leaving the labor force or could provide incentives for entering the labor market.[13]

The wage equation includes two new policy-related variables—the replacement ratio of unemployment benefits and the share of temporary workers in the labor force. The replacement ratio reflects the reservation wage of workers, and hence should have a positive impact on collectively bargained wages. It is not clear ex ante whether the presence of temporary workers would increase or decrease average wages. On the one hand, because temporary workers tend to be paid less than their permanent counterparts, there is a composition effect that would cause the average wage to decline as the share of temporary workers increases. On the other hand, the presence of temporary workers may exacerbate insider-outsider problems by making permanent workers less susceptible to redundancies (see Bentolila and Dolado (1994); Jimeno and Toharía (1993)). Finally, the minimum wage is included as with the basic model.

In estimating the employment equation, three policy variables were added to the variables included in the basic model. Two relate to labor market relations between worker and employers, one measuring days lost to strike action and the other measuring the coverage of trade union agreements. The strike activity variable reflects a clear nonwage cost to employers that could negatively affect their level of employment. The coverage of union agreements may also affect employment levels by constituting a direct labor cost, or, through wages, an indirect cost. The third policy variable, severance pay, measures the real value of severance pay settlements as a means of exploring the impact of dismissal costs on employment levels. In addition, in order to examine the effect of government policies on labor market taxation, the product wage variable has been split into its constituent parts—a real social contribution costs variable (TSS) and the real wage as perceived by employees.

---

[13]First-time entrants into the labor force are not eligible for unemployment benefits. Nevertheless, the future availability of unemployment benefits will certainly have a positive impact on the expected value of entering the labor force, especially since there has been a large amount of rotation between temporary jobs and unemployment since temporary contracts were liberalized in 1984.

Estimation Results

As with the model in the previous section, the policy model was initially explored in OLS, with regressions subsequently run in error correction form using, where necessary, instrumental variables and including cointegrating long-run relationships. The long-run relationships are shown in Table 8, with the error correction models of the individual equations shown in Tables 9–11.

Labor Force Equation

As seen in Table 8, wages and the labor force show a significant positive relationship in the long run, in contrast to the negative sign given in the basic model. The idea that higher wages draw more labor force participation is more intuitively satisfactory than the negative sign found previously. The positive long-run relationship between working-age population and the labor force is also strongly significant, as expected. The fact that the size of the coefficient is even larger than in the basic model probably reflects the accelerating trend of the incorporation of women into the labor force in the 1980s compared with the 1970s. Turning to the policy variables, there is a small but significant positive effect of the replacement ratio on labor force participation, while the generosity of disability pension benefits holds the expected negative correlation with participation. The unemployment rate showed no significant relationship, and was excluded from the preferred specification.[14]

The error correction version of the model is shown in Table 9. Wage growth has the expected significant positive effect on the labor force. The two policy variables also hold significant signs in the expected direction, with increasing disability pensions decreasing the labor force, while the growth replacement ratio increases it. The error correction term also has the expected sign. In contrast, short-run fluctuations in the working-age population paradoxically decrease the labor force. As in the basic model, changes in the unemployment rate have virtually no net effect.

An examination of the summary statistics on equation dynamics in Table 12 shows that the half-lives of the responses to permanent shocks are smaller than those for the basic model, while the speed of adjustment to temporary

---

[14]It should be noted, however, that the long-run regressions do not unambiguously cointegrate. See the footnote to Table 8.

Table 8. *Long-Run Cointegrating Regressions for the Policy Model*

Labor Force Equation

$\ln LF = -3.017 + 0.237 \ln W + 1.452 \ln WorkPop - 0.1703 \ln DPens$
$(SE) \quad (0.7534)(0.107) \qquad (0.1376) \qquad\qquad (0.08463)$

$\qquad + 0.01395 \ \ln RepR + 0.02548 \ \text{Seasonal}$
$\qquad (0.004754) \qquad\quad (0.01834)$

WALD test $\chi^2(5) = 1127.2 \ [0.0000]$ **

Tests on the significance of each variable

Variable	F(num,denom)		Value	Probability	Unit root t-test
ln LF	F(1, 43)	=	106.51	[0.0000] **	−3.8288 [1]
Constant	F(1, 43)	=	13.393	[0.0007] **	−3.6596
ln W	F(1, 43)	=	7.6414	[0.0084] **	2.7643
ln $WorkPop$	F(1, 43)	=	15.689	[0.0003] **	3.9609
ln $PensD$	F(1, 43)	=	6.4561	[0.0147] *	−2.5409
ln $REPR$	F(1, 43)	=	4.7291	[0.0352] *	2.1746
Seasonal	F(3, 43)	=	13.341	[0.0000] **	1.6176

Real Wage Equation

$\ln W = 2.2 - 0.004407 \ UR + 0.8892 \ln PROD + 0.368 \ln WMIN$
$(SE) \quad (2.393) (0.001611) \qquad (0.13) \qquad\qquad (0.1622)$

$\qquad + 0.03123 \ \ln RepR - 0.001464 \ Tempshare - 0.08182 \ \text{Seasonal}$
$\qquad (0.004906) \qquad\quad (0.0005428) \qquad\qquad (0.03824)$

WALD test $\chi^2(6) = 1212.5 \ [0.0000]$ **

Tests on the significance of each variable

Variable	F(num,denom)		Value	Probability	Unit root t-test
ln W	F(3, 42)	=	10.517	[0.0000] **	−7.8598**
UR	F(2, 42)	=	17.506	[0.0000] **	−3.1633
Constant	F(1, 42)	=	0.79076	[0.3789]	0.88925
ln $PROD$	F(1, 42)	=	53.676	[0.0000] **	7.3264
ln $REPR$	F(1, 42)	=	40.206	[0.0000] **	6.3408
ln $WMIN$	F(3, 42)	=	1.8698	[0.1494]	2.2322
$Tempshare$	F(1, 42)	=	9.9623	[0.0030] **	−3.1563
Seasonal	F(3, 42)	=	16.758	[0.0000] **	−2.3641

Table 8   (*concluded*)

Employment Equation

$\ln E = -2.298 - 0.1019 \ln W - 0.2949 \ln TSS + 1.016 \ln GDP$
(SE)   (0.7786) (0.08087)   (0.06779)   (0.03561)

$- 0.06734 \ln SEVER - 0.002626 \ln STRIKE - 0.01571 \ln Coverage$
(0.009573)   (0.001331)   (0.002264)
$- 0.01261$ Seasonal
(0.02735)

WALD test $\chi^2(7)$ = 1820.6 [0.0000] **

Tests on the significance of each variable

Variable	F(num,denom)		Value	Probability	Unit root t-test
$\ln E$	F(4, 37)	=	12.62	[0.0000]**	−5.6891**
$\ln W$	F(1, 37)	=	1.3874	[0.2464]	−1.1779
$\ln TSS$	F(3, 37)	=	11.238	[0.0000]**	−4.4591
$\ln GDP$	F(1, 37)	=	34.985	[0.0000]**	5.9148
$\ln Coverage$	F(1, 37)	=	14.286	[0.0006]**	−3.7796
$\ln SEVER$	F(1, 37)	=	17.064	[0.0002]**	−4.1309
$\ln STRIKE$	F(1, 37)	=	4.1322	[0.0493]*	−2.0328
Constant	F(1, 37)	=	6.8657	[0.0127]*	−2.6203
Seasonal	F(3, 37)	=	6.9233	[0.0008]**	−0.44946

Notes: One asterisk means significant at the 5 percent level and two asterisks mean significant at the 1 percent level.

Both the significance tests and the t-statistics should be taken as only rough guides to significance, since they do not make the adjustments necessary for Phillips-Hansen (1990) fully modified estimation of cointegrating relationships.

[1]The critical value for this test is about 3.9, so there is not conclusive evidence of cointegration. Nevertheless, the same model without the inclusion of the dummy variables does unambiguously cointegrate. On this basis, and in light of the characteristics of the residuals to the regression, cointegration is accepted.

shocks is somewhat longer. The speed of adjustment to shocks in the labor force itself seems to have improved significantly. This phenomenon appears for all of the policy model equations, as well as for the dynamics of the system as a whole (see section on structural change and unemployment). This apparent improvement should not, however, be interpreted as reflecting better real adjustment; rather, the structural variables included reduce the coefficients on the lagged dependent variables because they are accounting for some of the causes of delayed adjustment.[15]

[15]In the basic model, own variable persistence and responsiveness measures capture the adjustment effects of the structural features of the labor market that are separately modeled in the

Table 9.   *Policy Model Results for the Labor Force Equation, 1981–93*
(Lags shown in parentheses)

Variable	Coefficient	Standard Error	t-Value	t-Prob	PartR^2
Constant	−0.0040603	0.0026636	−1.524	0.1353	0.0549
$D \ln W(3)$	−0.034878	0.016465	−2.118	0.0404	0.1009
$DUR(7)$	−0.0022275	0.0012352	−1.803	0.0789	0.0752
$DUR(8)$	0.0026690	0.0013203	2.021	0.0500	0.0927
$D \ln WorkPop(3)$	−2.4973	0.63070	−3.960	0.0003	0.2816
$D \ln REPR(3)$	0.0018743	0.0014475	1.295	0.2028	0.0402
$D \ln REPR(4)$	0.0035148	0.0015403	2.282	0.0279	0.1152
$D \ln LPENSD$	−0.053779	0.030614	−1.757	0.0866	0.0716
$LFECM2(1)$	−0.20421	0.046137	−4.426	0.0001	0.3288
Seasonal	0.0036653	0.0034986	1.048	0.3011	0.0267
Seasonal(1)	0.0075809	0.0041596	1.823	0.0759	0.0767
Seasonal(2)	0.016190	0.0032696	4.952	0.0000	0.3800

$R^2 = 0.737506$ F(11, 40) = 10.217 [0.0000] $\sigma = 0.00239251$ DW = 2.31
RSS = 0.0002289640177 for 12 variables and 52 observations

AR 1–4 F(4, 36)	=	0.98292	[0.4291]
ARCH 4 F(4, 32)	=	0.18011	[0.9470]
Normality χ^2 (2)	=	3.7685	[0.1519]
χ^2 F(19, 20)	=	0.52641	[0.9161]
RESET F(1, 39)	=	0.54023	[0.4667]

Notes: Dependent variable is $D \ln LF$, estimated by OLS. None of the endogenous variables was significant in contemporaneous variables, so the estimation was done with OLS rather than IV.

Real Wage Equation

The long-run determinants of wages (Table 8) show the expected strong positive correlation between productivity and wage growth. In

policy model. To illustrate this effect, consider the comparison between a simple autoregression versus an autoregressive equation with additional structural variables. If one calculates the adjustment speed of the simple autoregressive model compared with the model that includes structural variables, the autoregressive model will necessarily show slower adjustment (that is, higher coefficients on the lagged terms) because the autoregressive terms are picking up some of the effects of the persistence of the omitted structural variables. One should not, however, conclude that the impulse response functions shown in the basic model are useless because they come from a model that suffers from omitted variable bias and is therefore misspecified. By that criterion, virtually every VAR would also be classified as useless as a result of misspecification because VARs do not include potentially important structural variables. Rather, the impulse response functions should be seen as illustrative of the adjustment time required as a result of a shock given the "average" underlying levels of the structural variables over the period of the regression.

Table 10. *Basic Model Results for the Real Wage Equation, 1971–93*
(Lags shown in parentheses)

Variable	Coefficient	Standard Error	t-Value	t-Prob	PartR^2
Constant	0.013066	0.015687	0.833	0.4096	0.0162
$D \ln W(3)$	−0.23414	0.087457	−2.677	0.0105	0.1458
$D \ln W(4)$	0.34891	0.10150	3.438	0.0013	0.2196
$D \ln PROD(3)$	−1.0042	0.52678	−1.906	0.0635	0.0796
$DUR(1)$	0.013594	0.0047158	2.883	0.0062	0.1652
$DREPR$	0.030792	0.0082032	3.754	0.0005	0.2512
$D \ln WMIN(2)$	−0.31806	0.097096	−3.276	0.0021	0.2035
$Dtempshare(3)$	0.0021394	0.00096377	2.220	0.0319	0.1050
$LWECM2(1)$	−0.66090	0.12613	−5.240	0.0000	0.3953
Seasonal	−0.068184	0.022547	−3.024	0.0042	0.1788
Seasonal(1)	−0.0021800	0.022236	−0.098	0.9224	0.0002
Seasonal(2)	0.029393	0.020928	1.405	0.1675	0.0449

$R^2 = 0.983182$ $F(11, 42) = 223.21$ [0.0000] $\sigma = 0.0132199$ $DW = 2.23$
$RSS = 0.007340122792$ for 12 variables and 54 observations

$AR\ 1–4\ F(4, 38)$ = 1.5174 [0.2166]
$ARCH\ 4\ F(4, 34)$ = 0.2956 [0.8788]
Normality $\chi^2(2)$ = 1.2894 [0.5248]
$\chi^2\ F(19, 22)$ = 0.34389 [0.9890]
$RESET\ F(1, 41)$ = 3.1949 [0.0813]

Notes: Dependent variable is $D \ln W$, estimated by OLS. None of the endogenous variables was significant in contemporaneous variables, so the estimation was done with OLS rather than IV.

contrast to the basic model, the coefficient is less than 1, implying that not all productivity improvements are translated into wages. This result is consistent with the general increase in profit margins experienced in Spain in the 1980s. Unemployment has a significantly negative effect on wages, although the size of the effect is small. The minimum wage continues to have a positive effect on real wages; however, the size of this pass-through effect is smaller than in the basic model. Turning to the policy variables introduced in this version of the model, increases in the replacement ratio increase wages as expected. Interestingly, the share of temporary workers in the labor force on balance exerts a moderating effect on wages, suggesting that the composition effect of lower wages paid to temporary workers dominates the insider-outsider effect that more temporary workers could have on wage bargaining.

Table 11. *Policy Model Results for the Employment Equation, 1981–93*
(Lags shown in parentheses)

Variable	Coefficient	Standard Error	t-Value	t-Prob
Constant	−0.00013265	0.0025914	−0.051	0.9595
$D \ln GDP$	0.24073	0.13816	1.742	0.0910
$D \ln GDP(3)$	−0.61608	0.15212	−4.050	0.0003
$D \ln W$	−0.040610	0.019300	−2.104	0.0433
$D \ln W(1)$	0.035554	0.014486	2.454	0.0197
$D \ln E(1)$	0.39297	0.082871	4.742	0.0000
$D \ln E(3)$	0.21376	0.094120	2.271	0.0300
$D \ln E(6)$	−0.24854	0.057618	−4.314	0.0001
$D \ln TSS$	−0.26215	0.041517	−6.314	0.0000
$D \ln TSS(1)$	0.30460	0.039048	7.801	0.0000
$D \ln TSS(3)$	0.096461	0.046362	2.081	0.0456
$D \ln TSS(4)$	−0.16525	0.044189	−3.740	0.0007
$D \ln STRIKE(2)$	−0.00095640	0.00033149	−2.885	0.0069
$D \ln STRIKE(4)$	0.0014214	0.00033737	4.213	0.0002
$D \ln COVER(1)$	−0.0094967	0.0024831	−3.825	0.0006
$EmpECM2(1)$	−0.44459	0.052754	−8.428	0.0000
Seasonal	−0.0089656	0.0045113	−1.987	0.0555
Seasonal(1)	0.013916	0.0041862	3.324	0.0022
Seasonal(2)	0.0073756	0.0019385	3.805	0.0006

Additional instruments used:
$D \ln SEVER$ $D \ln TSS(2)$ $D \ln GDP(1)$ $D \ln COVER$ $D \ln E(5)$ $D \ln W(2)$
$D \ln W(3)$ $D \ln SEVER(1)$

$\sigma = 0.00176823$ $DW = 2.02$
$RSS = 0.000100052243$ for 19 variables and 51 observations
3 endogenous and 17 exogenous variables with 25 instruments
Reduced form $\sigma = 0.00155334$
Specification $\chi^2(6) = 10.587$ [0.1020]
Testing $\beta = 0$: $\chi^2(18) = 1157.8$ [0.0000] **

Testing for error autocorrelation from lags 1 to 4
$\chi^2(4) = 1.4692$ [0.8321]
IV error autocorrelation coefficients:

	Lag 1	Lag 2	Lag 3	Lag 4
Coeff.	−0.05538	0.1402	−0.1866	−0.1426

$ARCH$ 4 F(4, 24) = 0.94264 [0.4564]
Normality $\chi^2(2)$ = 0.40163 [0.8181]

Notes: Dependent variable is $D \ln E$, estimated by IV. Two asterisks mean significant at the 1 percent level.

Table 12. *Indicators of Labor Force Equation Dynamics, Policy Model*

	Response of a 1 Percent Shock to					
	Wages	Unemploy-ment rate	Working population	Replace-ment ratio	Pension	Labor force
Permanent shock						
Long-run elasticity	0.237	0	1.452	−0.333	−0.17	1
Half-life (quarters)	6	—	11	10	3	5
Responsiveness (percent)	−5.62	—	−13.3	−15.29	−3.35	−4.91
Temporary shock						
Maximum deviation	0.0482	0.0031	−2.27	−0.124	−0.054	1
Half-life (quarters)	7	10	8	11	2	5
Persistence (percent)	0.236	$7*10^{-8}$	1.478	−0.331	−0.169	4.887

The error correction version of the real wage equation, shown in Table 10, provides stronger results than those of the labor force equation. Real wage increases tend to perpetuate themselves into the future, as demonstrated by the net positive impact lagged wage growth has on current wage increases. The error correction coefficient is large and highly significant, suggesting a rapid adjustment to the long-run real wage path. Changes in the replacement ratio have a significantly positive impact on wage growth, as in the long-run relationship. The share of temporary workers in the workforce has a short-run positive effect compared with its long-run negative effect. Changes in the unemployment rate, in productivity, and in the minimum wage have short-run effects that also run counter to their long-run relationship with real wages. Unemployment growth lagged one quarter is positively linked to wage increases, while the coefficient on lagged productivity is of only marginal significance statistically.

As with the labor force equation, the real wage equation of the policy model shows faster adjustment than with the basic model, as demonstrated by the shorter half-lives and less negative responsiveness numbers (see Table 13). This is particularly true of the response of the real wage to a real wage shock. Temporary shocks, in contrast, tend to have longer half-lives than in the basic model. This is a result of the functional form of the equation, which induces a behavior that oscillates around the final values. These oscillations take time to settle down, hence the long half-lives despite small net persistence statistics.

Employment Equation

One of the most striking results of the long-run regression on the employment equation is the weakness of the relationship between wages and employment (Table 8). Although the variable has the expected negative sign (unlike in the basic model), it is not significantly different from zero according to standard t-tests. Social security contributions, in contrast, demonstrate a strongly negative effect on employment. GDP holds a pos-

Table 13.   *Indicators of Real Wage Equation Dynamics, Policy Model*

	Response of a 1 Percent Shock to					
	Produc-tivity	Mini-mum wage	Unemploy-ment rate	Replace-ment ratio	Tempo-rary share	Wages
Permanent shock						
Long-run elasticity	0.8892	0.368	−0.0044	0.031	−0.00146	1
Half-life (quarters)	6	4	15	1	9	2
Responsive-ness (percent)	−2.55	−3.314	−4.518	0.508	−2.867	−1.52
Temporary shock						
Maximum deviation	−0.927	0.242	0.011	0.031	0.002	1
Half-life (quarters)	16	16	11	6	13	2
Persistence (percent)	0.897	0.371	−0.0043	0.031	−0.0015	1.512

itive relationship with employment of approximately one to one, implying little or no long-run labor productivity growth. The three policy-related variables included in the regression all maintain a significant relationship with employment. Severance pay is negatively related with employment, as is strike activity. The coverage of collective bargaining agreements is also related negatively with employment.

The error correction version of the employment equation is presented in Table 11. As with the real wage equation, the error correction term is large and highly significant. Changes in employment tend to persist over time, as evidenced by the positive net relationship between current employment growth and its lagged values. Social security taxes retain the negative relationship with employment in differences that they have in the long-run regression, while wages have a very small negative effect on employment growth. GDP growth has an unexpected negative relationship with employment growth over the short run. Changes in the coverage of collective bargaining agreements have a negative impact on employment growth, while strike action has a very small positive effect. Severance pay was not significant in the short-run regressions and was excluded from the preferred specification.

Table 14 shows a faster speed of adjustment in the policy model compared with that of the employment equation in the basic model. The time for one-half of the adjustment is less than one and a half years, although the oscillations in employment caused by shocks in several of the explanatory variables (for example, social security taxes, collective bargaining, and strike days) led to considerable overshooting that is not reflected in the summary statistics.

Results of the Policy Model

One important conclusion of the three equations in the policy model is that labor market structure does indeed play an important role in the underlying long-run equilibria of employment, real wages, and the labor force, as well as in the dynamics. In addition to confirming that increases in the minimum wage appear to contribute to upward pressure on overall real wages, there is also evidence that other key social and labor market policies of the government affect employment, wages, and the labor force. The policy effects can be summarized as follows:

- Higher minimum wages push up real wages overall.
- Higher employer social security contributions reduce employment.
- Higher average disability pensions reduce the labor force.

Table 14. *Indicators of Employment Equation Dynamics, Policy Model*

| | | Response of a 1 Percent Shock to | | | | | | |
	GDP	Real wages	Social security tax	Product wage	Collective bargaining	Strike days	Severance pay	Employment
Permanent shock								
Long-run elasticity	1.016	−0.1019	−0.295	−0.397	−0.0157	−0.0026	−0.0673	1
Half-life (quarters)	2	5	4	4	2	3	3	3
Responsiveness (percent)	−2.28	−1.338	−1.251	−1.273	−0.295	−0.26	−1.453	−1.451
Temporary shock								
Maximum deviation	0.438	−0.04	−0.261	−0.301	−0.0164	−0.00261	−0.0298	1
Half-life (quarters)	7	5	6	6	3	4	5	4
Persistence (percent)	1.014	−0.101	−0.293	−0.394	−0.0156	−0.0026	−0.067	2.253

- Increases in the generosity of unemployment benefits contribute to higher unemployment by increasing the labor force and also help generate higher real wages.
- The liberalization of temporary contracts has dampened wage increases.
- Higher severance pay reduces employment.
- More labor conflicts (as measured by strike days) reduce employment.
- Greater coverage of collective bargaining agreements reduces employment.

Each of these effects is statistically significant. The impression that institutional variables are crucial to understanding the Spanish labor market is reinforced by the fact that the policy model equations are much more econometrically stable than those of the basic model. Comparing the basic model, run over the same sample period, with the policy model confirms that much of the slow adjustment captured in the basic model is due to the effects of the institutional variables included in the policy model.

The second key insight emerging from the policy model is the lack of responsiveness of the Spanish labor market to traditional market clearing forces. Unemployment has little effect on the decision of potential workers to enter the labor force, nor does it have much impact on moderating wages (the coefficient is significant but small). Even more striking is the fact that the expected negative effect of real wages on employment is not strongly present. The variable has the expected negative sign, but it is not statistically significant. Thus, not only are real wages insensitive to the level of slack in the labor market, but employment itself does not unambiguously respond to the wage.

Structural Change and Unemployment: Persistence and Responsiveness

So far in this chapter, the static and dynamic characteristics of each equation in the three-equation model have been analyzed separately. This exercise yields interesting information, but it ignores the possibility that changes in one equation could feed back into other equations in the model, prolonging the adjustment process. The specifications chosen for both the basic model and the policy model provide several channels for such interequation effects: changes in employment generate effects in wages via the unemployment rate; changes in the labor force affect unemployment, which feeds into the wages; changes in real wages could affect both the labor force and employment, and so on. Recognizing the endogeneity of GDP to this labor market model, additional avenues of feed-back become apparent. Output and employment are simultaneously determined and, through labor productivity, they affect wages. To test the importance of these feedback effects and obtain a more complete idea of the overall speed of adjustment of the labor market to shocks, simulations were conducted for the system as a whole for both the basic and policy models following the methodology of Snower and Karanassou (1995).

To simulate the model as a complete system, it was necessary to develop a simple equation for GDP. A simple Cobb-Douglas style output equation was estimated as follows:

$$\ln GDP = a_o + 0.75 \ln E + 0.25 \ln K + a_1 t, \tag{7}$$

where K is the capital stock and t is a simple trend term. For the purposes of the simulations, increases in real wages are assumed to affect both the consumption wage and the level of social security contributions (effectively assuming that social security contribution rates remain constant).

Using this four-equation system, a shock was administered to the model so that the persistence and responsiveness measures for the full system could be observed. In these simulations the employment equation was shocked by 1 percent, and the Snower-Karanassou measures of persistence and responsiveness for the level of unemployment itself were calculated. For the basic model, a temporary shock yields a persistence of 32.6, with a half-life of 32 quarters.[16] A permanent shock has a persistence measure of −1,439, with a half-life of 22 quarters (Chart 2). The chart confirms that a significant proportion of the adjustment takes place several years after the initial shock. Indeed, for a permanent shock, it takes 80 quarters (20 years) for 90 percent of the final impact of the shock to appear, while for a temporary shock it takes nearly as long—75 quarters (18.7 years).[17] With the recovery period from shocks lasting considerably longer than the average business cycle, the dynamics of unemployment become extremely complex, with the unemployment effects of one recession beginning before the effects of the previous one have become fully manifest. With this dynamic pattern, the whole concept of "natural" rate of unemployment can be called into question.

---

[16]The Snower-Karanassou persistence measure used here is slightly different from that used in the measures of persistence used for shocks to the individual equations in previous sections. See the appendix for details.

[17]Once again, it should be emphasized that the exact values of the adjustments should be treated cautiously owing to the inadequacies of the basic model; nevertheless, it is safe to conclude generally that adjustment is extremely slow and that adjustment times lengthen when interequation effects are taken into account.

Chart 2. *Spain: Basic Model: Impulse Response Graphs for the Model as a Whole*
(Index, initial position = 0)

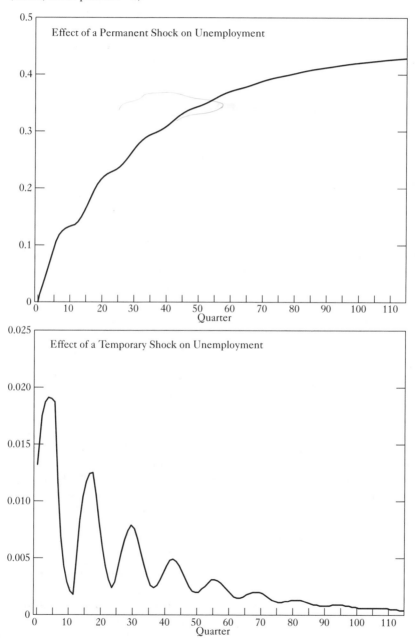

The results of the basic model confirm the central assertion of this chapter—that feedback both within and between equations produces a situation where the adjustment to labor market shocks is extremely slow in Spain. The additional delays in adjustment from the interaction among equations can be clearly seen by comparing the 32-quarter half-life for an employment shock as a whole with the 7-period half-life of a temporary employment shock on the employment equation alone. The shock to employment affects output, which feeds back to employment and wages (through a countercyclical increase in productivity); higher wages affect the labor force and, through product wages, feed back into employment, maintaining the high unemployment rate.

The adjustment to shocks is not only slow relative to the adjustment of the individual equations, it is also slow relative to other European countries discussed in other chapters. For a temporary shock, a comparison of the persistence and half-life measures with those of the other major European countries shows that the half-life is longer than those for Germany (six and a half years), Italy and the United Kingdom (five years), and France (three years). The persistence measure is also the highest, tied with the United Kingdom and well above those for the other major EU countries. For a permanent shock, the same conclusion holds—the adjustment time for Spain is significantly longer than for the other major European economies.

Turning to the policy model, there appears to be either a contradiction with the basic model or a marked improvement in the speed of adjustment of the Spanish labor market in the 1980s and early 1990s compared with that in the 1970s (reflected in the basic model)—a persistence of 10.3 with a half-life of 13 quarters for a temporary shock. As shown in Chart 3, the pattern of both the permanent and temporary shock dynamics is similar to the basic model, but the size of the reactions is smaller and the time scale is compressed. For a permanent shock, responsiveness is –102.4, with an adjustment half-life of 11 quarters. While it remains true that adjustment is slower for the system as a whole than for the individual equations (13 quarters versus 4 for the employment equation alone), the Spanish results now compare reasonably well with those for the other major European countries. This does not mean that adjustment is quick. To achieve 90 percent recovery from a temporary shock, it still takes eight and a half years, while 90 percent adjustment to a permanent shock takes six years.

These speeds of adjustment, while considerably faster than in the basic model, are slow enough that they do not alter the qualitative conclusions of the basic model. Furthermore, as argued above, the contradiction is more apparent than real. Under the policy model, adjustment to "equilibrium"

Chart 3. *Spain: Policy Model: Impulse Response Graphs for the Model as a Whole*
(Index, initial position = 0)

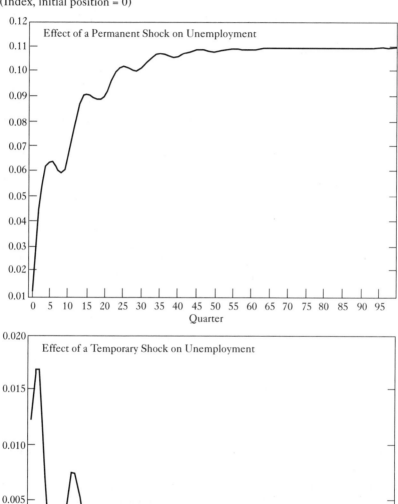

unemployment is indeed more rapid than under the basic model, but it is an adjustment to an equilibrium level that is driven higher by the inexorable increase during the 1980s of labor market policies that induced unemployment to persist. In other words, the basic model indicates that unemployment persists in Spain; the policy model indicates that this persistence is due to the persistence (and even increasing rigidity) of labor market institutions (including unemployment benefits, severance pay, minimum wages, and social contributions).[18]

Conclusions

This paper has presented two main contentions. First, it was argued that the dynamics of labor market adjustment constitute an important part of the explanation of the size and persistence of unemployment. This is amply demonstrated by the results of the basic model, where an external shock can take eight years just for one-half of the eventual effects to manifest themselves—the slowest adjustment rate among major European countries.

The second main conclusion points to the causes of this observed persistence in unemployment and the associated poor adjustment dynamics of the labor market. Profound structural changes have affected the economy, as have long-term sociodemographic factors (indicated by the significance and greater-than-unity size of the coefficient on the population variable), as confirmed by the results obtained in the empirical analysis. The comparison of the basic model with the policy model suggests that the persistence of unemployment observed in the basic model is due to the persistence of certain variables linked to the structure and policies governing the labor market in Spain (such as labor taxation, replacement ratios of unemployment benefits, minimum wages, collective bargaining, and the share of temporary contracts). Furthermore, the evidence on the importance of the policy variables in the regressions suggests that policies themselves have played a role not just in sustaining, but in generating high unemployment beyond the role of any external shocks.

Only a significant change in these features of the labor market generating and sustaining high unemployment can lead to a substantial reduction in Spanish unemployment. The Government made a start in 1993–94 with significant reforms in unemployment benefits, changes in certain rigidities

---

[18]The models of the other countries used in the comparison are actually more similar to the basic model than to the policy model, so that the basic model is the more appropriate reference point.

in hiring and firing, and improvements in the flexibility in using the work-force. These reforms are slowly bearing fruit in terms of lower unemployment and more flexible real wages, but it is likely that many additional changes will have to be undertaken if unemployment in Spain is to fall to the European average or below.

Appendix: Simple Measures of Cross-Persistence and Cross-Responsiveness

Snower and Karanassou (1995) define unemployment persistence as the sum of the deviations of unemployment from its initial value from an employment shock as follows:

$$\pi = \sum_{t=1}^{\infty} \frac{u_t' - u_t}{\Delta\varepsilon_0},$$

where $\Delta\varepsilon_0$ is the shock in period 0. To obtain a measure of persistence for shocks in explanatory variables, this indicator must be modified since it is unclear what the denominator would be because the shock is the domain of a variable different from the reaction. To solve this, it is normalized by the equilibrium value of the dependent variable rather than by the shock itself. Thus, the cross-persistence measure of deviations in the dependent variable, y, owing to a shock in variable x, is as follows:

$$\pi_{yx} = \sum_{t=1}^{\infty} \frac{y_t' - y_t}{y_0},$$

where y_0 is the value of the dependent variable before the shock to x. Where persistence is measured due to a shock in the dependent variable, π_{yy} is related to Snower-Karanassou persistence (π_{sk}) by the following relationship:

$$\pi_{yy} = [(y_1 - y_0)/y_0]\pi_{sk}.$$

For responsiveness to a permanent shock, the Snower-Karanassou measure is

$$\sigma = \sum_{t=0}^{\infty} \frac{u_t'' - \overline{u_t''}}{\Delta\varepsilon_1},$$

where u'' bar is the long-run equilibrium value. Here again, the Snower-Karanassou measure has to be modified to measure the cross-responsiveness effect of one variable on another, although here the modification is more minor. The difference between the initial and final equilibrium values is used to normalize as follows:

$$\sigma_{xy} = \sum_{t=0}^{\infty} \frac{y_t'' - \overline{y''}}{y_0 - \overline{y''}}.$$

For responsiveness to shocks in the dependent variable in a single-equation error correction model, this measure would be identical to the corresponding Snower-Karanassou responsiveness measure (although this might not be true for a system of equations where feedback effects from other equations could cause the long-run change in the dependent variable to be larger than the shock).

References

Bean, Charles R., 1994, "European Unemployment: A Survey," *Journal of Economic Literature*, Vol. 32 (June), pp. 573–619.

Bentolila, Samuel, and Juan J. Dolado, 1994, "Labour Flexibility and Wages: Lessons from Spain," *Economic Policy: A European Forum*, Vol. 9 (April), pp. 53–99.

Bianchi, Marco, and Gylfi Zoega, 1994, "Unemployment Persistence: Does the Size of the Shock Matter?" CEPR Discussion Paper No. 1082 (London: Centre for Economic Policy Research).

Blanchard, Olivier, and Lawrence Summers, 1986, "Hysteresis and the European Unemployment Problem," *NBER Macroeconomics Annual 1986* (Cambridge, Massachusetts: MIT Press), pp. 15–78.

Booth, Alison, 1995, *The Economics of the Trade Union* (Cambridge, England; New York: Cambridge University Press).

Dolado, Juan José, and others, 1996, "The Economic Impact of Minimum Wages in Europe," forthcoming in *Economic Policy*.

Dolado, Juan José, and David López-Salido, 1996, "Hysteresis and Economic Fluctuations (Spain, 1970–94)," CEPR Discussion Paper No. 1334 (London: Centre for Economic Policy Research).

Franks, Jeffrey R., 1994, "Explaining Unemployment in Spain: Structural Change, Cyclical Fluctuations, and Labor Market Rigidities," IMF Working Paper No. 94/102 (Washington: International Monetary Fund).

Friedman, Milton, 1968, "The Role of Monetary Policy," *American Economic Review*, Vol. 58 (March), pp. 1–17.

Jimeno, Juan F., and Luis Toharía, 1993, "The Effects of Fixed-Term Employment on Wages: Theory and Evidence from Spain," *Investigaciones Económicas*, 27(3).

Karanassou, Marika, and Dennis J. Snower, 1993, "Explaining Disparities in Unemployment Dynamics," CEPR Discussion Paper No. 858 (London: Centre for Economic Policy Research).

Oswald, Andrew J., and Peter J. Turnbull, 1985, "Pay and Employment Determination in Britain: What Are Labour Contracts Really Like?" *Oxford Review of Economic Policy*, Vol. 1 (No. 2), pp. 80–97.

Pesaran, H., and Y. Shin, 1995, "An Autoregressive Distributed Lag Modelling Approach to Cointegration Analysis," DAE Working Paper No. 9514 (Cambridge, England: University of Cambridge, Department of Applied Economics).

Phillips, Peter C.B., and Bruce E. Hansen, 1990, "Statistical Inference in Instrumental Variables Regressions with I(1) Processes," *Review of Economic Studies*, Vol. 57 (January), pp. 99–125.

Snower, Dennis J., and Marika Karanassou, 1995, "A Contribution to Unemployment Dynamics," CEPR Discussion Paper No. 1176 (London: Centre for Economic Policy Research).

The Authors

S.G.B. Henry is Professor of Economics at the London Business School. He has contributed extensively to the literature on empirical macroeconomics.

Dennis J. Snower is Professor of Economics at the Birkbeck College of the University of London. A well-known authority on labor market issues, he has on several occasions been a Visiting Scholar with the IMF.

Charalambos A. Christofides is an Economist in the Southern European Division I of the IMF's European I Department.

Jeffrey R. Franks is an Economist in the Southern European Division II of the IMF's European I Department.

Karl F. Habermeier is Senior Economist in the Western European Division of the IMF's European I Department.

Marika Karanassou is a graduate student in economics at the University of London.

Paolo Mauro is an Economist in the Southern European Division II of the IMF's European I Department.

Tessa van der Willigen is Deputy Division Chief in the IMF's Policy Development and Review Department.